Life's a Trip
Shortcuts to Making the Most of Your Journey

Amity Carriere, RN, BSN

&

Karen Kelliher, RN, BSN

Life's a Trip: Shortcuts to Making the Most of Your Journey

Copyright © 2014 Carriere, Kelliher
All rights reserved.

No part of this publication may be reproduced, distributed, or transmitted in any form or by any means, including photocopying, recording, or other electronic or mechanical methods, without the prior written permission of the publisher, except in the case of brief quotations embodied in critical reviews and certain other noncommercial uses permitted by copyright law. For permission requests, write to the publisher at the email address below.

Although every precaution has been taken to verify the accuracy of the information contained herein, the author and publisher assume no responsibility for errors or omissions. No liability is assumed for damages that may result from the use of information contained within.

Cover Design: **Laura Casentini**
Editor: Lisa Bovee
Interior Design: Green Pen Editing
Photography: **Paula Casentini**

Shortcut PublishingAustin, Texas
lifesatrip.shortcuts@gmail.com

Printed in the United States of America
Life's a Trip: Shortcuts to Making the Most of Your Journey.
Amity Carriere & Karen Kelliher
ISBN 978-0-9862849-0-8
10 9 8 7 6 5 4 3 2 1
1. Self-Help
2. Spiritual

DEDICATION

This book is a result of an ongoing friendship between two girls (now women) who honored and supported each other's strengths and challenged each other's weaknesses. It is a relationship that allowed us the freedom and courage to grow and change. Relationships we share with others allow us to explore the potential of what we were put on earth to do: love ourselves, be of service, and have some fun in the process. We would like to dedicate this book to our beautiful daughters. It is our greatest wish that you live fearlessly with compassion, become all that you desire to be, and fully discover the magnitude of how uniquely special you are. Mothering you has been one of life's greatest adventures. Thank you. We love you and hold you most dear to our hearts.

CONTENTS

SECTION I: Life's a Trip 2

Chapter 1: How About Some Shortcuts? 5

Chapter 2: Meet Your Back Seat Drivers 9

SECTION II: Know Your Vehicle – YOU 14

Chapter 3: Mechanical System – Mercedes or Dump Truck? 15

Chapter 4: Electrical System – Hot-wired or Hard-wired? 29

Chapter 5: Navigation System – Who's Driving? 42

Chapter 6: The Key – Uncovering the True Self 52

SECTION III: Rules of the Road 64

Chapter 7: Rule #1 – Take Radical Responsibility 65

Chapter 8: Rule #2 – Be Grateful 75

Chapter 9: Rule #3 – Let Go of Control 85

Chapter 10: Rule #4 – Be Present 99

Chapter 11: Rule #5 – Love Yourself 115

Chapter 12: Ready, Set, Review 128

SECTION IV: Creating Your Journey – The Road Map 130

Chapter 13: Step 1 – Know What You Want 132

Chapter 14: Step 2 – Watch Your Thoughts 142

Chapter 15: Step 3 – Change Your Thoughts 154

Chapter 16: Step 4 – Feel 182

Chapter 17: Step 5 – Believe 192

Chapter 18: Step 6 – Perceive 202

Chapter 19: Step 7 – Participate 209

Chapter 20: Step 8 – Receive 218

SECTION V: Roadside Assistance 229

Chapter 21: Unscheduled Stops, Detours & Breakdowns 230

Chapter 22: Grand Tales From the Trenches 261

Chapter 23: Happy Trails 277

ACKNOWLEDGMENTS
(CONTINUED ON PAGE 280)

Collectively, we express our great appreciation for the many people who have been part of our journey in producing *Life's a Trip*. This book would not exist without the stories and inspiration from our friends and family. Their willingness to share the intimate details of their lives with us is an ultimate privilege. We would be in no position to write this book if it weren't for the many authors and teachers that we studied throughout the years. Many are mentioned throughout, but most notably Louise Hay, Deepak Chopra, Wayne Dyer, Eckhart Tolle, Caroline Myss, Sonia Choquette, Brian Weiss, Joe Vitale, Miriam Williamson, Scott Peck, Bruce Lipton, Gregg Braden, Michael Singer, Panache Desai and Joe Dispenza.

Many thanks to our "A Team" for all of your unwavering support. You know who you are. The friendship and advice you freely shared fueled us with encouragement. Several people generously gave us their time to review our work. Hollace Beard-Hunting, Carol Albee, Jennifer Proffitt and Nikki McDaniel, we sincerely appreciate your time and attention.

A special thank you to Dan Caro for including us in your Hay House adventures and giving us the opportunity to meet some of our favorite authors. The times we traveled together are some of our favorite memories. Thanks also to Lori Anderson for lighting the path to completion. It was great to share the process of writing our first book with such a cherished friend. The beautiful photography and artwork were generously provided by Paula and Laura Casentini, respectively. We are blessed to have our book touched by your creativity. Thanks also to Jennifer Hawthorne who helped us edit our book proposal early on and our lawyer, Pete Kennedy, for the clarity and confidence.

Lastly, a huge shout out to our editor, Lisa Bovee. We are so glad fate brought us together in perfect time. It was an honor to have our work in your skillful and talented hands.

SECTION I
LIFE'S A TRIP

Inherently, we all know what is truly important in life: our family and friends, rewarding work, having integrity, being true to ourselves, and living our values. However, it's hard to focus on those things with all the crap we have to do. One thing is certain, we are all looking for a meaningful, satisfying life. For most people, life could use some new direction. Something seems to be missing, something just isn't right.

Where do you turn? What can you do? Unless you have an on-site, on-call coach or spiritual guru, you're like the rest of us – lost in the sauce of life. It's for this reason we decided to write this book; we share our experiences trying and applying everything and anything we could get our hands on to learn how to live fulfilling, meaningful, and satisfying lives. This book represents the best and most practical solutions we have read, studied, and practiced in our twenty-something year journey from misery to happiness.

Welcome to *Life's a Trip: Shortcuts to Making the Most of Your Journey,* the quick fix, how-to guide to getting the life you want in *shortcut* form, so you can chunk it down and put it into action. The book is divided into five sections, each with a Shortcut, a Tool Kit, and a quotation from a highly experienced driver:

Section I: Life's a Trip
The concept of shortcuts. Meet your back seat drivers.

Section II: Know Your Vehicle – You
Understand and maintain physical and mental health.

Section III: Rules of the Road
Natural laws that govern the flow of life.

Section IV: Create Your Journey – The Road Map
The Law of Attraction. Convert thoughts into a better reality.

Section V: Roadside Assistance
Obstacles to progress and how to overcome them. Plus Tales from the Trenches: adventures in applying many of the strategies in this book and miracles that played out right before our eyes.

Life's a Trip is designed as a reference guide, like the car manual you keep in your glove box. Feel free to read it cover-to-cover or go to the section that interests you most. Keep it close and pull it out whenever you need a little extra inspiration or a friendly kick in the ass.

1
HOW ABOUT SOME SHORTCUTS?

Life's a Trip. How is yours going? Are you enjoying the ride? People everywhere are feeling dissatisfied with their lives. Most of us have a nagging underlying feeling that there should be more to life, things should be different, or life just isn't fair. This epidemic of discontentment leads to feelings ranging from apathy to agony. Fulfillment and enthusiasm remain mysteriously elusive.

Are you so accustomed to that black cloud that hovers over your head that you justify your misery by telling yourself everyone lives this way? Are you spinning your wheels trying to have a better life, but it feels like nothing ever changes? The same old problems keep hanging around and showing back up. Perhaps you've tried positive thinking. Maybe you really try hard to look at the bright side and think you are doing okay, but somewhere deep inside, you have a desire for a life with more joy, more adventure, more satisfaction. Do you feel like you have tried it all, but life hasn't gotten any better?

If so, you are not alone. Millions of people feel unhappy. Life has sucked for us too. We got passed over for the promotion. We've had our hearts ripped apart and stomped on. We have been restless, broke, unhappy – not to mention lied to, screwed up in the head, and devastated by loss. Unfortunately, there's no magic pill to fix all of life's problems. Trust us, if there were, we would have tried it! If drinking, or partying, or traveling, or someone, or someplace could have made us feel better we would still be doing it, or them. We thought our lives sucked. Not anymore!

We have spent many hours, days, weeks, and years searching for meaning in our lives. And we have found it! We have read the books. We have done the research. We have tried and applied all the latest and greatest information on how to live a better life. We know what works and which strategies are worth the effort. We know how to make the most of our journey because we are living it. Lucky for your hectic lifestyle and short attention span, we are going to share what we have learned in shortcut form. This will help you avoid the time-consuming onslaught of information you'd have to chew through to assimilate it all. Why not take the fastest route and benefit from some road-tested shortcuts?

Today, we live in a world that is fast paced and hectic. We have been trained by our culture and our televisions to interpret eight seconds as an eternity. This reality is reflected in our society by innumerable drive-through food joints, HOV lanes, microwave ovens, text messaging, and countless other examples. Many call the "quick fix" the disease of the twenty-first century. We call it a necessity! We are busy as ants marching through life, working to get ahead, juggling social activities, navigating family dramas, staying current with changing technology, enduring the constant media barrage, checking our countless online accounts and remembering all those darn passwords! Add to that, managing kids and their abundant needs. Or perhaps the necessities of navigating the exciting (yet occasionally disturbing) realities of the single life! It's a wonder any of us can keep up, much less better ourselves along the way. Somebody please, hook me up with a shortcut!

Let's be honest. We all love a good shortcut. Our hurried lives demand it. We invite you to learn from our journey in shortcut fashion. But please, don't misinterpret what we mean by *"shortcut."* Shortcuts are gained by knowing the road thoroughly and by having the courage to find alternative, more efficient paths to travel. They are forged through hard work and determination. Occasionally, we got lucky and these shortcuts were created through happenstance, fate, and perhaps a little grace.

Shortcuts are what you make of them. Some of us can learn from the experience of others. Alternatively, others are determined to flog it out themselves. Whichever learner you choose to be, it never hurts to hear another's tales from the trenches. It may spark something meaningful in you and help you make the most of your journey. Partner with us, and other people in your life, to bring out your best Self and learn to enjoy the journey! There is a reason you are holding this book in your hands. There is a better, more meaningful way to live and always room for improvement.

 **Shortcut**

→ Learn from someone who knows the road.

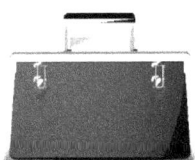 **Tool Kit**

→ Use this book as a reference guide and refer to it often.

> "What Romantic terminology called genius or talent or inspiration is nothing other than finding the right road empirically, following one's nose, taking shortcuts."
>
> ~ Italo Calvino

2

MEET YOUR BACKSEAT DRIVERS

If you use and apply the information in this comprehensive reference guide, it will lead you to a life of happiness and fulfillment. To help you stay on track, we have decided to crash your road trip and come along. Consider us back seat drivers. After all, we've taken this route before, and our insight will help guide you through the detours, roadblocks, and wrong turns to navigate your journey as painlessly and efficiently as possible. Who are these two wild and crazy back seat drivers? We thought you'd never ask! Allow us to introduce ourselves:

Karen's Story: The "Fix it Queen"

Karen is the kind of girl who gets things done. She can fix anything: quickly and efficiently. She rarely sits still. She is a mother of three tall, blonde and beautiful girls. She has a short attention span, and, if tested, she would most certainly carry an ADD diagnosis. She likes things fast and to the point. Karen doesn't consider herself to be intellectual, although you would never know it by her competence and street smarts. She is an RN who scratched her way through a bachelor's degree hopped-up on coffee and a budget tighter than her hand-me-down designer jeans. Raised by a struggling single mother, Karen learned some serious survival skills. She can take care of herself and everybody else.

Early in her life, Karen was self-directed and self-centered. She was a successful achiever and expected that money could buy her happiness. Although this mindset was productive and lucrative, Karen repeatedly found herself dissatisfied with life and always looking outside herself to find fulfillment. At 37, the good job, the nice big house, and the Super Mom mentality just weren't translating into empowerment, and she couldn't figure out why. She had done and achieved everything she thought would ensure a life of fulfillment, yet felt empty, lonely and unhappy. In a state of crisis, she finally opened her ears to what her friend and co-author Amity had been saying all along, "YOU CAN FIX THIS."

The "Fix It Queen" got inspired, and Amity began sending her shortcuts from all the books she had acquired and read over the years. Together they experimented with practical ways to change behaviors and reprogram their obsolete negative thought patterns. During this process, Karen began to shift her focus from "What am I getting?" to "What am I giving?" She also got real with herself about her need to control and manage everything and everyone around her. Karen's perspective began to change as she practiced new ways of thinking. Her relationship with her husband improved, she started having more fun, and she began to manifest things in her life that she never before thought possible.

Experiencing the amazing results from the work she'd been doing, Karen had no problem taking her newfound awareness to the next level, which continues to unfold in new and exciting ways to this day. She is a passionate advocate of how changing your thoughts will change your life. She truly believes that anyone has the power to create the life of their dreams. It is with this passion, and her gift of getting things done, that she convinced Amity to get off her butt and partner with her to produce *Life's a Trip: Shortcuts to Making the Most of Your Journey.*

Amity's Story: Expert Driver

Your other back seat driver is Amity. She is gifted with the ability to understand complex concepts and will make sure we get through our journey in a methodical, safe and thoughtful way. In college, she graduated with honors in nursing despite being far more concerned with spirituality, drinking beer, and chasing some hot ass. Love, friends, and opportunities came easily. She had a life plan and knew where she was headed: graduation, marriage, career, and a kid or two. Life seemed to be on cruise control until the day she learned that the boyfriend, who was part of this grand plan, had been killed in a motorcycle accident. In an instant, all that she knew of her life and her future was gone. The years following were plagued with self-pity, anger and loneliness.

After the devastating shock had eased, Amity began reading and studying philosophers, old and new, in an effort to heal and find meaning in life. It was through this search she discovered life is much more than she had ever known, and she eventually came to understand herself in a completely different way.

Over time, Amity has developed the habit of healthy self-reflection. She *enjoys a deep and satisfying internal life. Throughout her careers – cosmetology, nursing, sales, training, business ownership, yoga instruction, public speaking and writing – Amity has cultivated the ability to communicate easily and loves to inspire people with new information. Her passion is to encourage and empower people to seek deeper understanding of themselves and others.*

Amity is content reading about new ideas to play with and really enjoys being somebody else's back seat driver. Highly analytical, she can get lost in the details of planning a trip but finds less and less satisfaction arriving at a destination, instead preferring the ride. Amity has the knack for knowing which obstacles are approaching and, during our journey, provides us strategies to navigate around them. She has the foresight to see what lies ahead and the knowledge to help us get out of the ditch if we crash. Her understanding of the road is priceless.

We are very excited to embark on this life-changing journey with you. If you embrace the concepts offered in this book and try some of the practical shortcuts we offer, then your days of discontentment will be a thing of the past. Let's face it: what you have been doing isn't working. Why not shake it up and try something new? It is time to choose to change! Our goal is to provide you with a reference guide and a road map to help you live a more fulfilled, enjoyable life while expressing and celebrating your True Self and knowing that everything that's happening in your life has been created by you for your benefit. You will also learn that you have the power to deliberately create anything and everything you want out of life. It's a life you'll love, so pack your bags and load the car. It's time to put the pedal to the metal. Life's a trip. Let's take a ride!

Shortcuts

→ Keep an open mind and keep on reading.

→ Choose to change.

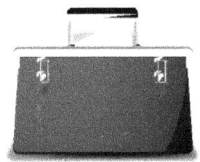
Tool Kit

→ Listen to your back seat drivers.

> "Is there anyone so wise as to learn by the experience of others?"
>
> ~ Voltaire

SECTION II

Know Your Vehicle
YOU

Before we start out on our journey, it is important to have information regarding the vehicle you will be using for your trip. That vehicle is YOU! Once you have a deeper understanding of your vehicle, you will realize the importance of why it needs to function at peak performance.

Chapter 3: Mechanical System – Mercedes or Dump Truck?

Chapter 4: Electrical System – Hot-wired or Hard-wired?

Chapter 5: Navigation System – Who's Driving?

Chapter 6: The Key – Uncovering the True Self

3

MECHANICAL SYSTEM MERCEDES OR DUMP TRUCK?

It is time to take a good hard look at yourself. Do you treat yourself like a Mercedes or a dump truck? If you are a Mercedes, you'll be filling up with premium fuel, going in for regular maintenance, and spit shining that baby. On the other hand, if you are a dump truck, you are more likely hoping to avoid your next breakdown. You are procrastinating doing regular maintenance, ignoring all the warning signs, and rationalizing a list of priorities that will cost you more in the long run. Be honest. Mercedes or dump truck?

If you want your vehicle to perform better, you need to invest in it by making sure you get adequate maintenance. The better you keep your car, the better it will perform for you. Think of it this way: You don't just take your car to get it washed before you set out on a trip, do you? No, you take it for a tune up, change the tires, check the brakes, and service the engine. You'd better be servicing the outside and the inside of the car or you are asking for trouble. The same holds true with your body. To have maximum performance, we need to examine the entire car, inside and out.

Fluids

Let's begin with a maintenance check. The first thing we need to do when inspecting our vehicle is to check the fluids and make sure they are topped off. The biggest bang for your buck in the maintenance department is to DRINK MORE WATER. It is easy to do, and it is free. If you decide to make just one change after reading this book, let it be this.

Drinking more water will make a significant difference in the way you feel. Water is what keeps all the body's systems running smoothly. It is so vital to the human body that it only takes three days without it for brain damage to occur, and without water for seven days you will die. Even mild dehydration can drain your energy, cause you to lose focus, and make you tired.

Drinking water is the simplest and easiest change you can make. Quit or cut back on drinking anything else. If this sounds impossible, then at least drink a glass of water every time you drink something else. Try carrying a water bottle with you everywhere you go as a reminder. Increasing your water intake can help you lose weight, improve mood, increase cognitive ability, flush toxins out of vital organs, carry nutrients to cells, and even make you stink less.

The amount of water you need to drink per day varies depending on your body weight, activity level, and the temperature and altitude of the environment you live in. Most experts say to drink eight ounces of water eight times a day. We say pay attention to your body's variable needs, and make sure you are tinkling often enough. If your pee is cloudy and smells like the coffee you drank this morning, drink more water! Urine should be light yellow and clear. Drinking sufficient water is extremely important for your body.

Fuel

Next up on our maintenance list is to make sure there's fuel in your tank. For our bodies that fuel is food. Food is required to keep all systems running. Most people don't eat the right foods often enough. We know that we should, but faced with all those aisles filled with yummy crap at the grocery store, we tend to buy what is easy, quick, and cheap rather than what is healthful.

If you are looking for a jump-start to changing your eating habits and getting your vehicle in better shape, simply eat more fresh fruits and vegetables. Eat less of everything else, especially processed foods. Our hectic lifestyles and abundant grocery store choices delude us into buying food that is processed instead of fresh natural foods. The next time you go food shopping or eat, ask yourself, "Is this processed food?" Pasta, crackers, yogurt, lunchmeat = processed food. Fresh fruit, vegetables, nuts = non-processed. Assessing your food is trickier than you think. Many foods we assume are good for us are still processed. The next time you go to the store to stock up on groceries try shopping the perimeter. Non-processed foods are more likely found on the outside aisles of the grocery store, and most of the processed foods are found in the center aisles. Processed foods are also more likely to come in a wrapper. Stay away from food in wrappers.

Another shopping shortcut is to make a list of healthy meals prior to going to the store. Write out each meal for the week with all the ingredients needed. You may find that your ingredients get used multiple times, so your shopping cart is a lot emptier. Follow your meal plan! Your list will help repel the lure of placing tempting and unnecessary items into your cart.

Lastly, in case your mama never told you, always go to the store on a full stomach. You are much more likely to lose control and go for a gut-building moon-pie if you are hungry. A full shopping stomach will help prevent impulse buys and save you money too! Armed with these shopping shortcuts and some discipline, you will soon experience the rewards of fueling up on fresh and natural foods.

Here's the dreaded disclaimer: Eating good food alone will not make you totally feel better. You can't stuff your face with healthy food and expect to just miraculously be healthier. You need to eat the right food in the right amount to attain and maintain a healthy body weight. This is a struggle for us too! When we get off track and pig-out or pound-down a quart of ice cream, the B*tch in the bathroom, aka the scale, gives us a quick warning that we are headed in the wrong direction. On these occasions, we find that keeping a food diary helps us to quickly snap back into shape. We've tried it and it works! Write down everything you eat and drink each day for at least a week. Everything! Even a nibble of sandwich crust needs to be written down. Next, calculate the number of calories in each item you ate. Calories can be located on the wrapper or container of the items you are ingesting, but if you need to know the calories in a banana for example, you can find online tools to help you total up all your calories for the day. The recommended caloric intake for the average adult is approximately 2,000 calories a day. To lose weight, you must cut your daily caloric intake. Most calorie-tracking tools will tell you exactly how many calories you need to eat based on your age, weight, and exercise amount. If you are motivated to lose weight, there are many apps like MyFitnessPal or personal fitness devises like Fitbit or Nike Fuel Band that can help you keep a close eye on your fitness goals and count calories too.

Load

If you are one of the millions of people who want or need to lose weight, be realistic about what you are up against. When your body begins to shed pounds, levels of the hormone Leptin begin to drop. The decrease in Leptin sends a message to the brain that the body's fat storage is shrinking. Our primal brains perceive this as starvation. In response, the brain sends out messages to preserve calories and the metabolism drops. Meanwhile, other brain signals simultaneously send out hormones to stimulate the appetite. The combined result of losing weight is that you lower your metabolism and stimulate your appetite. What does this mean? Basically, after you have lost weight you will need to eat less to maintain that weight loss than someone who is the same size who hasn't lost weight. For example, if you weigh 160 pounds and get down to 130 pounds, you can't eat as much as your friend who has always weighed 130 pounds. This is the whole reason why diets don't work! Here's your shortcut: Don't diet! You have to make a lifestyle change to eat smaller portions of live and natural foods. Before you start crying over the reality of weight loss, there are some fun tricks to help offset those low Leptin levels and increase your metabolism. Once a week, you can have a cheat day. This will become your favorite day of the week where you can eat whatever you want. Having a meal high in fat on cheat day satisfies your primal brain to reassure it that you are not starving somewhere on a deserted island. Sure, you will still have to process those calories, and it may be a minor setback, but your metabolism will process at a higher rate for the rest of the week. And more importantly, that yummy food will help you keep your sanity and make a lifestyle change more attainable.

Mileage

Cars need regular maintenance to run efficiently, look good, and last long. A car that sits idle can have minor and sometimes major problems. The same goes for the body. Your body needs exercise! People have different expectations for how they want to look and feel, so their exercise needs vary accordingly. In order to have a healthy body, you should be raising your heart rate for at least 20 minutes a day. We, however, are firm believers in one hour a day of moderate exercise. If you refuse to believe that you can carve out time in your day, then you will need to ramp-up the intensity of your workouts. Many recent studies show you can accomplish the same or better fitness results with short bursts of high intensity sprints with short recovery breaks in between. If shorter duration, high intensity exercise is your style, check out the book *PACE: The 12-Minute Fitness Revolution*, by Al Sears, M.D. Amity has tried this work out with rapid results. Karen prefers a high intensity cross training style of cardio workout.

In the long run, any exercise is tremendously better than no exercise. Consider the findings of researcher Nicola Lautenschlager of the University of Western Australia. She found that elderly people who did just twenty minutes of moderate exercise a day statistically improved their memory, language ability, and attention compared to a sedentary peer group. Take the stairs, park far away from the door, walk the dog and get off your butt and get your body moving. The benefits are worth the effort.

Perhaps time is not the issue but you just feel too tired to exercise. Here is the catch: you are too tired to work out, but working out is what will ultimately give you energy. Believe us, we aren't excited to go to the gym either. We drag our pale faces and stiff bodies out of bed to go exercise. When we leave the gym, we are glowing and ready to take on the day. If we focused on how we felt before we exercised, we would never go. The shortcut is to focus on how you will feel after the workout is complete. You will feel a sense of accomplishment, vitality, and alertness. A recent study showed that just by exercising three days a week, twenty minutes a day for six weeks, persistently tired people increased their energy levels. Six weeks is going to go by anyway, so why not help yourself feel better?

Regular exercise is amazing for your body. It improves the functioning of all body systems including your cardiovascular system, metabolism, respiratory health, digestion, skin, and musculature. In fact, Daniel J. Siegel, M.D. says, "If you spend 5% of your waking hours on fitness (1 hour/day) the return on investment is that your risk of heart disease falls by 50%, your risks of stroke and dementia decrease, and your quality of life, mood, and energy level improve."

Exercise isn't just good for your body; it is good for your mind as well. In *The Happiness Project* author Gretchen Rubin reflects on Nietzsche's wise words, "All truly great thoughts are conceived while walking." She states "His observation is backed up by science; exercise-induced brain chemicals help people think clearly." Even more profoundly, recent studies have shown that regular exercise is as effective, or even more effective, than antidepressants for treating mood disorders! Harvard Health Publications reports that the effects of exercise on depression can last longer than those of antidepressants without the negative side effects or the expense associated with drugs. So stop with the depressing excuses of why you don't have the time to exercise. You can do it if you want to and should do it even if you don't want to. Getting off your butt to exercise will have amazing effects on your mind and body.

If you are not convinced that exercise is tremendously important, here are some recent projections where the rubber meets the road. Mark Huffman, Assistant Professor of Preventative Medicine and Cardiology at Northwestern University, has calculated that if Americans stay on the same track, the current 32% of men and 34% of women who are overweight and obese will increase to 83% of men and 72% of women by 2020! Not only will we be a nation of fatties, almost half of us are projected to be diabetic. If those numbers don't make you lose your appetite, we hope at least you will be motivated to exercise!

It is simple. If you are not exercising, your body is in the process of decay. You will get fat, weak, and tired. If you exercise, you will improve your quality of life, look better, feel more vibrant, and be in a better mood. The advantages of exercising are worth the return on investment. Go get yourself a workout outfit and just do it!

Recharging

Cars don't run 24 hours a day / 7 days a week and neither can your body. Sleep is another extremely important aspect of your regular maintenance. A recent Swedish study has correlated level of attractiveness to the amount of sleep a person gets. It turns out that "beauty sleep" is not just a cliché. Another common saying has scientific backing: "Sleep on it" refers to the findings of a Harvard University study that shows you are 33% more likely to make connections between distant related points if you sleep on new ideas, proving that adequate sleep helps foster a creative mind.

Research suggests the average adult should sleep 7-9 hours a night. Most adults sleep 20% less than in 1900. Not only will a lack of sleep make you cranky as hell, there are serious consequences to not getting this required amount.

Short sleep cycles can contribute to:

→Increase in body mass index – a greater likelihood of obesity due to an increased appetite caused by sleep deprivation

→Increased risk of diabetes and heart problems

→Increased risk for psychiatric conditions including depression and substance abuse

→Decreased ability to pay attention and react to signals or remember new information

→Increased risk of motor vehicle accidents

Another study published in the *Annals of Internal Medicine* looked at the function of fat cells in individuals who received seven to nine hours of sleep in a lab for one week compared to the same individuals a month later who were receiving less than five hours of sleep. The study found that inadequate sleep has a harmful effect on fat cells, reducing their ability to respond to insulin by about 30%. That is a huge amount. Over time, this decreased response could set the stage for Type 2 diabetes, fatty liver disease, and weight gain. The scientific evidence on the damaging effects of sleep deprivation continues to mount. Getting good shut-eye is serious business.

Getting a good night's sleep can be challenging. Calming the body and the mind are essential to being able to fall asleep soundly. Go to bed on an empty stomach, eating your last meal or snack at least 3 hours before bed. Digestion requires energy and can stimulate the body and mind, making it hard to settle down. Avoid caffeine and alcohol before bed. It may also help to make your bedroom comfortable and dark. Even the slightest light from a clock radio produces optical stimulation for your brain to process. This of course includes TVs and computers, which should be removed from your sleep space altogether.

The body responds well to routine. Do your best to establish a consistent bedtime and try to use your bedroom only for sleep and sleep related activities. Sleep-related activities include reading a book before bed, slow rhythmic breathing through the nose, and orgasm. Yes, you heard us, orgasm! Orgasms release a cocktail of brain chemicals including Oxytocin and Endorphins, which can relax the body and induce sleep. Try it. It may help you sleep like a rock!

Pollution

A few last words about maintenance. SMOKING IS UNACCEPTABLE! If you smoke, slap yourself and go throw your cigarettes in the trash. You cannot love yourself and kill yourself with cigarettes at the same time. Half of all smokers will die from cancer or other related smoking diseases. That is one out of two! Look to your left or right on your smoke break or flip a coin – worse odds than Russian roulette! No more excuses – quit! If you think you need help, it's everywhere. Smokefree.Gov for starters.

DRINKING TOO MUCH IS UNACCEPTABLE too! No one except a date-rapist likes a drunk. Besides being unattractive, too much alcohol is poisonous to your body systems. Keep your alcohol consumption at two drinks or fewer, per occasion, and you and everyone around you will be happier. If you find yourself doing the walk of shame after a night out drinking, it may be time to consider checking out aa.org.

Notice the lifestyles of healthy, happy people around you. They put effort into maintaining their bodies. It may look like a lot of extra work, but for those who do it, it becomes just part of what they do and who they are. You too can create a healthy lifestyle for yourself and enjoy it!

Amity's Story: Smokey Treats

Shortly after college graduation, I was driving down the interstate in my packed-to-the-gills, little white Escort, affectionately named "Snowball." I was on my way to start a new life in Atlanta, Georgia. After a few hard years in the climate of Western New York, my mind wandered with possibilities for my future in the South. The familiar feeling of nicotine craving was creeping on, so I reached for my pack of Marlboro Lights. As I began to light up, I paused in my daydream and wondered, "How the hell did I become a smoker?" Once I was released from having to live in the dorms, I moved in with my newly found friend Sue. Sue was a smoker. I was a drinker. The two went together like peanut butter and jelly.

Although I would never have identified myself as "a smoker," I found myself moving from the occasional cigarette during a night out, to a cigarette with my morning coffee, to one on my way to class, to more during study time, blah, blah, blah – forget about when I was stressed. And here I was trucking down the highway enjoying a smoke, but at the same time uncomfortable with the notion of labeling myself "a smoker." I did like to smoke. I liked lots of things about it: the smell, the distraction, the social interaction with other smokers, and the way it gave my fingers something to do. I guess that was the real problem. I liked it. But liking it went against my better judgment, my self-image, and all that I had learned in nursing school.

Atlanta is famous for being an outdoorsy city where people love to exercise and enjoy hiking and biking. Day dreaming about my glorious future as a young professional living and working in Atlanta, I just couldn't see myself as a smoker. I wondered if smoking had already affected my athletic ability. I contemplated how many smokers vs. non-smokers there would be in such a young city. I mused at the irony of not wanting to meet a boyfriend who smoked. As I got deeper into my future as a smoker I wondered how long my ovaries would hold up in the oxygen-deprived environment my smoking was creating in my body, a fact I had learned in my women's health studies. And then the shocking, most horrific thought crossed my mind. "What would I look like when my bright red lipstick would bleed through all those smoking crinkle, wrinkle lines around my smoker's mouth?" F@#* that!

In that moment, with my future self in mind, I threw my half-smoked cigarette out the window. A split second later, the rest of the pack followed. Despite the littering foul, it was the best decision I could have made for myself. At the ripe old age of twenty-two, I certainly did not know all there was to know about loving myself. In fact, I am quite certain the topic had probably not crossed my mind. I did, however, make the decision that I loved my unwrinkled, unstained lips more than I loved that cigarette, and I quit cold turkey!

It wasn't easy. I was as cranky as a starving baby, and I had dreams about chain smoking with a smile on my face, but I never gave in. Not one drag. Not one puff. I liked it too much to mess with that kind of temptation. Two decades later, I can't imagine what life would be like – and, God forbid, what I would look like – if I'd kept smoking! The other really important thing I learned in nursing school about smoking is: It is never, and I mean NEVER, too late to quit. The lungs have an amazing capacity to heal from damage caused from smoking. If you happen to be one of the last smokers left in America, I promise you, it's worth it to quit. Just find something you love about yourself, more than you love about smoking. The answer may be something as simple as YOUR LIFE!

Shortcuts

→ Drink more water.

→ Eat more fresh fruits and vegetables.

→ Avoid processed foods.

→ Get regular exercise.

→ Don't diet.

→ Sleep 7-9 hours a night.

→ Don't smoke.

→ Don't drink – or drink in moderation.

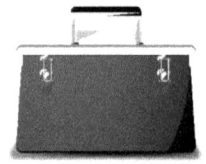 **Tool Kit**

→ Carry a water bottle.

→ Shop the perimeter on a full stomach with a list.

→ Avoid food in wrappers.

→ Use a food diary.

→ Move more.

→ Focus on the "after work out" feeling.

→ Make a bedtime routine.

→ Create a comfortable, dark sleep space.

→ Enjoy only sleep related activities in the bedroom.

> "A man's health can be judged by which he takes two at a time – pills or stairs."
>
> ~ Joan Welsh

4

ELECTRICAL SYSTEM
HARD-WIRED OR HOT-WIRED?

Now that we have completed a thorough assessment of our vehicle, we need a greater understanding of how this bad boy works. Every car on the road has an electrical system and so does your body. Your electrical system is made up of billions of neurons in the brain and miles of nervous tissue, but it is more than just the hard wiring. Your body's electrical system is also hot-wired. Every cell of your body emits an energy wave that sends signals and interacts with the environment. You are not just your physical body. You are also an energetic being. You are energy!

Consider this. Each beat of your heart is produced from an electrical charge in your heart muscle. That is why when someone's heart stops they try to "shock" it back into action with a machine called a defibrillator. The defibrillator sends an electrical impulse through the body that literally jump starts the heart.

Our hearts, which beat approximately forty million times a year and keep blood pumping through our veins uninterrupted for the entire duration of our lives, are more than mere machines. Our hearts actually produce an electromagnetic field just like cell phones and radio transmissions. According to research being done at the Institute of HeartMath in Boulder Creek, California, "The heart's electromagnetic field is by far the most powerful produced by the body; it's approximately five thousand times greater in strength than the field produced by the brain." This electromagnetic field communicates with your brain and is hypothesized to include its own intelligence. That sounds far out, but consider the fact that in utero a baby's heart develops and beats before the brain even starts to develop. That fact challenges the notion most of us have that the brain runs the body. Maybe it is the other way around! Also, consider how you felt when you suffered a great loss or got dumped by someone you were in love with. Remember the pain, the ache that actually emanated from your chest? For centuries, cultures from every part of the globe have universally referred to the heart as the organ that gives us guidance and leads us in the right direction. There must be some intrinsic intelligence of the heart that drives us as human beings. We are just now on the verge of being able to study and understand the mysteries of the heart.

Our body's energy is not just internal. It also exists externally beyond the boundary of our physical body. We all maintain an energy field around us, which surrounds us like a bubble. The HeartMath researchers, and others, have used magnetometers to measure the electromagnetic field that extends beyond the body, proving that this field can radiate up to eight to ten feet away. This is what the sixties hippies referred to as "vibes."

Imagine being in a great mood and walking into a funeral. Or conversely, imagine feeling depressed and entering a room with a raging party for all of your favorite friends. After some time, the energy emitting from the others in the room starts to have a profound effect on your emotional state, and eventually you will be uplifted or depressed to match the mood of the room. This happens because your energy extends beyond your physical boundaries, and it has the ability – negatively or positively – to affect those around us.

The people around, the thoughts we have, the beliefs we hold, and the emotions we convey all affect our body's energy field. When you feel angry, upset, frustrated, jealous, or sad, you are emitting negative energy. When you feel happy, generous, compassionate, or loving, you are emitting positive energy. This field of energy has tremendous power. Understanding your energy body and how it works is a critical part of making the most of your journey!

Physics also provides some explanation of the concept that our bodies are energetic beings. Before you start feeling too special, bear in mind that physicists would describe everything that exists as being made up of energy: people, furniture, buildings, diamonds, wind, you name it! Think back to middle school science class where we first learned that everything is made up of atoms. In case you don't remember, an atom is a basic unit of matter made up of a nucleus that contains protons and neutrons and is surrounded by a cloud of electrons. The electrons are bound to the nucleus by an *electromagnetic force*. Translation – energy! All matter is composed of atoms. This means all matter has physical energy.

Quantum physics, the branch of physics that uses quantum theory to describe and predict the properties of the physical world, is also helping to shed some light on the science involved with our expressions as energy beings. Quantum physics uses a mathematical description of energy and matter in its dual particle-like and wave-like behavior. WTF??? CAT scans, PET scans, and MRIs are all practical examples of how quantum physics is applied in the real world. These non-invasive machines are used to detect disease in the body by measuring unique energy signatures emitted by tissue. Diseased tissue sends out a different energy wave than healthy tissue. The machines then translate the energy waves into visual images for interpretation and diagnosis by health care professionals.

Bruce Lipton, author of the groundbreaking book *The Biology of Belief,* explains, "Quantum physicists discovered that physical atoms are made up of vortices of energy that are constantly spinning and vibrating; each atom is like a wobbly spinning top that radiates energy. Because each atom has its own specific energy signature (wobble), assemblies of atoms (molecules) collectively radiate their own identifying energy patterns. So every material structure in the universe radiates a unique energy signature." Further, Lipton states, "Matter can simultaneously be defined as a solid (particle) and as an immaterial force field (wave). When scientists study the physical properties of atoms, such as mass and weight, the atoms look and act like physical matter. However, when the same atoms are described in terms of voltage potentials and wavelengths, they exhibit the qualities and properties of energy (waves)." Everything and everybody in the universe emits energy.

Energy signatures don't just emit, they interact. When energy signatures converge, they can complement each other, which increases the collective energy called harmonic resonance. Or they can be destructive, which decreases and discombobulates the energy, called interference. A great example of how constructive interference is used in the medical field is through the use of ultrasound technology to treat kidney stones. The ultrasound uses harmonic frequency to interact with the atoms in the kidney stones causing them to vibrate so feverishly that they explode and dissolve.

The work of Japanese scientist Dr. Masaru Emoto also demonstrates that our thoughts emit a vibration frequency that influences the world around us. Dr. Emoto photographed frozen samples of polluted water before and after prayer was done over the water, and he photographed distilled water before and after exposure to various kinds of music, such as heavy metal and Beethoven. He also taped words to containers of distilled water such as, "You make me sick; I will kill you" and "love and appreciation." He states, "The energies from beautiful words and thoughts, even if only written, created exquisite snowflake–like patterns in the water. The negative energies created images of disorder and toxicity. Even a simple, 'thank you' produced a lovely crystalline pattern." Our bodies are made up of approximately 70% water; just imagine how the vibrations of our thoughts and emotions can impact our bodies and others.

You may assume it takes the modern scientific world to explain our physical reality, but the Chinese experienced their environment in energetic terms when they developed the practice of Feng Shui, nearly five thousand years ago. Feng Shui (pronounced "fung shway") acknowledges the concept that everything has energy. It uses color and placement of furniture to attract and enhance life energy called Qi, pronounced "chee." Feng Shui is the practice of managing the free flow of Qi by properly arranging furniture to avoid blockages in energy, which are believed to create problems and discord. The Chinese believed, if practiced correctly, Feng Shui could help a person create a better quality of living by enhancing their love life, health, wealth, happiness, and success. Feng Shui is still practiced throughout the world today. If you are interested in learning more, check out the best-selling book *Move Your Stuff, Change Your Life* by Karen Rauch Carter.

By now we hope you are getting the picture that everything, including you and the entire universe, is emitting energy that is constantly interacting with other energy. Let's bring that back down to earth and expand on the concept of emotional energy. Positive energy energizes; negative energy wipes you out and leaves you exhausted. Think about how you feel when you meet someone who has the same interests as you. You feel an immediate kinship with that person. Energized! Now think about how you feel after an argument.

You probably feel wiped out! The differences are subtle exchanges in energy. People are generating frequencies of energies at all times. Like the force field out of a *Star Wars* movie, your body's energy is flowing through you and around you interacting with everyone else and the environment. Your electrical system perceives all of these signals and sends messages to your brain. Your brain then decodes the information and decides what energy *it* wants to have. If you are not aware of yourself as an energetic being, then most likely your brain did its hard wire job and just took on the energy around you. Bingo, your day sucked because you unknowingly let someone else's energy affect you. Or you can consciously develop the ability to perceive yourself as an energetic being and learn how to create, protect, and preserve your positive energy.

If you are interested in doing an easy in-home experiment to test the energy emitted by your body, you can make an energy-testing device out of regular metal hangers. Our friend and mentor, Carol Albee, taught us how to do this, and we have had wild fun with it. Take two wire coat hangers and fashion an "L" shape out of each one. The long leg of the "L" should be 18 inches long and the short leg of the "L" about 5 to 6 inches long. Slide the short side of your hangers into a cardboard tube like the rod you would find on wire trouser hangers. If you don't have that available, drinking straws will do. With your elbows bent by your sides, hold your rods by the cardboard or straws with the long ends pointed out in front of you so the rods are able to move freely side to side. Clear your mind and attempt to hold them steady, giving them a moment to settle. Have another person across the room at least 15 to 20 feet away approach very slowly while you hold the rods steady. Once the approaching person's energy field reaches the tips of the wires, you will see distinct movement in the rods. They may cross or widen, but the movement will be noticeable. You can also play with these rods individually to test your own energy field. Try holding the rods steady and look straight ahead. Think a positive thought, like gratitude, and feel that thought through your entire body. Most likely you will find the tips of the rods will move away from one another, opening, representing the expansion of the your energy field while thinking a positive thought. Conversely, if you hold a negative thought of something painful or unpleasant, the ends of the rods will point towards each other and may even cross, representing the contraction of your energy field under negative influence. Go ahead. Try it! It will satisfy your need to know and just might become your favorite party trick. It is an easy and fun way to heighten your perception of your energy field.

Finding people and situations that resonate with your positive energies is one of the most important factors in making the most of your journey. What makes us feel good is different for all of us. What energizes us may exhaust you or vice versa. We encourage you to familiarize yourself with your own energy patterns. In doing so, you will be able to more clearly identify who resonates with you and who drains your energy. It is really simple. Who makes you feel good? When you can answer that question, you are ready to build an A-Team! Your A-Team is your inner circle of people who pump you up, help you discover your true inner beauty, and challenge you in positive ways to become a better person. Hanging around groups of like-minded, positive people is documented to be one of the most meaningful contributors to being happy and feeling energized.

Your body is much more than just its physical parts; it is also electrical, made up of millions of electrical impulses and energy waves. We are as much "energetic beings" as we are physical beings. Beam me up, Scotty!

Kim's Story: Massage Message

Our friend Kim became a massage therapist when she was twenty-three years old. Very kind and empathetic, she was drawn to helping people and the healing arts. The training was basic and focused primarily on anatomy, physiology, pathology, and kinesiology. The program also covered business strategies, eastern and western massage techniques, and of course, clinic work. In clinic work, Kim quickly honed her ability to objectively touch and treat the human body without engaging in any assumptions regarding her clients. Throughout her schooling she was never taught, nor did it ever occur to her, that someone else's energy could impact her in anyway.

Immediately after her training, Kim went to work in a well-established day spa and accepted as many clients as she could physically serve. At work all of the employees were required to wear scrubs and lab coats to maintain a professional and clinical appearance. She loved her work and was enjoying the process of learning about herself and her profession. Kim found that while performing massage and maintaining an attitude of selfless service, she would slip into a kind of moving meditation that felt constructive and gratifying.

Kim's career as a massage therapist was progressing better than she had ever expected, and each week her clientele was growing. Then it all changed. One afternoon a middle-aged man called to schedule an appointment. Kim was very comfortable accepting new clients so she thought nothing of it as she prepared the necessary intake forms. Upon their first meeting, Kim felt uneasiness in the pit of her stomach as she walked him back to the therapy room. She immediately disregarded her feelings and chastised herself for her lack of professionalism and pushed through. As the massage began, Kim was uncharacteristically uncomfortable and was trying desperately not to make assumptions. The man's body was completely shaven and abnormally tanned. He also talked incessantly, mostly about his time in the gym and his physical appearance. On more than one occasion, he asked Kim to compare his body to that of her other clients and wanted her to rate his appearance. Kim was doing her best to keep the conversation clinical, and to a minimum, while she desperately tried to manage her mounting discomfort. At the halfway point Kim asked her client to turn over on his back while she took extra care to give him complete privacy with the sheet. As the man adjusted himself on the table, he reached and pulled the sheet to the top of his groin, bending his knee up and then opening it to the side, exposing his hairless man sac! Kim was mortified! In an awkward state of disbelief, she readjusted the sheet and continued working. Needless to say, Kim never did get into that selfless altered state. Instead, she labored through an anxiety attack fueled by her feelings of shock, disgust, and disbelief.

For the sake of Kim, I wish I could say it was just one hell of a bad day at work, but unfortunately for her, it was much more than that. That evening Kim got sick. She felt as if she contracted the flu. A week later her flu-like symptoms subsided, and she was able to return to work but now during every massage she was in acute pain. Her back ached, and the joints in her hands hurt. Kim assumed that in time she would return to normal, but her condition worsened to include strange neurological symptoms. Despite seeking help from various physicians and being tested for everything under the sun, the best diagnosis the doctors could come up with was possibly a rare form of reflex sympathetic dystrophy which is an unexplained constant firing of nerves that can cause pain and swelling with no known cause. After six months of working in extreme pain, Kim finally quit doing massage. It took her three months to recover enough to go back to work in a completely different industry.

For the next decade, Kim continued to have intermittent neurological symptoms. In the absence of any effective medical treatment or guidance, Kim sought to improve herself through her mind-body connection and through emotional and spiritual development. During her self-improvement journey, Kim discovered Louise Hay's book *You Can Heal Your Life*. In the back of the book, Louise includes of list of physical ailments and diseases and their probable mental and emotional causes. Interestingly, in this list, problems with nerves "represent communication" and pain in the hands is correlated to "grasping and letting go." After reading this book, Kim realized that she was holding on to the energy in that negative experience, and her refusal to let it pass through her was keeping her sick. Over time Kim began to understand and respect how energetically sensitive she is. She also recognized the importance of learning how to protect herself from other people's negative energy. For Kim, this meant developing the skills of expressing herself instead of stuffing her feelings, and better controlling her environment. She also had to learn to stand up for herself and draw healthier boundaries in her relationships.

Today, Kim is completely symptom free. She definitely attributes her illness and neurological symptoms to an exchange of energy initiated by the interaction between her and that creepy client years ago and her inability to process the event. Unfortunately, Kim's condition was not medically understood or explainable, but her story underscores how intensely we can interact with one another on energetic levels and what an impact those exchanges of energies can have on our quality of life.

Shortcuts

→ Your body is more than physical.

→ Think of yourself as energy.

→ Your energy field extends beyond the physical boundaries of your body.

→ Your energy field is constantly interacting with the energy patterns of others and the environment.

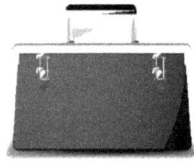
Tool Kit

→ Become aware of your energy and what you are emitting.

→ Become aware of the energy in your environment.

→ Be aware of other people's energy, how you react to it, and how it can affect you.

→ Create your "A Team."

→ Spend time on things that make you feel good.

> "I do not take a single newspaper, nor read one a month, and I feel myself infinitely the happier for it."
>
> ~ Thomas Jefferson

5

NAVIGATION SYSTEM
WHO'S DRIVING?

There is another very important component of your vehicle: the navigation system. For your car it's a device that tells you where to go and does the thinking for you. For YOU, this navigation system is your MIND. As we discuss the mind, we will divide it into three different areas: the conscious mind, the subconscious mind, and the ego.

Our conscious mind is in action when we are "aware" of what we are thinking. When we *decide* to think a new thought we are using our conscious mind. The conscious mind is what gives us free will and separates us from lower order mammals. It is the part of the mind that helps us plan and make decisions. It can think about the future and the past and is responsible for our self-image and our ability for self-reflection. The conscious mind's processing center lives in the prefrontal cortex area of the brain, right behind the forehead, and according to the book *The User Illusion*, the mind is able to process 40 environmental stimuli per second. Many people think this is the part of the mind that's driving the car, but that's not really the case.

The subconscious mind is the one running the show. It has the staggering processing power of 20,000,000 environmental stimuli per second and only operates in the present moment. Its processing power draws upon a series of ingrained habitual patterns (learned behaviors) that occur when we're not paying attention. The subconscious functions just below the level of awareness and drives an enormous amount of our behavior. It takes the chosen route based on beliefs, past experience, and previous choices, good or bad. The subconscious mind just reacts. It needs no input or influence from the conscious mind to do its business.

Most of our subconscious was etched in our minds as children. If your parents told you that you could do anything, you grew up believing you *could* do anything. If you never felt loved as a child, chances are you grew up looking for love in all the wrong places. Our parents unknowingly did a major mind job on us. As children our brains absorb and process information differently from adults. This has been proven through electroencephalogram (EEG) brain wave measurement. As reported by Dr. Rima Laibow in *Quantitative EEG and Neurofeedback*, the brains of children from birth to two function predominantly in Delta, the lowest EEG frequency of 0.5 to 4 Hz (cycles per second), which is the same brain wave frequency exhibited in adults in deep sleep. From ages two to six, the predominant brain wave frequency increases to 4 to 8 Hz, or Theta, which is the same brain wave pattern hypnotherapists strive to achieve when attempting to reprogram patients' beliefs and behavior patterns. As we age, our brain wave frequency increases and fluctuates through Alpha (calm consciousness) to Beta (active or focused thought) to Gama waves (peak performance). In a nutshell, up until the age of six years old we are in a highly suggestible and programmable state, absorbing and beholding all as truth from our environment.

In this context, the subconscious mind can easily look like the culprit in all of our self-sabotaging behavior and limiting belief systems. It is also probably true that these beliefs and behaviors – given to us by our parents and other people – may not be in line with the expectations and goals of our current conscious awareness. But before we go blaming all of our bad behavior on our subconscious, let's keep in mind it is the subconscious that also does a darn good job of keeping us alive and successful as a species. It's this mind that blinks your eye for protection before you know what happened and moves your body out of the way of danger before your conscious mind has time to react. The subconscious assimilates an unfathomable amount of information from our environment, teaching us though observation what is safe and unsafe and translating that information into survival skills. No one has to tell you to take the stairs instead of jumping off the sixth floor balcony. You just instinctively know that. The subconscious mind deserves to be respected for the magnitude of its power.

The subconscious and conscious minds are constantly at work, driving our decisions and behavior. The subconscious is the Goliath. The conscious mind is the David. A recent study done by Stanford University professor Baba Shiv and recounted in the book *How we Decide,* by Jonah Lehrer, suggests that the conscious mind needs as little as seven digits to overwhelm its capacity and give way for the subconscious mind to take over driving your behavior. That is a very small amount of information. Basically, if you are trying to remember something as little as a phone number, your subconscious mind springs into action. There are no warning signals, no beeping dashboard lights. Your subconscious takes over with programmed behavior while your conscious mind is focusing on something else. Imagine driving your car and having an intense conversation; then miles down the road you realize you haven't been paying attention to where you were going. Who was driving the car? Your conscious mind was engaged in the discussion while your subconscious mind effortlessly handled driving the car.

The navigation device in your car is only as good as its programming. The same holds true for your subconscious. Don't fret. With time and effort even the subconscious can be reprogrammed. Without reprogramming, don't be surprised if you end up at the same destination over and over again. We will give you shortcuts on how to make those reprogramming changes and chart a new course throughout the remainder of *Life's A Trip*.

The conscious and subconscious are not alone with each other in our mind; the dominating force of the ego joins them. The concept of ego, as we refer to it here, is not the traditional narrow meaning of "inflated sense of self" or "arrogance," but rather the concept of the way the mind *identifies* itself. For example, your ego is who you *think* you are. The ego loves to define itself with labels: mother, brainiac, friend, comic, employee, hot shit tambourine girl, and many others. Without labels, the ego believes it would be nothing.

The ego is constructed of personal beliefs and our self-concept. Author Dan Caro in his inspiring book *Gift of Fire*, describes the ego as a "blinded sense of self that can act like a spiritual anchor by fastening any of us to petty concerns and blocking our creative force."

The ego's job is to pull you out of the current moment, where your True Self lives, and put you into the past or the future. The past helps the ego define itself and gives it self-worth based on previous experiences and accomplishments. The ego especially attaches to psychological traumas and old wounds, which it creatively weaves into our personal stories. Some people carry these stories around with them their whole lives. It's these stories that perpetually taint our current perceptions and constantly reinforce the ego. The future, on the other hand, creates all kinds of glorious possibilities for fantasy. The ego loves to engage in worry, fear, uncertainty, and lack of security and creates make-believe events that almost never play out the way we imagine.

The ego's favorite pastime is to create and engage in problems. In many cases, the problems don't even exist in reality. It is the part of you that fantasizes *I should have said that* or *I am going to do this*. It ruminates, deliberates, and engages you in mindless thought about things that haven't even happened and are quite statistically unlikely to occur. Worrying is a great example of how the ego hijacks thoughts and creates make-believe distractions for us to focus on.

The ego always has an opinion and hates to be wrong. It's your inner critic. It loves to compare and contrast to make itself feel better or more worthy. The ego judges situations, people, and events in an effort to keep your focus external. When you're focusing on what others are or aren't doing, that's one red flag to know the ego has surfaced. The worst offense the ego can suffer is to be humiliated. It drives the ego mad! You will find yourself going to great lengths to disprove, deny, avoid, or avenge any such assault.

The ego also has an insatiable need for approval. There is nothing sweeter than a compliment for the ego to devour. Eckhart Tolle in (one of the best book ever written) *A New Earth* reminds us that the peak elevation we feel when given a compliment is exactly the inverse of how low we can feel when receiving an insult. Unfortunately, external reinforcements never truly satisfy the ego. It always needs more.

As we discussed, the ego has the capacity to distract us from our True Self by means of repetitive thinking patterns and obsession with past and future events by creating drama for the mind to analyze, fantasize, and obsess about. The ego's constant need is to reinforce itself with praise. How does this ego engage us so thoroughly and completely? It uses fear as its weapon of choice. Fear is the root of all negative emotion. If you analyze why you or someone you know is angry, behind the anger is fear of something. Example: I am angry with my husband because he didn't call and tell me he was going to be late. Fear: I am fearful that something happened to him or that he is doing something I would not approve of – fear of loss. Anytime you are feeling a negative emotion, consider that your ego is probably driving your car. Chase that negative emotion back to its root and you will find fear. Unless you are actually being stalked by a gunman, or under real threat, you can bet your ego is conjuring up some fantasy to keep your True Self undercover.

Without your consent or awareness, your ego has appointed itself your "protector" and will spring into action whenever someone calls you out or challenges you. When your ego flares, it does so in varying degrees. Occasionally, the ego goes off the hook and engages in tyrannical escapades. We affectionately call these "Evil Twin episodes." Your Evil Twin is the worst exaggeration of your ego. This Evil Twin abandons all rational thought in the heat of an argument and convinces you to say things you know you shouldn't and will regret later. This Evil Twin goes for the low blow and relishes in the pain it causes. It is the darkest aspect of the ego, and it lives in the depths of your personality. The Evil Twin usually needs to be provoked into action but certain situations and influences can make you more susceptible to its surfacing. It likes to appear when you are under stress, have had too many cocktails, didn't get enough rest, or feel threatened or hurt. The Evil Twin lives in fear of being recognized, not wanting you to gain the knowledge or power of awareness to send it packing.

So how do you control the ego and stop the Evil Twin from driving you off a cliff? It's simple – all you need to do is observe it and catch it before it becomes too powerful. If you are angry, upset, hurt, scared, or frustrated, the ego is in the house. Under observation, the ego will dissipate. The darkness cannot survive the light of awareness; the same way the darkness in a room vanishes when the light switch is turned on. Spiritual masters across the ages have written volumes on how to eradicate the ego. You could spend a lifetime watching, uncovering, and learning about your ego.

We prefer the shortcut approach of taming, not abolishing the ego. It's easier, more practical, and a lot more fun. Sonia Choquette, writer and spiritual intuitive, demonstrates an excellent example of taming the ego in her workshops and writings. We attended one of Sonia's seminars where she asked each of us to identify our ego as our pet. We were challenged to pick the dog breed that best represented the characteristics of our ego. The next step in the exercise was to give it a name. When we started it was tempting to claim that our pet ego was a yellow lab named Buddy, but as we dug deeper we realized that we were describing our personality, not the ego's true identity. After a hilarious, light-hearted bit of soul searching, Karen identified her ego as a German shepherd named Heidi, quick to attack when provoked and trained to kill. Amity's was Trixy, a black standard poodle who has a keen sense of superiority and feels entitled to the finer things in life. Sonia used the analogy of a trained or untrained dog to demonstrate a well-behaved or badly-behaved ego. Put into this perspective, watching and training the ego became fun. While our egos were in training, we did let them off the leash long enough to go ahead and name our husbands' egos too: Dick the Doberman and Buster the Bulldog.

Learn how to operate your navigation system. Recognize and understand all the components and how they work. A smooth trip is in order. Let's get this Road Trip started!

Amity's Story: Future Fantasy

Eckhart Tolle suggests in his book *The Power of Now* that you become acquainted with your ego by monitoring your thoughts and assessing whether you are spending time thinking about the past or the future. After practicing this for a week, my ego and I were incredibly relieved and proud to discover that I spend most of my time in the future – about eighty percent future, twenty percent past. The future, in my head, consists of many different scenarios ranging from, "when I am at the store later…" to "my calendar this week looks like…" to "when I build my dream house someday…" to "when I see that person I'm going to say…." The past in my head was mostly made up of fleeting thoughts like "I should have said…" or "I hope I didn't say anything stupid after all that wine."

I was quite content being future-minded. It appealed to my sense of empowerment and drive. At minimum, I thought it preferable to living in the past or desperately trying to hold on to my bygone glory days, both of which, seem emotionally inept and desperately pathetic.

After completing the exercise for the week, I continued reading Tolle's book. I was shocked to discover that my preferred method of futuristic-thinking was even more absurd than my past thinking. The defining thing that makes future thinking more ludicrous than past thinking is the fact that the past has actually happened. The details of the future are pure fantasy.

Ruminating in the past or future is just the ego doing its job, distracting you with incessant repetitive thought patterns.

Tolle makes this point by drawing a comparison between the ego ruminating in the past or future and an insane person walking the streets talking to themselves. The only difference, he points out, is that the supposed non-crazy person's lips aren't moving! How's that for a reality check? The only thing separating me from needing a straightjacket is the movement of my lips!

Shortcuts

→ Be aware of your mind: subconscious, conscious, and ego.

→ Bringing awareness to your ego will tame it.

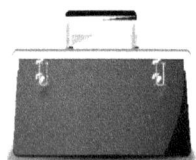

Tool Kit

→ Try to have more positive, conscious thoughts.

→ Recognize that when you are having negative thoughts the ego is driving.

→ Name your pet ego and characterize its breed.

Two Wolves

One evening an old Cherokee told his grandson about a battle that goes on inside people. He said, "My son, the battle is between two wolves inside us all. One is Evil – It is anger, envy, jealousy, sorrow, regret, greed, arrogance, self-pity, guilt, resentment, inferiority, lies, false pride, and superiority. The other is good – it is joy, peace, love, hope, serenity, humility, kindness, benevolence, empathy, generosity, truth, compassion, and faith." The grandson thought about it for a minute and then asked his grandfather: "Which wolf wins?" The old Cherokee simply replied, "The one you feed."

~ Author Unknown

6

THE KEY
UNCOVERING THE TRUE SELF

Now you are ready to hit the road. Your car has been through a complete maintenance check, your engine and electrical system are functioning at peak performance, and you just learned how to operate your navigation system. That's a great start, but unless you have the key, you're not going anywhere. The key for your vehicle, and for your journey, is finding your True Self.

The physical self, the energetic self, the mind, and the ego are all accessories of the True Self. The True Self is the essence of who you are: your spirit, the spark of life that exists in all of us and connects us to all that is. It's the True Self that peers through your little eyeballs and interacts with the world. The more we know and experience our True Selves, the more we can align our lives with our unique individual gifts. The more we express our unique gifts, the more satisfying and content our lives will be.

Unless you've been down this road before, you're like the rest of us, unsure of the essence of your True Self and certainly unaware of how to find it. Finding your True Self is somewhat of an oxymoron because it is totally impossible for you to lose it in the first place. Finding your True Self is really more like an uncovering or reconnecting with your divine nature. Being in touch with your True Self is what holds the key to having it all.

From our experience we have found a few ways to get reacquainted with your True Self. First, remove all the labels your ego has adorned you with: mom, daughter, partner, sibling, employee of the month, bitch, teacher, superstar athlete, friend, badass musician, hot lover, whatever. Notice, even as your thoughts are orchestrating a list of labels to describe your life, your ego is probably getting a bit agitated. Gently tell your ego to get back in the trunk; there is no need to panic. Now that the labels are removed, check out what's left. Are you drawing a blank and still struggling to figure out the essence of who you really are? That's fantastic. Try becoming comfortable sitting in the vastness of the question. Don't chase the question around in your mind. Remember you are already there. Just be, feel your inner being, and let it happen. The more comfortable you become in the blank space, the more pregnant that space will become. This is the True Self emerging. Next, try asking yourself some questions and feel for the answers. What kind of person are you? Are you loving and kind? Do you find joy in doing for others? What inspires you? If the answers elude you, try envisioning the life you desire. What kind of person would you be in that life? Make a list of your attributes and write them down.

Again, notice if your ego or her Evil Twin is getting restless with this exercise. Is the ego sensing that you are looking inside yourself and starting to panic? If so, you may hear a little voice inside your head saying, *This is confusing, I'm bored, what a waste of time.* That is your ego getting pissed. It is so paranoid you will find out who you really are that it will continually try to distract you at every opportunity. The ego knows that when the True Self is at the wheel, the ego has no power, and without power it fears nonexistence. Don't be surprised if you find your ego acting up as you go through the adventure of uncovering the True Self. It is a normal and healthy part of the learning process.

Finding your True Self does not just involve stripping yourself of labels or saying good things and being a good person. It involves living a life where you've aligned yourself with who you really are. We all have special qualities that make us different and unique. It is up to YOU to figure out what those are for you. Here is a shortcut to keep in mind: when you are doing your special thing, it feels different from the rest of what you do. Time flies by and you are energized when you are using your unique gifts. Lord Michael Nolan sums this up best, "There are many things in life that will catch your eye, but only a few will catch your heart…pursue those."

Are you using your special unique qualities and talents? This is what you were born to do, and this is your gift to the world. Your ego may hate to hear it, but your special gift may not be anything complex or earth shattering. It may be something as simple as baking birthday cakes or being a good listener. It is the thing you do that makes you feel great. With no effort required, you do your thing naturally, with love.

Align yourself with your gifts, and watch your world change. Don't talk yourself out of living your bliss with practical mumbo jumbo, like "I have bills to pay." You are not required to do your special thing for your job. Most people don't have that luxury. However, you can practice your special gift as a hobby if you haven't yet found a way to make a living from it. Are you in a sales job in the corporate world but always loved planning parties? Find a way to do what brings you joy as a hobby, and look for ways to incorporate it into your everyday life. Plan parties for yourself or your friends. Keep notes and take pictures to catalogue your parties so you can easily reproduce and share with others. Finding your gift will align you with what feels good. Doing what feels good will bring out more of your unique gifts. Don't be surprised as new avenues unfold before you as you start living your True Self.

On an energetic level, each one of us has a distinct

vibration associated with our True Self. It is as original as a snowflake or a fingerprint. Aligning with your True Self is a metaphor for creating coherence with your individual energy pattern. Panache Desai, a very cool modern day spiritual master, calls this original vibration your "Soul Signature." If you are up for experiencing an energetic shift toward aligning yourself with your True Self, we highly recommend Panache's audio series called, "Reclaiming Your Soul Signature." You can find it at www.panachedesai.com.

How will you know if the key is in the ignition and your True Self is at the wheel? You will feel good. You will feel happy. Other people won't be able to dictate how you live your life. Your inner compass will be steady, and despite other people's expectations, you will feel joy and deep inner peace. You will laugh easily and be open to new ideas and experiences. You will also feel compassion toward yourself and others. Most importantly, life will flow effortlessly and roadblocks will dissipate. Amazing synchronicities will pleasantly surprise you. The whole universe will conspire to support your journey. Uncover your True Self, and you've found the key to making the most of your journey.

Dan's Story: No Hand Man

During our very first Toastmasters meeting, my husband and I (Amity) met Dan Caro. In case you are unfamiliar with Toastmasters, it is an international nonprofit educational organization that operates clubs for the purpose of helping people improve their communication, public speaking, and leadership skills. I decided to attend the meeting that day because I thought joining Toastmasters would help me keep my presentation skills sharp and fill some dead space on my resume. Recently, I had decided to leave the corporate world and stay home with my second child. It was a decision I was not yet comfortable with and I was searching for a way to stay as professional as possible. Kevin and I filled out our nametags and settled into our seats not knowing what to expect. A customary part of a Toastmaster meeting is for a member to practice giving a speech to the group. That fateful day it was Dan's turn. His speech was about tenacity and hard work.

Dan wasn't your ordinary guy. He was covered from head to toe in thick scar tissue caused by a terrible accident when he was two years old. While his mother was mowing the grass, Dan went into the garage after a toy and accidentally kicked over a gas can. The gas and the fumes filled the garage and eventually reached the pilot light on the water heater. In one giant fireball explosion, Dan's skin, diaper, and shoes instantly melted.

Miraculously, the first responders were able to extinguish the flames and save Dan's life. His burns were so severe that no one, not even his parents, expected Dan to survive. A family friend convinced them to seek medical care in Boston at the Shriners Hospital for Children, and within thirty-six hours of the accident, Dan was in the care of one of the world's best pediatric burn care units. Roughly eighty percent of Dan's body was severely burned. His nose, his ears, his lips, and even his eyelids were burned off. Perhaps most painful of all, Dan's parents bore witness to their little boy's charred fingers and toes pealing off during the bandage changes. Against all imaginable odds, the risk of infection, and the severity of his burns, Dan survived.

Dan went on to endure almost eighty reconstructive surgeries. One of those surgeries proved to be life changing. The Shriners were able to fashion Dan with a thumb, of some sort, out of the remaining bone fragments on his hand. His hand functions more like a shallow pincher and his thumb is about four times the size of an average person's. Thanks to this procedure, Dan was eventually able to grasp things with his left hand. This seemingly small enhancement was a game changer.

At the beginning of Dan's speech, I knew nothing of Dan's accomplishments. I had never before seen anyone this burned, and my nursing background provided me with a host of assumptions regarding his physical limitations. I was in awe as he opened his speech in silence. Dan stood in the front of the room with his foot perched up on a wooden bench. He then began to slowly and deliberately tie his shoe! With his left hand he pinched a shoelace and wrapped it around his right wrist; then he carefully picked up the other shoelace and methodically twisted and turned the strings into a functional bow. Dan tying his shoe would be the equivalent of you or me tying our shoes with chopsticks! He later explained that tying his shoes was the single most meaningful accomplishment in his life, and it only took him about 2,555 days to learn. So what's a handless guy supposed to do after he learns to tie his shoes? As if survival, and then learning to tie his shoes, wasn't extraordinary enough, Dan decided to learn to play the drums. One of the many challenges that Dan would have to face in order to play the drums was to first figure out how to hold the sticks. On his right hand he rigged up a contraption using sweatbands and rubber bands. This mechanism allowed the drumstick to vibrate naturally against the drum skins as if it were held in a normal hand. Dan was adamant about learning to hold the other drumstick in his reconstructed left hand, or nub, as he affectionately calls it. When he started, just one strike to the drumhead would send the stick flying out of his hand. It took years for him to build up enough strength to maintain a beat. He relentlessly practiced for at least five hours a day. Through unimaginable hard work and an insane amount of determination, Dan not only became a drummer, he became one of the best jazz drummers in the United States of America. Dan concluded his speech that day by playing the drums. Kevin and I were completely flabbergasted. We shot each other a glance that said, "Oh, we are definitely gonna be friends with this dude!"

Immediately following the speech, we introduced ourselves to Dan. He explained in detail the years it took him to find his preferred method of playing by strapping a drum stick to his right hand and the strength required to grasp the stick in his left. Within minutes we began talking about conscious living and how life's a trip. Kevin had just finished reading Wayne Dyer's *Power of Intention* and recommended it to Dan whole-heartedly. A long friendship began, and for the next couple of years, Kevin and Dan would talk regularly about the latest Dyer material they were learning and assimilating.

Dan had accomplished so much in his life: tying his shoes, mastering the drums, and functioning like a "normal" human being in the world. All of these things, though astounding, were purely accomplishments of his personality and therefore, only temporarily satisfying. Dan was longing for more. He was embarking on an inward journey, a journey to uncover his True Self.

The years that followed were nothing short of remarkable. In the fall of 2009, Dan had a chance meeting with a woman who would change the course of his life. He met her at a pizza joint not far from his home in Mandeville, Louisiana, which is a small town across Lake Pontchartrain from New Orleans. It should come as no surprise that Dan would be found frequenting the local pizza joints since eating pizza requires no fingers for consumption. The woman was born in the area but had left home years earlier. She was back with her daughter to visit family for the week and was intrigued to meet someone as unique as Dan in her small hometown. Upon their meeting, the woman was eager to hear Dan's story and listened with amazement as he described the accident, his recovery and the mind-blowing music career that followed. The woman was astonished and told Dan that she wanted him to meet her boss. She told Dan that her boss was an author – but he lived in Hawaii. Pondering this information, Dan couldn't help himself but ask, "Your boss wouldn't happen to be Wayne Dyer, would he?" Startled, she replied, "YES! How did you know?" By now, Dan was a huge Wayne Dyer fan and had read and listened to everything the man had ever written or said. The woman checked her schedule and told Dan that Wayne would be in Florida in November, and she would arrange for them to meet.

As it turned out, Wayne was headlining an "I Can Do It" event in Tampa put on by Hay House, his publishing company. Dyer was promoting his new book *Excuses Be Gone*. As fate would have it, Dan was scheduled to be in Tampa to speak at a Shriner's convention that very same weekend!

Dan recruited Kevin to go to Tampa to meet Wayne. Words can barely describe the elation the two of them felt as they drove to Florida. It seemed surreal as they reflected on the fact that years earlier, in their very first conversation, they bonded over one of Wayne's books, and now they were venturing across the Southeast to meet Wayne in person! We could hardly wait to see what would happen next.

Wayne is not an easy man to meet. He has an incredibly busy schedule, droves of fans, and many handlers to keep those fans off him. Somehow, Kevin and Dan were able to get close enough to get his attention. Once Wayne saw Dan, he recognized him as the man his assistant wanted him to meet and invited them backstage. Their friendship began, and ultimately Wayne asked Dan to be an example for his new book *Excuses Be Gone* as Dan was a shining example of someone who never used the excuse of HAVING NO HANDS to keep him from PLAYING THE DRUMS!

After receiving a few standing ovations during Wayne's talks, Dan was invited to do a cameo appearance on Wayne's nationally televised annual fundraising event for PBS. He also got a book deal from Hay House. Dan was ecstatic and so were we. To make it even more special, Dan invited us to join him and his parents at the live taping event in California. We were thrilled and the night was a huge success. We watched as Dan told his story in front of his parents for the first time. You could hear a pin drop as Dan worked his way behind the drum set to play. I think the audience would have been thoroughly impressed if Dan could hold a simple beat, but to the astonishment of the crowd,

Dan rocked the house down! There was not a dry eye in the place. It was one of the most beautiful moments I have ever witnessed. Who could have imagined that an even bigger miracle was on its way?

We didn't sleep much that weekend, high on the excitement of the event. On Sunday, we fetched Dan from his high-roller hotel and headed for the airport. We all had a sense of "Pinch me. Did that really happen?" During the ride, we talked of the book to be, the upcoming airing of the PBS show and how best to maximize Dan's newfound opportunities. None of us had any experience in media or promotions, so we decided the best course of action would be to get a hold of the person who appeared with Wayne the year before on PBS and pick her brain about what to expect. That person was Immaculée Ilibagiza, a Rwandan holocaust survivor who wrote the beautiful book *Left to Tell*. The problem was that none of us knew how to get a hold of her or where to find her. Dan figured he could ask someone at Hay House, and we whole-heartedly encouraged him to do so.

The next morning came too early as we awoke from a hard night's sleep in the comfort of our own beds. Kevin left for work while I finally disabled the snooze alarm to sleep in. About an hour later I got a frantic call from Kevin. His voice was as smooth as velvet as he started, "In case you are secretly trying to convince yourself that all of this was just a coincidence.... You won't believe this.... Pay close attention.... This will blow your mind.... Are you ready for this?" One of his employees had called in that morning saying he would be late for work because he had promised his wife he would attend "a thing" at church. Not long after, he called Kevin back and said, "Hey, weren't you guys just in California for the PBS taping? I am over at Mary Queen of Peace, and there is a chick speaking here who said she was discovered by Wayne Dyer and that she was on that show last year."

Immaculée was in Mandeville! She was signing books as we spoke at the church right next to Kevin's office! Dan was already on his way and Kevin hurried across the parking lot to hold a place in the line for Dan until he arrived. As they approached the table where Immaculée was signing books, she looked up and caught a glimpse of Dan. With astonishment she slowly rose from her chair and motioned him to the front of the line. They broke into tears as their outstretched arms turned into embrace. She was flabbergasted to see Dan standing right in front of her. She had just received a call from a friend the night before who had attended the PBS taping and told her all about Dan's inspiring performance. Neither knew that Immaculée's tour would lead her right to Dan's inquiring mind the very next day! Dan was uncovering his True Self, which was conspiring with the entirety of the Universe to bring his story to the masses. Dan's book *The Gift of Fire* was released in 2010.

Shortcuts

→ Seek your True Self.

→ Recognize what you express and do effortlessly.

→ Follow your inner compass.

→ Energetically align with your individual "soul signature."

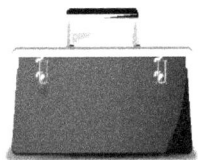

Tool Kit

→ Make a list of your characteristics.

→ Reflect on your life – what brings you joy?

→ Do more of the things that bring you joy.

→ Share your unique gifts.

> "Getting in touch with your true self must be your first priority."
>
> ~ Tom Hopkins

SECTION III

RULES OF THE ROAD

Some people hate rules. Other people worship rules (you know who you are). Whether you love 'em or hate 'em, some rules are just part of life. Road signs, speed limits, and laws of the land are essential rules to obey on any road trip. For our life journey there are fundamental *Rules of the Road* that we must respect and follow also. These five *Rules of the Road* will help make your trip an interesting and meaningful adventure rather than a treacherous escapade. Keep these crucial *Rules of the Road* consciously in mind throughout your entire journey. These essential rules of life apply at all times.

Rules of the Road:

    Chapter 7: Rule #1 – Take Radical Responsibility

    Chapter 8: Rule #2 – Be Grateful

    Chapter 9: Rule #3 – Let Go of Control

    Chapter 10: Rule #4 – Be Present

    Chapter 11: Rule #5 – Love Yourself

    Chapter 12: Ready, Set, Review

7

RULE #1
TAKE RADICAL RESPONSIBILITY

Take radical responsibility. When you get behind the wheel you are taking responsibility for your car, yourself, your passengers, and everyone around you. You have carried this sense of responsibility with you since the day you got your driver's license. We challenge you to expand the feeling of responsibility beyond the construct of your car to encompass your entire existence. Radical responsibility is all about you!

Hey, isn't it about time that everything is about you? That is probably music to your ego's ears, but put that Evil Twin in check and let's take a deeper look into the concept of radical responsibility.

Radical responsibility is the willingness to accept that everything that happens in your life and everyone who is interacting with you - good and bad - is created by you and for your benefit. Yes, EVERYTHING, even if you are too blind, attached, invested, or just plain stupid to see it. It is a very large concept to grasp. Certainly most people don't create tragedies or accidents in their lives on purpose. We are not suggesting that anyone would agree to do so. But we already know there is much more going on in our lives than what we are consciously aware of (refer back to Chapter 5). Not only does our subconscious play a role in what happens daily, but there may be a myriad of other factors that influence the events that unfold in our lives – like fate, karma, and lessons our souls were sent here to learn. It may require some amount of faith to stomach accepting that the good, the bad, and the ugly are all created by us, for our best interest, but we promise if you adopt the attitude of radical responsibility your life will change for the better. You will become one of those people whom you admire, who can roll with the changes and handle life gracefully no matter what comes along. Remember, you can take radical responsibility for everything good in your life too! With radical responsibility you will build character and learn all kinds of juicy and interesting things about yourself.

The first step to shifting into radical responsibility is to stop blaming others – even if they suck! If you are blaming others, it is because you feel victimized in some way. We have all done it to some extent. Some people are subtle in their blame-game; others play it up in dramatic fashion or prefer to play the martyr. What is your style? A pandemic favorite is to point the finger at your crazy mother or your dysfunctional family. Another common pitfall is to be a victim of circumstance or substance abuse. When you point the finger at anyone or anything outside of yourself, you are assigning blame and using it as an excuse to avoid radical responsibility. Get real and empower yourself. You are going to have to give up the victim mentality and identity. The victim mentality is weak and pathetic. You can get what you want and need in much more productive and empowering ways.

The next shift into radical responsibility comes from deciding to stop making excuses. You can simply start by substituting the word "choice" for "excuse." Was it your choice to go to the gym this morning, or did you choose to sleep in?

Did you choose to snap at your kids for being slobs, or did you make the choice to stay calm and ask them to pick up after themselves? Every situation has a multitude of outcomes. Instead of focusing on someone or something that you think is screwing up your world – STOP! You have the power to take responsibility for this situation. If you're in a bad relationship, you can leave or you can stay. If you choose to stay, regardless of reasons or excuses why, you have to take responsibility for the decision. It's all about stepping up. So, if it applies, go ahead and say it, "Yes, I made the choice to stay with a loser." No one forced you – you decided! And don't think that not deciding is a way out of taking responsibility. Doing nothing is also a choice. Doing nothing may be a way of avoiding taking responsibility, but choosing to do nothing may actually be a very smart choice if it provides the time for situations to fall into place and become clear. Radical responsibility doesn't have to be about all the wrong choices in your life. It's simply about being able to recognize our choices. In the must-read book, *Excuses Be Gone,* Wayne Dyer sums this up by saying, "In spite of your history, the one and only place that your excuses originated is in you. Regardless of the age you were when these ideas were implanted; how contagious your early family conditioning was; how frequently you were exposed; and how potent the diseases were in your home, school, church and culture, the responsibility is yours. To live a totally excuse-free life, you must be willing to state: "I adopted these behaviors – I chose all of it. I may have been a child, and I may not have had the skills or natural abilities to resist early influences, but it was still my choice. I take full responsibility for any and all excuse making that I've engaged in." It only hurts a little bit at first. Trust us.

The other way to shift into radical responsibility is to use the principle of "The Mirror." The Mirror suggests that everything you see and experience on the outside is just a reflection of what is going on inside your spirit. You see hate because you have hate in you. You see love because your heart is filled with love. If you ARE love, you only SEE love. It's kind of like when you are in the market for a new car and you have your eye on a certain make and model, all of the sudden you see them everywhere. The awareness in you sees that reflected in the environment. This is a tough one to swallow, we know! We continue to struggle with this on a daily basis. Grasping it is like falling down a rabbit hole into knowing and understanding yourself better. When someone or something is yanking your chain, try to define specifically what is bothering you about that person or situation. Then take that specific and turn it inward and look for the significance inside yourself.

An example is when one of Amity's guy friends introduced her to his baby-mama. She was nice and smart and always made a big effort to be Amity's friend. Something just didn't sit right with Amity about her, besides the fact that she didn't use protection. Whatever it was bothered Amity at a deep level, and her disdain for this girl did not match the situation. Amity could not pinpoint what it was so she prayed about it. In her meditation she realized she felt this person was selling herself short by putting up with her friend's bad behavior in their relationship. When Amity applied the mirror principle, she recognized that it was not the person she did not like; it was the aspect of herself that she had recognized in this woman that made her so incredibly uncomfortable. She actually reminded Amity of a time in her life when, as a young woman, she sold herself short and tolerated abuse from a boyfriend. Once she recognized the root cause was her own feelings about herself and her past, the animosity toward her new friend evaporated.

Next time you look at someone or something and you don't like what you see, turn that awareness inward as if looking in the mirror. Search yourself on the inside for what you don't like on the outside. Recognizing you see things in others because they exist in you is taking radical responsibility.

We are asking you to look in the mirror and choose an attitude of radical responsibility. Specifically say to yourself, "Everyone I meet, every situation placed before me, every problem, every triumph is there for a reason. I have created it. I have chosen it. It exists so that I may gain a greater understanding of myself." Your job is simply to remain open to whatever it is. It may be a challenge for you to implement radical responsibility in your life, but if you do, from this moment forward you will make the most of your journey. You have the knowledge to take full and radical responsibility. You are gaining the knowledge through this book to change your behavior. Remember, not making a decision to change is still making a decision. So don't just watch life throw you curve balls. Man up, get to the plate, be your best, and do your best. Take responsibility for hitting a home run or striking out. Own it!

Taking radical responsibility and using the mirror principle will open your mind to all kinds of possibilities for self-discovery and experiencing life in a different way. Author Bruce Lipton states, "You are personally responsible for everything in your life, once you become aware that you are personally responsible for everything in your life. Once you become aware of this information, you can begin to apply it to reprogram your behavior." You don't have to look much farther than your mirror to know who can take responsibility. The sooner you take radical responsibility, the faster you will stop making excuses and blaming others for your situation and the quicker your situation will change for the better.

Karen's Story: Is Anybody Listening?

I find it very easy to see other people's weaknesses, to see their problems and know how they can fix themselves. However, I have always found it a challenge to look at myself or recognize how I can improve. Every January for the last five years, my husband and I have made out a list of things we wanted to accomplish in the upcoming year. This list often includes financial goals, household updates, trips we want to take, and ways we want to improve ourselves, and our relationships. My goal in 2010 was to undertake some major self-improvement projects and clean up my act. I wanted to attend more yoga classes, meditate more often and become a better listener. The most challenging of these was the listening part. After years of hearing it from my husband and friends, I finally was willing to recognize that I was a terrible listener. Up to this point in my life, my concern had always been about being heard. I felt like people didn't listen to me, or perhaps I wasn't able to find the words to make people understand what I was trying to say. I was aware of my need to work on this area of my life for about two and half years and with that awareness I began to notice how I bullied in conversations. As my awareness grew so did my frustration. I spent a lot of time reflecting on what I should or shouldn't have said. Unfortunately, my reflection wasn't doing anything to help me when I was in the heat of discussion. I needed to change my behavior!

After I made the conscious decision to do the work in 2010, it was like a bright light was shining on my listening problem. I couldn't help but notice my overwhelming desire to interrupt the other person while we were having a conversation. I desperately wanted to spew my own point of view. I rarely heard what the other person was saying. I would get lost in my thoughts and then have trouble finding the words to make my crucially important point.

Meanwhile, I was in the midst of full-blown mommyhood: part-time work, homework, dinners, laundry, and seemingly endless errands. I felt the ceaseless cycle of meaningless jobs held no reward. Sure it was great to spend time with my children, but doing tasks such as homework and their dirty laundry were highly overrated and didn't give me much satisfaction. The feeling that my kids and my husband weren't listening to me or my requests continued to build. If they would only listen, perhaps I would feel better about my daily routine. I pleaded for them to pitch in, pick up their rooms, pick up their backpacks, and without resistance, they agreed. Predictably, their cooperation lasted about one day! I found myself pestering, nagging, and feeling a growing resentment that no one valued what I was saying. Did they not hear me? Hello? Am I irrelevant? My requests were falling on deaf ears. I would repeat myself two or three times. I was pissed off and my nagging was even starting to drive ME crazy. Fantasies of going on Mommy Strike were playing loudly in my mind.

While escaping to Facebook for a well-deserved break from the chaos, a post grabbed my attention. It said, "The negativity and anger you see in others is actually inside of you." Instantly it snapped me out of my frustration and back into "My Mirror." I went for a run where I always do my best processing. It's the combination of the exercise and being outdoors that helps me put everything into perspective. While running, I recognized that during the first lap through the neighborhood I was still focusing on the behavior of my husband and kids. I had rampant thoughts of going home to make chore charts and implement punishment and reward systems. Then it dawned on me that again I was focusing externally about how to fix my family. I stopped and figuratively got out "My Mirror" and decided to take a look at how that Facebook post could be all about me. I replayed the quote in my head a few times, rounded my second lap, and then there it was. With warm sun beaming on my face, a beautiful blue sky in my view, I felt clarity. It was so simple. How could I have not seen it? I laughed out loud to myself and giggled the rest of the way home. When I reached the house, I ran inside to tell my husband my new revelation.

"Guess what!" I said excitedly to my husband. "I know why you and the children aren't listening to me." Puzzled and apprehensive, he asked, "Why?" With exclamation I confessed, "BECAUSE I'M NOT A GOOD LISTENER!" We laughed and laughed. I immediately made a conscious effort to be a better *listener. Now I actively force myself not to think of my next sentence before someone else has finished theirs. And guess what happened? My children and hubby miraculously got better. They started listening. The children responded when I asked them to do something and tasks got done even without having to raise my voice. "The Mirror" offered me a simple revelation that helped me initiate a small change, which led to such a big payoff. So simple, yet so transforming.*

Shortcuts

→ Take radical responsibility.

→ Know the world is a reflection of what is going on in you.

→ "Be the change you want to see in the world." ~ Gandhi

Tool Kit

→ Point the finger inward instead of outward.

› Give up victimhood. Choose empowerment.

→ Make "Choices" instead of "Excuses."

→ Stay in front of "The Mirror," figuratively not literally.

> "Be willing to say these words and mean them: 'I'm the product of all of the choices I've made in my life. I have no one to blame for anything that isn't going the way I'd like it to go, including myself.'"
>
> ~ Wayne Dyer

8

RULE #2
BE GRATEFUL

Gratitude is like having air freshener in your car. Being grateful makes life sweeter. Gratitude also aligns you with positive energy and as we discussed earlier, positive energy attracts more positive energy. Being grateful is a magnet to attract more of what you'll be grateful for. Gratitude is what keeps us in the auspicious flow of life. Being grateful is an attitude for your life's journey, an important rule of the road.

Being grateful is a habit. So is being ungrateful. It is a habitual product of the way our brains process information. To be more grateful simply takes practice. The more you do it, the more grateful you will feel, and being grateful makes you feel GREAT! In *The Happiness Project*, Gretchen Rubin explores how gratitude is important to happiness. She states, "Studies show that consistently grateful people are happier and more satisfied with their lives; they even feel more physically healthy and spend more time exercising."

One of the simplest ways to be grateful is to focus on what you have, not on what you don't have. Follow the Tenth Commandment: Thou shalt not covet. Coveting is a gratitude killer. Rubin goes on to say, "Gratitude brings freedom from envy because when you're grateful for what you have, you're not consumed with wanting something different or something more. That, in turn, makes it easier to live within your means and also be generous to others." If your attention is focused on what you don't have, let's say, a bigger house or a better-paying job, you are probably missing the good attributes about your home and the co-workers you enjoy. All the good stuff around you is taken for granted and you end up miserable. Instead, keep yourself consciously focused on what you have. Be grateful.

Looking on the bright side is another way to cultivate gratitude. It is a choice that can make the difference between misery and joy. One of Amity's cousins had a premature baby. Katie was only 1.3 pounds at birth. Her parents set up a webpage at CaringBridge.org within days of the delivery to keep friends and family informed about Katie and her mother. Despite the many challenges – surgeries, brain bleeds, infections, fevers, low oxygen level, and many other setbacks – they focused intently on the bright side. They posted almost daily about Katie's strength, her will to live, and her beautiful little body. With amazing fortitude they kept everyone up to speed on all the tests and procedures that were required and eloquently requested prayers for good outcomes. Five months later, little Katie was able to leave the hospital and come home. Her parents continue to focus on all the positives. No one knows at this point what the extent of Katie's disabilities might be, but her parents are committed to providing her with the best chance possible by giving her the best physical therapy and diligently attending to her medical, emotional, and physical needs. With this approach, they are able to enjoy the small strides Katie makes on a daily basis, and they relish in the amazing progress she has made. For them, having a sweet baby to hold in their arms is the brightest joy they could have hoped for.

Appreciation is another form of gratitude. We challenge you to tell people what you appreciate about them. Start with your family or anyone you live with and don't get discouraged if you feel awkward at first. Look them in the eye and say it with conviction and authenticity. Once you become comfortable doing this with family members, start to expand your appreciation compliments to your friends and co-workers. Soon you will be a natural, and you can try it on the perfect strangers who serve you throughout the day at the store, the local post office, or gas station. Go ahead. Have fun with it. It's like casting a magic spell on people. It will help them feel good about themselves, and they will smile. They will do their jobs better and work harder to please you and other people. They may even be nice to someone else. Why? Because it feels good to be appreciated and people like it! You will find the magic isn't just limited to the person getting the compliment. You, yourself, will also be positively affected. It feels good to make someone's day, and you will smile too. It also helps train your eye to see the best in people, and when you spend your time focused on the positives, the negatives just don't seem so apparent as they once did. You will start to like people more, and they will probably like you back. And best of all, by reinforcing people's good behavior you will get more of that good behavior! People will become what you reinforce. So why not make it positive? The magic of wielding your appreciation will help others, including you, become their best and experience more gratitude.

There are some shortcuts to help you increase your sense of being grateful. One simple tool is to keep a gratitude journal. Before going to bed each night, jot down at least three things that you were thankful for that day on a note pad. This will force you to make a conscious effort to look for things to be grateful for in your daily life. The other benefit is your brain will marinate in gratitude all night. When your gratitude journal is overflowing, and you find yourself filling pages and pages every night, you'll know you've got the hang of it. Another way to build expressing gratitude into your day is to give thanks at mealtime. Try giving thanks for your food and then take turns going around the table to share what each person is thankful for that day. If you are alone, do it silently to yourself. It still works. Building it into a part of your daily routine will help establish expressing gratitude as habit, and you will begin to live in gratitude.

World-renowned, mind-body healing pioneer Deepak Chopra says, "When you want something you have to give it." Give someone something to be grateful for, and you will also experience gratitude. Another practical shortcut to elevate gratitude in your life is to give of yourself and help others. There is plenty of evidence to show that when people give to others, they experience a genuine boost of happiness and gratitude. Researchers at the National Institute of Health suggest that altruism activates the same regions of the brain that light up when we have pleasurable experiences like sex and eating chocolate. Go ahead and donate your time, your attention, and your talents. You can do this through big organizations like nonprofits, schools or hospitals or you can give in equally important ways to your friends, your neighbors, and your family members. Try to do one small act of kindness a day even if it is as small as holding a door for someone or picking up a piece of trash. Doing good deeds and being generous help increase your sense of gratitude naturally. Researchers from Harvard University and the University California, San Diego, found that the influence of generosity extended three degrees of separation. In other words, each time you commit an act of kindness you will influence three other people to do the same who will influence nine others to do the same and so on. Generosity, therefore, is exponential. Now *that* is something to be thankful for.

If you are having trouble feeling gratitude in your life, or if you simply want more of it, here is an exercise that will help you actually experience the feeling of being grateful and even intensify it. Sit or lie down with your spine straight. Calm and relax your breathing. Now think of something you are grateful for, thankful for, or something you appreciate about a person, place or thing. Feel that thought in your head. With intention, move that thought from your head, down your neck and into the center of your chest. Now feel that grateful, thankful, or appreciative thought with your heart. Be still. Imagine the thought feeling warm or like a bright light in your chest. Assign a color to it and bask in it. Enjoy the feeling. Now expand that feeling from your chest, down your arms and through your hands, down your torso, down your legs, through your feet, up your neck into your shoulders and down your arms, up into your face and through the top of your head. Imagine the light and warmth throughout all the cells of your body. Then imagine the feeling growing more intense and spilling beyond the boundaries of your body, expanding beyond your physical body and filling the room, consuming the building and then pouring out into the world. A few minutes of this simple exercise will radically transform negative energy and thought forms. It will leave you feeling relaxed, centered, and rejuvenated. Go ahead, put down the book and try it! Your back seat drivers will wait.

Actively cultivating gratitude will urge you to consciously look for reasons to be grateful. Studies suggest that people are significantly happier when they practice gratitude. Soon you will find yourself turning lemons into lemonade and seeing the best in everyone and everything. Gratitude will become a habit and your natural state. You will find millions of little things to be grateful for. You will see the beauty in nature and be thankful for it. It will help you see the best in other people and in yourself. Being grateful just takes a little effort and practice.

Best of all, in gratitude, you will start experiencing why… **Life's a Trip.**

Amity's Story: Act of God

I can't remember exactly how in the hell I let my husband convince me to quit my job, but I am sure if I had been paying closer attention to our financial situation, I would have put up a bigger fight. In all fairness, having our second child, owning a salon, and starting a new company made it pretty unrealistic to continue my traveling employment. We bit the bullet, gave up the benefits, and joined the ranks of the self-employed. It hurt. It took awhile to get over longing for my old jet-setting, sushi lifestyle but I handled it pretty well. Our friends were taking lavish vacations, buying vacation homes, and getting promoted. Still, we remained committed to the risks we had decided to take and the payoff that we hoped would someday come.

During this time in our lives my husband, Kevin, fell in love with this green technology product. He signed a contract to be a commission-only sales representative. The technology reduces power consumption and results in lowering power bills 9 to 15%. What could be easier to sell, right? Large companies could save millions with this product. Not so fast. These were the Bush era days of no global warming, and Louisiana, where we lived, was just getting its head around recycling. It proved to be a long, hard process. Fortunately, when my husband falls in love with something, he is not easily deterred. Two years later, Kevin was getting close to his first million-dollar deal with a large well-respected US company. The account was estimated to save 15 to 20 million a year if they rolled out nationwide, and we had an enthusiastic guy on the inside championing the project. After months of testing the product in various locations, the results were looking stellar. Based on the preliminary test results and savings alone, I thought it was a done deal. The last test was scheduled to end on August 29, 2005. We knew it would be a fateful day.

The test was going exceptionally well, and the corporation was pushing the project through all the layers of red tape. We were finally at the contract phase. Kevin was giving me daily updates. When the deal was done, I would have a lot-o-money and I could taste it. I started looking at fashion magazines and dreaming of building a house again. Kevin could almost smell the leather in the new car he desperately needed. We knew that once this deal was done, the next one would be easier and then the next, and the next, and the next. Soon I would be living large. The excitement mounted. One day Kevin came home from work with a smile on his face I will never forget. In his hand was a SIGNED CONTRACT!

I was off the hook! Credit card in hand, at the starting gate, I was just waiting for the sound of the gun. All the things I was coveting would be mine!!!!!! Our fateful date was fast approaching. We already knew the results would seal the deal and move us into the installation phase, which meant mucho dinero for Mamma.

It never happened. On Monday, August 29th, while we were all set to finish the test the equipment was now 12 feet under the ravenous waters of Hurricane Katrina. It turned out that our fateful day was more fateful than expected. The corporation cancelled the entire contract, citing "unforeseeable acts of God." Our champion inside the organization suddenly had much more important business to worry about than dealing with us. He lost his house and retirement home, had a heart attack, and retired. It was over. No deal.

I was crushed. All the shiny new things I would buy – gone, done. Under the stress of living in a federal disaster area, losing the contract and trying to rebuild our businesses destroyed by Katrina, I had some of my least proud moments, the culmination of which was my threat to cut my husband's balls off in the middle of the night if he ever mentioned that damn product again!

Busting my ass, covered in hair with my feet killing me, I was forced to face the reality of working long hours in our salon to try to stay afloat while our town, our businesses, and our hopes for our future were decimated.

So how does one recover? The only way I knew I could do it was through gratitude. I pulled myself together and decided to force myself into being grateful. It's actually not that hard to find something to be grateful for in the midst of a disaster. Compared to other people, at least I had a roof over my head, right? Tree damage starts to look good when you compare it to water damage. We still had our salon. We just needed to wait long enough for the people to come back to get haircuts. My parents even let our kids stay with them and go to school until our schools reopened. I was so grateful! The gratitude was pouring in. Even the little things would make me weep. We had MREs (meals ready to eat) from the military, and they weren't as disgusting as you might expect, thanks to our little jar of Tabasco. The list could go on and on: hot water, electricity, beer, make-up, my husband, our health and safety.... But, through gratitude, I found my center again. With the exception of my basic needs, nothing shiny could make me any more or less happy.

P.S. Occasionally, my husband reminds me how lucky I am that I never made good on the threat to cut off his family jewels.

Shortcuts

→Be grateful.

→Being grateful is a habit.

→People who express gratitude are happier.

→Express your gratitude.

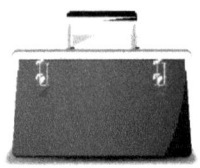 **Tool Kit**

→ Focus on what you DO have, NOT on what you don't have.

→ Look on the bright side.

→ Express appreciation.

→ Keep a gratitude journal.

→ Give thanks before meals.

→ Give of your time and attention. Perform a service to others.

→ Practice the gratitude meditation.

> "The unthankful heart... discovers no mercies; but let the thankful heart sweep through the day and, as the magnet finds the iron, so it will find, in every hour, some heavenly blessings!"
>
> ~ Henry Ward Beecher

9

RULE #3
LET GO OF CONTROL

We have a confession to make. Karen is a control freak. She is not alone. Many of us like that warm fuzzy feeling of knowing exactly how things will happen. We like the notion that somehow we are directing The Road Trip. We believe that by reading the map, following a plan, and listening to our Navigation System we are in control of when and where we will arrive. Newsflash: being in control is a delusion. This delusion is created by the ego, our darling Evil Twin, who thinks it controls all the details in the universe, which in turn makes us feel safe. The ego creates an illusion of safety by using its weapon of choice: control. Here's the reality check: You cannot control anything or anyone but yourself! The more we buy into the notion of control, the more we feed and reinforce our ego instead of our True Self.

Control and controlling behavior are not like an on and off switch. They are more like the volume dial on your car radio. A small amount of volume is pleasing to our senses, just as a small amount of control in life is necessary to function. When applied to ourselves, in the form of self-control, it is considered discipline.

Discipline can help us live healthy, productive lives.

However, when we seek to control others or we attempt to control things that are beyond our control, we create misery for ourselves and for those around us. Just like the volume dial in your car, a little bit is nice, but an excessive amount of control (or volume) can be flat out abusive to others and our selves.

To understand how this really works, we need to look at a subcomponent of control: attachment. Attachment is all the ways we think someone or something should be. When we use the word "should" it is a verbal expression of our individual opinion and nothing more. The problem with this opinion is that it is always emotionally attached, in some way, to an expectation. When our expectations are not met, we feel discomfort and pain. Unfortunately, most of our expectations are not rooted in reality anyway. So stop yourself!

Here is a common yet simple example: You're sitting in traffic and you're getting angry. Hopefully you're sane enough to realize it would be a ridiculous notion to think you could control the traffic — but perhaps not. Regardless of the rational argument, your frustration continues to mount. In your mind, you hear yourself saying, *}#&! *This traffic shouldn't be here at this hour. I should have left earlier.*

Look deeper at why you are about to explode. The frustration is not coming from the traffic itself. That would be redonkulous (extremely ridiculous); the frustration is coming from the attachment to when you need to be somewhere or the attachment to how you think your day should go. Fueled by our attachment, we attempt to control the traffic. Beware! Attachments and expectations can make us crazy. When your blood starts to boil, pay attention! You'll most likely find an unrealistic attachment or expectation underneath.

An easy way to recognize if you are having unrealistic expectations is to start noticing when you speak the word "should." When you hear yourself say it or think it, take a step back and evaluate what expectation that "should" is attached to. Psychologist Clayton Barbeau refers to this as "shoulding on yourself." It sounds a lot like "shitting on yourself" for a reason. Once you have mastered the skill of catching yourself "shoulding on yourself," then you can start to consciously let go of those judgments and expectations. This is the beginning of the process of letting go of attachment and ultimately letting go of control.

Letting go of the attachment and realizing our true lack of control go hand in hand. We cannot control other people, situations, or outcomes. So for all the control freaks out there...what can we control? We can only control our own reactions and ourselves. We can know what we want and set our intentions. The rest is out of our control.

Karen's Story: Adventure in Home Sales

While living and working in Michigan, my husband got a job offer that would move us back to his home state of Florida. Feeling confident about his new opportunity and returning to familiar territory, we decided to buy in Tampa before selling in Michigan. Bad move. Not only did we buy at the top of the market in Florida, the real estate market was starting to slide in the North.

We had sold homes before, so we knew exactly what to do and were not worried. We contacted realtors, painted walls, manicured the lawn, and researched the market to price the house right. The house was on a cul-de-sac and in good condition, so there was no reason to think that we would have any problem selling the home. It was a beautiful house with a great yard, and plenty of young children lived in the neighborhood. There was a two-mile stretch of dirt road to travel in order to reach our paved subdivision, but this was very common in the town so we thought nothing of it.

Despite my well-laid plans and preparations, our house sat on the market for months. Because we had already bought a new home in Tampa, we were forced to use up our savings and 401k to make both mortgage payments. I was getting nervous. For showings I baked cookies and put out fresh flowers, and we lowered the price below the competition's. There was no detail unaccounted for. We were eager to do anything to sell the house. Not only was I motivated by paying two mortgages, but my husband's departure date to Florida was rapidly approaching. I would soon be alone with three small children.

My thoughts were consumed with why people were not interested in the house. I became obsessed with scrutinizing every detail. I scrupulously monitored what my realtor was and wasn't doing. I wanted more open houses, more marketing strategies — and again we lowered the price, now far below the original price and our competition. The realtor speculated that the dirt road was a deal breaker. Soon after, anytime someone came to look at the house I immediately thought *that dirt road is going to ruin it for us; this house won't sell.* My family offered all kinds of advice about what to do to sell the house, including the Catholic tradition of burying a statue of St. Joseph in the front yard.

Willing to try anything, I immediately rummaged through our Christmas decorations to find St. Joseph. To my chagrin, I found him glued tightly to the Nativity. Now, I really thought that burying this statue would help sell the house, but I didn't know if forcibly removing him would also initiate some unknown curse. After a millisecond of consideration and a decision to plead ignorance, I got down to business. A few hard whacks, a handy handsaw and some elbow grease was all it took to liberate St. Joseph. Next, he went headfirst into the front yard.

I went to bed that evening thinking *now the house will sell*. But it didn't. I tried more ideas, praying to various saints and performing a Novena (Catholic ritual of praying for 9 consecutive days). In the back of my mind I knew that dirt road was a problem. I continued to relentlessly control the situation mentally. After many months of worrying, obsessing, and making myself sick, I finally decided to give up. I said my prayers that night and told God I was over it. I was done worrying, done thinking about it, and done trying to do something about it! I gave up and turned it over to God. He would handle it, the right person would show up at the right time, and He had it under control.

Three weeks later a young couple came to look at the house. Ironically, the agent who showed them the house decided to buy it.

In retrospect, the moment Karen decided to give up control of the situation was the moment she got out of her own way, and the universe began to conspire for her highest good. The St. Joseph statue has worked for many people. Perhaps that is precisely why so many Catholics swear by it. For Karen, burying the statue did not accomplish the goal because she was unable to let it go and trust the process. If religious symbolism helps you relinquish control and give it up to God (or the universe or whatever you call it), then go for it.

So how do we give up our controlling nature and release our attachments? First, we need to recognize what we are doing when it is happening. A good way to start practicing this is to notice when we are feeling uncomfortable (irritable, angry, impatient, negative, etc.) Then ask ourselves, "What is it that I need that I am not getting right now?" Once we can answer this question, it will provide us with an obvious path to what is creating that negative feeling. Once we are able to bring this into conscious awareness, we can replace those thoughts with a positive affirmation, phrase, or mantra.

Here is a simple example: *I am feeling angry while I do the dishes.* Recognize that you are uncomfortable and angry. Ask yourself what you are not getting right now that is causing you to feel uncomfortable. *I recognize that I am not getting help from my family to keep the house in order. I have an expectation that is not being met.*

Now you can separate yourself from the uncomfortable feeling and decide to change your expectation, or you can decide to ask for help. Perhaps no one is home at the moment and you are wasting your energy fantasizing about controlling other peoples' behavior when they're not even home. Or perhaps you just need to clearly express your needs and expectations. Either way, going through this exercise brings awareness to control and attachments. This diffuses the emotional energy, which is really just a symptom of the core issue. Once awareness is established, you can then replace the controlling thoughts with a positive affirmation. *I am doing the dishes because I enjoy a clean house.* Repeat. Repeat.

Letting go of control is serious business. People express varying degrees of control in all aspects of their lives. Exerting control at work may be very productive but exerting control in your personal life may be smothering to those you care about. It is our individual responsibility to increase our awareness of the ways in which we attempt to control situations and other people. It requires honesty and courage to let go of expectations, attachments, and control. Sometimes it is downright scary! Best selling author, Daphne Rose Kingma, describes it like this: "Letting go is scary. It's a free fall, an act of surrender. It's releasing ways of being and things you thought were important, and then being okay with the fact that they're gone. Though it can feel like passivity, letting go is in fact a shift in consciousness that's a critical part of how you will solve the problem."

The fear created by the ego is what makes it difficult for us to let go of control. Faith is great medicine for fear. You have heard it before, "Let go and let God." We need to trust that despite our own best efforts (or in many cases our worst) there is a greater force at work in our lives. Call it God, call it the exchange of energy, call it karma, call it chaos or maybe even fate. It is all the same thing, and it is out of our control.

If this thought makes you feel uncomfortable, out of control and/or scared, remember fear is born in the ego, not the True Self. The truth is, with our limited perceptions, how could we possibly know what is best for us? It takes time, space, and a larger perspective to realistically interpret the events in our daily lives. What you may be dealing with now will undoubtedly look like a different animal later.

In art there is a great example of what limited perspective looks like. Have you ever seen a photo mosaic created from hundreds of smaller pictures? From far away, it looks like an image of a flower or a portrait of someone famous, but when you get up close you discover that the entire picture is really made up of many tiny individual pictures. Our daily lives, in present time, are like one of the many little pictures. We are only focusing on one tiny piece. As we gain perspective through getting older and wiser, we are able to take a step back and see a bigger picture. The big picture is made up of all the little circumstances, people, and details that make up our lives.

Even when we strive to live consciously and seek to see the big picture, it is impossible to see the true reality. It takes time, including future events, for the meaning of our lives to unfold. This requires us to reserve judgment and keep an open mind and heart. Faith can calm the ego's desire to have it all figured out and misuse control. In Marianne Williamson's book, *A Return to Love*, she states, "When we stop trying to control events, they fall into natural order, an order that works. We're at rest while a power much greater than our own takes over and it does a much better job than we could have done. We learn to trust that the power that holds galaxies together can handle the circumstances of our relatively little lives. Surrender means, by definition, giving up attachment to results. When we surrender to God, we let go of our attachment to how things happen on the outside and we become more concerned with what happens on the inside."

Letting go and trusting in the natural order of things does not mean that everything is going to be rosy. Intuitively we know this, and that's probably why it's so scary to let go of control. Remember control is only a tool of the ego. Life is filled with unexpected events and crazy circumstances outside of our control. Universally, people report stories of great adversity that were beyond their control. During times of great despair, you wouldn't exactly see someone touting the benefits of their misery, but for many, that adversity turns out to be their greatest triumph.

On our road trip through life we can plan our destination, and we can plan our route. From there we need to learn to take what comes. We can't control if we get a flat, if the weather is treacherous, or if there is a twenty-car pile up. We can only control our own perceptions and how we respond to what our journey has to offer. Life is full of surprises! As you practice peeling away layers of your own controlling nature, we recommend using a mantra to support your efforts. A mantra is a phrase you repeat over and over to yourself. It will help you focus your thoughts and support the change you are seeking. For example, "I can only control my reactions, not other people" or "My greatest challenges may be my greatest blessings," or our favorite, "Just let it be."

Amity's Story: Birthday Gift

Madly in love with a former Marine, I had finagled my way into an academic scholarship to justify moving halfway across the country. I attended a Catholic University strategically located close to my crush. My parents didn't particularly want to pay for private out-of-state tuition, and I was not Catholic. I was, however, determined to live in close proximity to the man my dad referred to as "The Pair of Jeans." A damn, fine pair of jeans, as far as I was concerned.

I had met Frank in my hometown when I was 17 years old during a party while he was on leave from the Marine Corps. He was stationed with a mutual friend at Camp Lejeune in North Carolina. He held my hand while we stood around a bonfire, and I felt weak in the knees. That evening I broke my curfew to stay with him as long as possible, and we made plans to see each other the next night. Unfortunately, my parents had a different plan. I was grounded instead.

In the prehistoric days before email and cell phones, I relied on my friends to communicate my no show. Frank left town before we could exchange numbers or addresses. I didn't know if I would ever see him again, but I couldn't get him out of my mind. The mere thought of him would flip my stomach and give me goose bumps.

A few months later my friend Ann invited me to go on a road trip to Camp Lejeune to visit her boyfriend. I jumped at the chance. We put the word out through the grapevine to let Frank know we would be coming, and we crafted a plan that our parents would agree to. Off we went.

Fourteen hours later — and six hours late — we finally arrived. As we walked passed the window at the Denny's where we were meeting, I glanced in and saw Frank sitting at the booth with Ann's boyfriend. Every hair on my body stood on end. Ann's boyfriend was upset about how late we were, and they quickly started to argue. Frank suggested we take off and leave the two of them to their misery before their fight escalated into an abrupt end to our vacation. We spent a fantastic weekend together and our fondness grew. This time we parted with a promise to see each other again, and we stayed in touch through letters and occasional phone calls.

I finished up high school and started cosmetology school. I took one more trip to North Carolina to see Frank. We spent hours riding along the coast on his motorcycle. I etched the feeling of the wind in my hair and my arms around his strong body into my mind. I used that image throughout the coming months to soothe the longing to be with him.

Time was approaching for me to move out of my parents' house and get a degree. Frank had returned home to Jamestown, New York, after an honorable discharge. Somewhere along the line, probably during a "drunk dial" call in the middle of the night, Frank suggested that I move to New York to go to college. All I needed was the invitation, and with the blessing of my mother, I made it happen. I drove across the country, in the middle of winter, moved into my first apartment in the attic of an old house. It was a long, cold winter, and young love had its challenges.

Frank had many great attributes. He was intelligent, strong, determined, and most important to me at age 18, good looking. Despite all of his good qualities he, at the ripe old age of 22, was not so gentle, romantic, or amiable. Frank had grown up fatherless, despite the fact that his dad lived only a few short blocks away from him his entire life.

One evening, Frank and I had just left the grocery store. On the way home he informed me that we had been standing right next to his father in the checkout line. They never so much as acknowledged each other! Frank had been left to his own devices, combined with the influence of the U.S. Marine Corps, to define his own version of masculinity.

Frank showed his "strength" through a lack of tender emotion. One of the ways this presented itself was by never acknowledging birthdays. He would say that a birthday was just another day on the calendar invented by Hallmark, with the exception of his mother's, of course. I was not so lucky as to qualify. The first few years I protested, but eventually I gave up and learned to celebrate with friends or family.

Despite the turmoil of young love and both our shortcomings, we managed to stay together for five years. I planned for graduation, my career as a nurse, and a life with Frank. Everything was on track and under control.

The summer before my senior year, my roommate Sue and I set off on a road trip to Hot Springs, Arkansas. My parents had purchased their retirement home there and graciously offered to let us use it despite not being able to join us. When we arrived, I called my dad to let him know we had arrived safely and that everything was in good order. We talked for about a half hour and caught up with all of life's business. A few minutes after we had hung up, he called back. It seemed odd to me that he would call so soon after such a lengthy conversation, and I sensed that something was wrong. In his voice was a tone of seriousness and concern that I found disturbing and unfamiliar as he told me, "Frank was in a motorcycle accident." An air of denial washed over me as I turned to glance at Sue through the screen door. She stood frozen in fear, as if she already knew what my father was about to say, "He is gone, Amity, Frank is dead."

My eyes were locked with Sue's as my father's words tripped over my brain. Blackness crept into my field of vision. A few moments later, I felt my knees burning. Why were my knees burning? In an instant I popped back into awareness to find myself circling on my hands and knees, phone held to one ear, roving the living room carpet while Sue stood over me sobbing. Life as I knew it shattered in an instant. It just happened to be my birthday.

It took years to dismantle the attachment I had to how life was "supposed" to be. I was lonely, lost, and I believed I would never love again. In my despair and search to regain meaning in my life, I read many books about spirituality and learned from great spiritual teachers old and new. I scoured my soul, faced my inner victim, and slowly I changed. My heart opened, I began to live again.

Eventually I met and married my perfect partner. In him I found all the things I loved about Frank: intelligence, self-sufficiency, a love of music, and of course extra good looks. I also got everything else necessary to make a marriage complete: an occasional romantic, a sensitive but masculine man, a great husband and father, and most important, a best friend.

This story illustrates, in a dramatic way, just how unpredictable life is. Amity had her life totally planned out and then reality changed in an instant. During the grief and loneliness that followed her loss, she could never have imagined that the love she craved and the life she desired was organizing and making its way to intersect her path. All she could do was learn to release her attachment and expectations to embrace her new reality.

Shortcuts

→ Recognize your need or desire to control and let it go.

→ Don't control or excessively analyze the details.

→ Release attachment.

→ Have faith. Life events are part of the big picture.

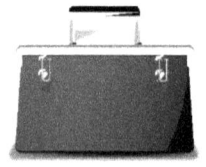 **Tool Kit**

→ Stop using the word "should."

→ Recognize your expectations.

→ Identify thoughts of control, attachment, or expectation, and reframe the situation into a positive affirmation.

→ Use a mantra.

> "Letting go doesn't mean we don't care. Letting go doesn't mean we shut down. Letting go means we stop trying to force outcomes and make people behave. It means we give up resistance to the way things are, for the moment. It means we stop trying to do the impossible – controlling that which we cannot – and instead, focus on what is possible – which usually means taking care of ourselves. And we do this in gentleness, kindness, and love, as much as possible."
>
> ~ Melody Beatie

10

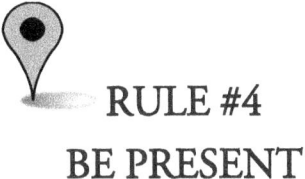

RULE #4
BE PRESENT

Being present while you are driving your vehicle is the most important factor to determining your safety and enjoyment on the road. The less distracted you are, the faster you can react to anything unexpected that may cross your path. Being present doesn't just keep you safe, but it also enhances your enjoyment while driving. Paying attention to the scenery, noticing people in the cars around you, and staying connected and engaged with your environment makes your trip more fun and memorable. Living in the moment accomplishes the same things in your life journey. When you are focused on the present, you are not expending energy on the past or the future, and thus, when life throws you mayhem, you are able to react more adeptly. Also, being present increases your well-being and your appreciation for life. Being present is being in the Now. It is the only moment that matters. The moment you are in is the only moment you can control. It makes the past and the future irrelevant and is the only place where truth exists.

To understand this rule of the road better, let's first

discuss what it is to NOT be present. Many of us go about our day in a task-oriented mode. We follow a to-do list moving from one task to another, crossing each off the list as we go. While we are doing one thing, we are thinking about the next. We hurriedly move toward the next thing we need to do. If you'd like a litmus test for how good you are at living in the present, notice how you handle waiting. How often do you feel like you are waiting? While you are waiting, how uncomfortable are you? An excerpt from *Practicing the Power of Now* by Eckhart Tolle states, "Waiting is a state of mind. Basically, it means that you want the future; you don't want the present. You don't want what you've got, and you want what you haven't got. With every kind of waiting, you unconsciously create inner conflict between your here and now, where you don't want to be, and the projected future, where you want to be. This greatly reduces the quality of your life by making you lose the present."

No one likes to waste time. The only real way you can waste time is to not be present in the current moment or the Now. This moment will slip away forever unused to its fullest extent, wasted, never to be recaptured.

In the fog of our task-oriented, self-directedness, we miss out on the life that is actually going on all around us. Our thoughts are consumed with problems and pressures, the past and the future. Michael Brown, author of *The Presence Process,* says, "By habitually dwelling in the mental state that enables us to reflect and project our attention into these illusory places, we are missing out on the very real physical and emotional experiences happening to us *right now.*" As we discussed earlier in Chapter 5: *Navigation System –Who's Driving*, our egocentric mind is constantly pulling us away from the current moment where our True Self lives. The ego is in constant competition with the moment of the Now. Remember, it is our job to train our ego to take a back seat to our True Self. We know the ego can be very useful in planning and strategizing, but the ego needs to be at our command; we need not be slaves to our ego. Instead of being distracted by planning dinner, thinking about the piles of laundry you have to do, or about the work emails you need to respond to, shift your thoughts to the present moment. Be where you are mentally, physically, emotionally, and spiritually. If you are doing laundry think about *doing laundry*. That sounds disturbing, doesn't it? We can hear you saying, "Surely there are more productive things to think about than laundry." But actually, intently focusing on mundane tasks is excellent practice to train yourself to be present! Feel the texture of the towels, concentrate on the folds, carefully carry the basket into your room, and diligently put the clothes away into drawers. Honestly, there isn't anything more productive or important than experiencing the current moment to its fullest.

This is why, once you start making a habit of being truly present – with the cashier at the grocery store, with your co-workers, with your spouse and children – you will begin to understand and appreciate that those moments matter most. The more you practice being present, the faster and more profoundly your perception will change. You will notice and behold beauty in a more vibrant way. You will experience your physical body differently and become more aware of your emotions and how you feel. With enough focused awareness, even breathing can feel good and satisfying. The relationships you have will deepen and become more meaningful. You will become more comfortable in your own skin, enjoy yourself easily, and laugh often. Creativity, inspiration, and intuitiveness will blossom. Once you deeply connect with the present moment, you may even begin to feel like you are connected to everyone and everything. When you fully experience the Now on a regular basis, you will feel good and at peace more of the time. When you feel good in the moment, you are putting out an energy that is attracting more of this good energy toward you, as we discussed in Chapter 4. It is what we are doing and how we are feeling in the current moment that is creating our experience in the future. In one of my favorite books *A New Earth,* Eckhart Tolle says, "There are three words that convey the secret of the art of living, the secret of all success and happiness: ONE WITH LIFE. Being one with life is being one with Now. You then realize that you don't live your life, but life lives you. Life is the dancer, and you are the dance."

It sounds lovely, doesn't it? So how the heck do we start dancing and get into this elusive moment of the Now? There are many tools we can use to help us stay focused and train ourselves to be present. First, make it a habit to notice your thoughts. Check in with yourself on a regular basis; we bet your mind will be wandering. Many people find it helpful to wear something like a bracelet or necklace to help remind them to check in on their thoughts. Next, after you catch yourself thinking God only knows what, replace that thought by tapping into your five senses. Bring your attention to one or more of your senses: seeing, feeling, hearing, tasting, or smelling. Here are a few shortcuts that have worked for us. Experiment with what works best for you or have fun making up some of your own.

<u>See</u> – Look intensely at your surroundings. This works very well if you can look at nature. Notice the different shades of green in the landscape or the different hues in the sky. If you are inside, you can do the same thing by visually assessing the different colors, textures, and materials in the space around you. One of Amity's favorite tricks is to visually experiment with trying to look at the space between the objects in her surroundings. Take a moment now and look up from your book and practice.

<u>Feel</u> – Feel your surroundings. Bring your attention

to the sensation of touch. If your mind is rambling when you are driving your car, check into the moment and feel the steering wheel. Really feel it: the texture, the temperature, the girth. If you are sitting in a chair, bring your attention to the material on the armrests or seat and really experience it. The next time you brush your hair, bring your full attention to the experience, and feel the texture and temperature. Take a moment and practice. Feel the book or iPad or whatever is in your hands at this moment. Put the book down for a minute or two and purposely feel what immediately surrounds you.

<u>Hear</u> – Listen intently to the sounds around you. Even in silence there is a tremendous amount of background noise. See how many sounds you can identify within the silence. If you are listening to music, see if you can hear deeper by focusing on the bass guitar or piano components. Hear more fully. Another more advanced listening tool is to hear the silent spaces between the sounds. It is the exact opposite of listening for sound. Instead, you listen for the silence. Try it – it's a mind bender.

<u>Taste</u> – Fully taste what you are eating. Chew slowly and be fully present to the taste, texture, temperature, and consistency of the food you are eating. You will be surprised at how much this simple exercise will enhance the flavor of your food and increase your enjoyment. At the same time, you will feel fuller faster and eat less. Not only will this connect you to the Now, it will also maximize your food experience and may even help you lose weight. Don't be surprised if fresh foods become more appealing than processed foods once you get the hang of it. Some people believe that we could single handedly solve our obesity problem with this one simple approach of conscious eating. Bon appétit!

<u>Smell</u> – Pay attention to all the different smells. Have you ever noticed that a certain perfume or cologne that

reminds you of someone can jog you right back to the old memories? The scent of Polo brings us right back to the antics of the 80s. We can smell it a mile away. Somehow we are always surprised when it's on some old guy because our brains fully expect to see some buff young stud in a half shirt, sporting a mullet. The smell of your mother's fresh clean laundry has no doubt also made an indelible imprint in your mind. Smell and memory are strongly linked in the brain. Take the time to enjoy the smell of a home-cooked meal. Let the smell of your coffee linger. There is good reason for the cliché "stop and smell the roses." Smelling forces you to slow down, to savor the moment, and cement meaningful memories for the future.

There are many other tools to staying in the present moment. Another favorite is eye contact – it's an art. Take a few days to notice the level of eye contact that you and those around you exhibit. Unfortunately, this art is at risk in our fast-paced tech-savvy society. It is amazing how much communicating we do without looking at one another. If you don't agree, go hang out where kids congregate, and count how many of them look you in the eye. With all the texting, cell phones, personal gaming devices, and computers, the ability to maintain eye contact is a precious resource. Consciously practice looking into another person's eyes during a conversation. It takes some finesse, but it will force you to be present. For nostalgia's sake, let's review the basics of good eye contact before you get all excited and start practicing and creep people out. Don't go probing people's eyeballs looking for their soul. That is the equivalent of French kissing with your tongue at the back of someone's throat. Instead feel centered inside yourself, and gently look the other person in the eyes giving them a look of genuine interest and attention. While you are connected to another person with genuine eye contact, it becomes very difficult for your mind to wander out of the present moment.

Tuning into your physical body is another way to bring yourself back into the present moment. A quick and easy way to do this is through conscious breathing. When you find your mind wandering, take a moment and draw in a deep breath through your nose. Feel the breath move into your lungs and fill your entire torso. Let go of your abdomen so you can fill the lower portion of your lungs and diaphragm. When we are caught up in our thoughts, we tend to take short shallow breaths, which rob our bodies and brains of the precious oxygen that helps us function and think clearly. Just a quick moment of really feeling the breath will help you center your thoughts and enable you to step into the present moment. Another shortcut to using the physical body to experience the Now is to take your pulse. You can accomplish this at the wrist or at the carotid artery of the neck by gently palpating with two fingers. Taking your pulse will bring your thoughts out of your mind and bring current awareness to your body, forcing you to slow down and bring your attention to the present.

A mantra, a phrase, or a sound used to evoke concentration is another great way to bring your thoughts back to the Now. When you find yourself wandering aimlessly in thought, have a mantra ready to roll. A useful one is, "Be here now" or "I am present." Some people prefer to use the name of the divine, like "Jesus" or "God." Considered the most sacred syllable in several Eastern religions, the sound "OM" is another favorite mantra. Pronounced (a-u-m), OM comes from the ancient Sanskrit language and means "all that is." OM represents both the un-manifest and manifest aspects of God. When you say OM slowly and drag out the sounds of a-u-m, you can feel it vibrate in your chest. This vibration is soothing to our physical bodies, and some say it can calm and reset our energy patterns. Repeat "OM" or any other phrase that helps you reel in your stray thoughts, center yourself, and bring awareness to what is actually happening in the moment.

The ultimate way to experience the current moment is through creativity. Music, art, and dance are all ways to get into the moment. Artists have reported losing all sense of time and space when they are immersed in their craft. Musicians access this state of presence and write music. Elite athletes experience this connection to the Now by "getting into the zone." Performers lose themselves in the current moment to create the reality we see on the stage and screen. You do not have to be a professional to access creativity yourself. Amity does it through cutting hair. Karen does it through exercise. Maybe you do it through scrapbooking, mountain biking, playing an instrument, or salsa dancing. If you don't have a creative outlet, get one! Experiment. Loosen up and find something that helps you get your groove on. Activating the creative centers in our right-brain forces our time-focused, analytical left-brain to take a back seat. It makes sense that while in a state of creativity we can slip into and experience the current moment where inspiration and the feeling of divine connection dominate to connect us with the Now.

Commit to practice being in the present moment, in the Now. Notice what you are thinking and how your mind habitually rambles, especially when you are doing mundane daily tasks like getting ready for work, cleaning, or driving. When you catch yourself mentally grazing, use some of these shortcuts and tools to force your thought back to the Now. It takes practice. This is perhaps the most challenging of all the Rules of the Road. We think so. You may do well for a few minutes or days and then forget about it for a while. Keep trying. The more aware you are of being in the moment, the easier and more natural it will become. It takes time, concentrated thought, and repeated practice, but it is worth it. Your quality and enjoyment of life will change for the better because, after all, *Life's A Trip*!

Karen's Story: Disney Trip

My husband, three daughters, and I went on a long-awaited family vacation to Orlando. We decided to stay at a nice condo with a pool, water slide, and an array of activities for the children and then see all the Disney parks in four days. Covering ground on four enormous amusement parks was no small feat with an eleven-, ten- and six-year-old. We thought the kids were at an age to handle action-packed, non-stop fun, and we were all looking forward to our big adventure.

We were right; the kids were able to handle pandemonium. Unfortunately, Mommy and Daddy, not so much! Mostly, Mommy. I did not have a good time. We ran nine hours a day through the hustle and bustle of the crowds, hurrying to get to our next ride, trying to pack it all in before the kids went on meltdown. It was a hot sticky 90 degrees outside the entire time. Even though we were prepared with a backpack full of sunscreen, water, and snacks, the kids always wanted more. At every corner one would be hungry, one would need to go the bathroom, and one would want some expensive trinket from the souvenir store. We went on all the rides at all the parks and accomplished all we set out to do. In the evening, after retiring to our hotel, we filled our bellies with more restaurant food. Thinking the day was over was a joke. After dinner the kids immediately wanted to hit the pool. They were relentless. There was no down time. Despite being exhausted, we would pack up the towels, dress the kids, and head to the pool. We mistakenly believed the pool would be a place to relax while the children released their remaining energy. Not a chance! Our brains were fried, and our feet were killing us from the long day. We were determined to do everything on our list and get our money's worth. My husband and I didn't speak for hours during the day in an attempt to keep our sanity and for fear of what might come out of our mouths. Each day of our "fun-filled" vacation continued in about the same grueling manner.

Sometime during the second day of all this fun, I noticed that my eldest was starting to butt heads with me. If I said white, she said black. She disagreed with everything that came out of my mouth. In my mind I was searched the many teenage parenting books I had read to help explain her bad behavior. Not wanting to ruin the vacation, I chose not to address it; instead, I relentlessly stewed on our conflict. I silently critiqued and analyzed every word that came out of her mouth. Despite being pissed, I kept the family train on the tracks, jamming in all the planned activities and sticking to my schedule.

Shockingly, we survived. On the ride home I couldn't tell if any of us had had fun. Back home, I was unable to wind down. I started the daunting task of unpacking, getting the school stuff ready, and figuring out what slop I could put on the table. I was exhausted, cranky, and overwhelmed. During dinner, we discussed our trip. It turned out that my husband and kids actually had a great time. I wondered why my perception of our vacation was so different from theirs. The next day, when my husband and I had some alone time, he asked me to consider whether my obsession for the schedule detracted from the enjoyment of my trip. I stewed on the possibility. A few days later, he sent me a link to Eckhart Tolle's newsletter, which included an article about how the ego pulls you out of the present moment. It explained that one criterion used to determine whether the ego is in charge is to recognize if there is any negativity. Anger, resentment, and irritation were used as examples of ways the ego distracts you from the present. Those were the exact feelings I experienced on our Disney trip. I was so consumed with getting the most out of every day, seeing and doing everything, that I viewed the "fun-filled days" as a blur of out of control, tiring, and exasperating activities. The bickering with my daughter was only adding fuel to the fire of my ego and taking me farther from the moment.

With emerging clarity, my mind started to open to possibilities. Did we really have to stay on such a tight schedule? So what if we missed one of the parks. I didn't enjoy the trip because I couldn't. I was too busy thinking about the next thing we were doing. I was on a mission to get to the next destination instead of enjoying what I was doing in the moment. I was busy doing, instead of being. In that state, my ego was in full control. No wonder I was butting heads with my daughter; my ego wanted to fight. What was the harm in letting her have a say in the day's activities? My daughter has been given a lot of responsibility in our household, and on vacation she was doing what I usually encourage. I was so out of the Now, I perceived everything she suggested as a challenge and an argument.

I recognized that by creating and adhering to such an intense schedule I forced myself out of the present moment and into the future. Not only did I miss out on the enjoyment of the vacation, I also ignited my ego, which lead to conflict with my family members. My ego was left unchecked because I WAS NOT IN THE

PRESENT MOMENT! So in retrospect this is what I realized:

- If I had been present, I would have enjoyed standing in line engaging in conversation with my family instead of planning the potty breaks and snack time.
- If I had been present, I would have noticed that it wasn't my daughter who was being negative. I, myself, was being negative and was just seeing the Mirror (Chapter 7 – Rule #1).
- If I had been present, my ego wouldn't have been in charge. I would have been connected to my True Self.

So what have I learned? I am now more aware of the need to be present. When I am out of my familiar environment, old patterns may reemerge. These are opportunities for practice. Presence takes practice! I need to check myself when I feel negativity or anger arising and make sure I am experiencing the current moment. This was an expensive lesson to learn and a lost opportunity for fun with my family. Maybe this was the universe's/God's way of smacking me in the head and saying, "Even though you thought you knew it, there is still room to grow!"

It is amazing how our thoughts and our ego can take us away from the present moment if we are not diligently aware of the present. Here is an extreme example of how it feels to be hijacked out of the Now.

Amity's Story: Ego Hijacking in the Shower

Years ago when I was working as a trainer in the pharmaceutical industry, I had just returned from a business trip to the corporate headquarters. It was a particularly challenging trip because I was joining a different department, which meant I would no longer be reporting to my former dynamic, creative, and visionary boss. I was leaving a team of women who put the company's goals above their own and all shared a similar vision of a cooperative work environment. We all had similar value systems and personalities. The division I was merging with had a very different concept of the company hierarchy. It was a difficult adjustment for me, mostly because I now had to work directly with the one guy in the company who gave me fits. Fred wasn't a bad guy; he was just exactly contrary to everything I stood for. No matter what the subject, Fred and I had the opposite opinion on everything. I knew I was right and he was wrong — and he felt exactly the same way. Oil and water. It was a recipe for major frustration and miscommunication, which started immediately.

The evening I returned home I slept fitfully. I awoke the next morning still stewing about Fred and our latest disagreement. I crawled into the shower. My mind was ruminating about what I should have said and what I was going to say to Fred. The shower was like a portal to another universe. All time, space, and reality were altered by my mind rant. I was gone. I was completely out of my mind. I know this only because my return to reality and the present moment was through the shock of embarrassment. Still in the shower, I noticed the feeling of someone or something standing close to me. The sensation of someone else being in the room was enough to snap me out of my mind rant just enough to notice where I was in space. To my surprise I was nowhere close to the stream of water coming out of the showerhead. Instead, I was standing well in front of it, naked, with my finger pointed straight ahead as if I were poking Fred between the eyes. As my awareness grew, I was horrified to recognize that I was fiercely mumbling a self-important, Fred-belittling monologue. Totally in character, I had pursed lips and a red face and was giving my best Bitch interpretation. Once I had a clear picture of how crazy I must have looked, I quickly slipped into a silent pleading prayer. "Please God, let that be the dog standing next to the shower door! Don't let it be a person watching me; let it be the dog! Please, please, please God!" With the anticipation of a horror movie, I turned toward the glass door in slow motion. Before we locked eyes, I heard my husband's booming voice, "What the hell are you doing?" I was out of my mind, out of the moment, and busted! I was having a totally ridiculous fictional conversation that existed in the past or the future with someone who wasn't there. I was wasting very real energy in a completely ludicrous fashion. From that point forward I knew I needed to make a big, big effort to be present. The last thing I needed to do was spend more time with Fred than reality really required. Besides, I looked like a jackass. Not even a dog should have to see that.

Shortcuts

→ Be present. Focus your thought on the current moment.

→ The pain or pleasure you feel while waiting is directly proportionate to your experience of the Now.

→ Living in the present moment will increase your creativity, inspiration, and intuitiveness.

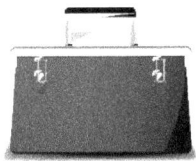

Tool Kit

→ Check in on your thoughts. Are you in the past, the future, or the present?

→ Engage your five senses: sight, touch, sound, taste and smell to ground you into the present moment.

→ Consciously make eye contact.

→ Take a deep breath and reconnect with your body.

→ Check your pulse.

→ Say your mantra.

→ Be creative: sing, dance, cook, paint, play music, write, build something.

"The art of life is to live in the present moment, and to make that moment as perfect as we can by the realization that we are the instruments and expression of God Himself."

~ Emmet Fox

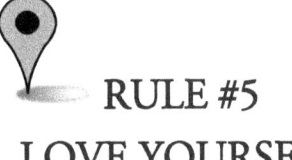

RULE #5
LOVE YOURSELF

Loving yourself sounds like a deceptively simple concept. To the contrary, self-love is multifaceted and extremely complex. Compare it to the battery in your car. The level at which you are able to love yourself is equal to the charge in your battery. With a healthy amount of self-love, your battery is fully charged. With lack of self-love your battery is low or even dead, rendering you helpless and vulnerable on your journey.

Your ability to love yourself has a direct correlation to your happiness, self-esteem, and capacity to love other people. There is a vast range of expression of self-love, or lack thereof, each with its own consequences and ramifications. The lack of self-love may present itself through unhealthy relationships, low self-esteem, co-dependency, perfectionism, negative self-talk, shame, guilt, neediness, and all kinds of other repelling common qualities. In the extreme, it may manifest as eating disorders, substance abuse, disease, self-mutilation and even suicide. At the other end of that scale, respectfully loving yourself results in attractive characteristics such as healthy boundaries, meaningful relationships, self-esteem, acceptance, compassion, and empowerment. Extreme self-love probably culminates in enlightenment. Let us know if you ever get there!

Most of us probably haven't given self-love much thought. We want to change that. Understanding and cultivating love for self is a foundation for making the most of your journey. It is a Rule of the Road, so listen up!

Let's pop the hood on our car and check out our batteries. Take a good look at the battery casing. Do you see any corrosion? Hating yourself is like corrosion on your battery. It is toxic and it will burn you, literally and figuratively. When you pop your hood and see yourself naked in front of the mirror, what thoughts go through your mind? Does this sound familiar? *I look fat. I hate my thighs. Yuck, loose skin. Where did all that cellulite come from?* That, my friend, is corrosion, aka, hating on yourself. Here are other self-decimating examples that may apply. Have you caught yourself thinking you couldn't do something? Have you have ever criticized yourself, made an excuse for your behavior, or felt unworthy? Do you wish to be better, more relaxed, or someone you're not? Newsflash – that is not loving yourself!

There are many other ways that lack of self-love results in our everyday behavior patterns. Do you put everyone else first? Do you meet everyone's needs but never find time to take care of your own – like exercise, rest, or solitude? Are you too busy doing for everyone else that you sacrifice yourself? Are you tolerating unhealthy relationships and settling because you don't think you can have any better? Do you abuse your body and soul with alcohol or drugs? Do you think your thoughts are wrong and inappropriate? In the book *Codependent No More*, Melody Beattie states this truth, "Many of us wouldn't dream of loving or treating other people the way we treat ourselves. We wouldn't dare, and others probably wouldn't let us."

Not loving yourself comes from "never feeling good enough" as Louise Hay tells us in her must-read book *You Can*

Heal Your Life. This self-criticizing wretchedness could have been programmed into your subconscious through toxic relationships, childhood experiences, or the way you were taught to look at the world. Having a "never good enough attitude" sets up a pattern to always try to be someone other than you. It results in a feeling of wanting to be better or different than you actually are. If only you were as smart as your brother or could play sports like your sister or were prettier or richer then everything would be wonderful, your parents would love you more, you would have more friends, and the world would be right. Wrong! Those low-lying, seedy statements we secretly tell ourselves are part of the problem. Let's get real. Spend some time accurately assessing how and where you lack self-love in your life.

An effective way to assess the charge on your self-love battery is to determine if you carry any resentment. When you have resentment toward another person or a situation, it is easy to point the finger to blame and complain about the other person. But as we learned in Chapter 7: *Rule of the Road #1 – Take Radical Responsibility,* you need to turn that finger back around and point it at yourself. The root of resentment is lack of self-love. In the book *The Art of Forgiveness*, Virginia Fair states, "As we move along the path of forgiveness, we eventually glimpse the self-hatred which is contained in resentment. We may be living a good life according to impeccable standards, and yet, if we have harbored any resentment, we will come to know our responsibility in the matter of self-forgiveness. We begin to see how we abdicated our responsibility and let things happen to us. We may not have "wronged" another, but the moment we denied our feelings and our expression, we committed a grievous "wrong" against ourselves. The many days, or months, or even years of bitterness, which followed, began in that very first moment of self-denial. And for that, we become responsible and need our own personal forgiveness."

Forgiveness is a shortcut for learning to love yourself. Self-development author Bryant H. McGill states, "There is no love without forgiveness, and there is no forgiveness without love." There are many things we can forgive ourselves for. The list is universal. We can forgive our negative self-talk and forgive ourselves for the times that we lost our temper and treated someone badly. Let's forgive our past and our participation in situations that disempowered us. Let's forgive ourselves for not doing what we should have done and then for "shoulding" on ourselves in the first place. Forgiveness is not about condoning behavior. It is about being willing to let go of resentment, anger, shame and guilt.

If you are at a loss for exactly how to forgive yourself, here are a few tips to get you started. First, you need to recognize and acknowledge the need for self-forgiveness. *The Art of Forgiveness* goes on to say, "When first beginning our efforts toward forgiveness, we may not realize that we have a need to forgive ourselves. But forgiveness is not complete without this 'act'. It is our gift to ourselves." After embarking on a self-forgiveness journey, you may want to try using the following mantra. "I forgive myself for ____. I love myself just as I am." Use your mantra every time you catch yourself having a self-defeating thought. Keep in mind the wise words of Louise Hay, "We do not have to know HOW to forgive. All we need to do is be WILLING to forgive."

Another tool for forgiveness is to use the grief process first described by Elisabeth Kubler-Ross. The stages in the grief process – denial, anger, bargaining, depression, and acceptance – can be applied to self-forgiveness. At first, you may deny your need to forgive yourself through minimizing or refusing to see the truth. Then, you may become angry at yourself for failing to recognize the situation or participating in it. After that, you may bargain with yourself for the need to take action. When you realize that there is nowhere to hide from this new level of awareness, depression can set it. Finally, resolution and forgiveness come with acceptance. These stages may proceed in order or may fluctuate back and forth. It may take seconds to process or it may take years. It depends on the magnitude of the situation and your propensity for self-love.

Compassion is also a tool you can practice to accomplish self-forgiveness and enhance self-love. Compassion toward self requires willingness and determination to be gentle with yourself. Here is an example of a gentle attitude toward self: If you are feeling guilt or shame about something in your past, you can focus on that in a self-hatred fashion, or you can choose to reframe the situation by realizing that your new level of awareness is causing the dreadful feelings. Most of us are really doing the best we can, based on our capacity. Once we recognize we can do better, it serves us no purpose to wallow in what was. It robs us of energy that we could use to focus on how to do it better the next time, now that we know the difference. Lesson learned, treat yourself with compassion.

Acceptance is another tool for self-love and forgiveness. All human beings have positive and negative aspects of their personalities, including you! Yes, you have a dark side. It's okay. It is very normal for people to have occasional unkind, malicious, perverted, or corrupted thoughts. It's how you handle the thought that counts. As we learned in Chapter 5: *Navigation System – Who's Driving?* the ego stirs up random thoughts for us to decipher. Detaching from and not acting on these thoughts result in right behavior; there is no need to judge or condemn yourself. Caroline Myss, author of *Sacred Contracts*, describes the "shadow side" and "light side" of our personalities. In order to truly experience self-love we need to acknowledge and accept our shadow side. Settle down. Acknowledging and accepting does not mean embracing and acting upon! Experiencing more of the light and accepting all aspects of ourselves is a great start toward self-love.

While you are experimenting with forgiveness, compassion, and acceptance of self, there are some other very simple tools to use in your daily life that will put you on the road to self-love. Start sharing your unique personal gifts. When you help others because you want to, not because you think you have to or because you want something in return, it will make you feel good. You will see how your special self makes an impact on other people's lives, and you will see yourself more lovingly. Another simple tool is to practice accepting compliments. When someone tells you that they like your shirt, don't say, "this old thing." Instead simply say, "Thank you, I feel great in this color," or "Thank you, that made my day." Once you pay attention, you may be shocked at how often you don't receive the offered compliment. It may feel strange at first to accept a compliment wholeheartedly. With practice, you will notice a shift to feeling more uncomfortable dissing yourself when you hear a compliment. Next, try keeping a self-appreciation list. Marci Shimoff, author of *Love for No Reason*, encourages people to write down three new things that they appreciate about themselves in a journal each night for at least thirty days. By the end of the month, self-appreciation and self-love will feel much more natural. Lastly, if you are going to love yourself, it is time to stop taking so much shit! There are numerous ways to gracefully and respectfully stick up for yourself. It's amazing how many people are talked down to by their spouses, kids, co-workers, and bosses. It happens so frequently that many people get used to it and don't even hear it anymore. Time to clean your ears out. The next time someone talks down to you, in your best "matter-of-fact" tone say, "Please don't talk to me like that," and walk away. Some of our other favorite canned responses include, "I would prefer it if you said, _____;" "I can't hear you when you talk in that tone;" and "That is not going to work for me right now." Practice makes perfect, so get to it.

If you are one of the lucky ones who already reaps the rewards of a fully charged self-love battery, we challenge you to take it to the next level and fall in love with yourself. WARNING: The following may sound extremely corny if your battery is running low. Stretch your imagination; this level of self-love is possible.

The next level in self-love is a full-on love affair. Imagine you just met yourself, and you are blindly infatuated with all of your own attributes. While infatuated with yourself, you can't see any of your flaws. You look great, you smell good, everything you say is clever and witty. There is a gentle breeze blowing through your hair, your skin glistens in the sun, and you are moving slightly in slow motion with background music setting the ideal mood. You are perfect. If this description fits a love interest, instead of yourself, you would act accordingly. You would want to spend time with that person. You would want to go on a date and do something special. Maybe you would buy them a gift, or go out of your way to treat them to something nice. How about writing a love note to express your fondness and inner feelings? You would certainly speak kindly to that person and cherish your relationship. Abracadabra, that person is you! What can you say to yourself that would make you feel loved? "I am beautiful and kind." "What I do does make a difference." Or "I am worthy; I deserve the best in life." Pick one or make one up on your own. How can you treat yourself to something special? Maybe a massage, a hot bath, or your favorite food? Take yourself on a date. Buy yourself flowers. Go for a walk during sunset. When you really love yourself, doing all of these things will feel really good. Try it!

There are huge benefits for increasing your self-love. When you love yourself, you'll look for healthier relationships because you'll know you're worth it and worthy of it. When you love yourself, you'll eat healthy foods and exercise so your body will work at optimal performance. You will be deserving and worthy of only the finest conversations and relationships. You will not tolerate mediocrity. You will accept only the best because you are worth it. Appreciate the greatness that lies within. Don't just appreciate your wonderful smile, how well you connect with small children, or your gift for being a quick learner, but love yourself completely. You are as you should be. Know that you are perfect, even with your "flaws." Yes! You are lovable just as you are, with your damaged past and annoying habits. So you're not a supermodel. Who cares? Melody Beattie says, "The people who look the most beautiful are the same as us. The only difference is they're telling themselves they look good, and they're letting themselves shine through."

Beyond increasing everything attractive about yourself, self-love will also increase your capacity to love others. In *The Road Less Traveled*, Scott Peck says, "We are incapable of loving another unless we love ourselves, just as we are incapable of teaching our children self-discipline unless we ourselves are self-disciplined. We cannot be a source of strength unless we nurture our own strength." As your capacity to love others grows, you will attract higher quality people into your life. As you quit judging yourself, you will stop judging others and be more compassionate. So look at yourself and appreciate the amazing person that stands before you. Once you abide by this – the most important Rule of the Road – you will be able to give love and receive love. You are loved, loving, and lovable.

Richard's Story: Love it or Lose it

Meet Richard. He was successful, athletic, and incredibly handsome. By age 40 he had it all: a six-figure career, a beautiful wife, three kids, a big house in the burbs, and a perfectly behaved dog. Life appeared ideal but beneath the surface, Richard was wrestling with his dark side. Silently he harbored resentment and felt unappreciated by his employer. He was irritable and perceived others as miserable. At a deeper level he never felt good enough. Richard was suffering from a lack of self-love. Perhaps it was because he never measured up to his parents' expectations like his older (bio-chemical engineer) brother did. Maybe it was because he had been labeled early on as the wild-child party guy. Or maybe it was because he never dealt with the death of his best friend, who passed away due to drugs and alcohol, or maybe because he never dealt with the pain and regret associated with the death of his father. Perhaps it was the guilt he carried from the heart-wrenching details involved in the breakup with his first love. Whatever it was, Richard was not into giving it much thought. He was in complete denial, using alcohol to numb out any feelings below the surface. He just kept plowing through life attaining more of what he thought would satisfy his family with no regard or understanding of his own happiness.

Richard missed the class on moderation. He drank hard and he smoked. No matter how severe the hangover, he would get up and exercise to the extreme in 100-degree heat. He believed that life was mind over matter, and he knew how to push himself. Over the years his wife had begged, threatened, and pleaded with him to quit smoking, stop drinking and be more present in their relationship. He would make the necessary adjustments to get her off his ass, and then he would gradually return to his old ways. In his mind he was doing it all right. He used his success as a provider to negate the need for any deeper relationship with himself or others.

Richard was also a big fan of beating himself down. He used it as a sadistic form of motivation. He would torture himself with negative thoughts, saying in his mind and sometimes out loud, "I'm an idiot, I suck," or "I am so stupid." If his own internal thoughts weren't enough to garnish action, he would turn to his wife and relentlessly instigate a verbal beat down from her. Usually that would do the trick. After being completely demoralized, he would gather the energy to get back on track and produce. It was a vicious pattern of self-abuse.

Richard's world began to crumble after his 41st birthday. It started with a pain in his right leg, which he attributed to mild arthritis. A few months later his legs began to ache and tremble with weakness. A battery of tests followed until the doctors delivered the crushing news. Richard was diagnosed with Primary Progressive Multiple Sclerosis (PPMS), a progressive degenerative neuromuscular disease with no treatment or cure. The prognosis involves a 75% chance of loss of mobility, sometimes as rapidly as within one year of diagnosis. Richard was potentially facing a wheelchair. For a man who ran 4 miles a day and seemingly had it all, this was devastating. This was a beat down he never expected.

Immediately, Richard recognized that there was nowhere to hide, no way to keep denying a deeper inner truth. He knew he was living a charade. Richard's family and friends had been trying to tell him for years to be kind to himself, to live in moderation, and to respect his body and spirit. But now, with this diagnosis, it was a message that no longer could be rejected. His mind, his heart, and his ears were wide open as he set off to make radical changes in his life.

After intensely researching and studying all the medical information he could find, the first thing Richard did was to fundamentally change his diet. Right away he gave up red meat, wheat, dairy and sugar, eating only fresh fruits and vegetables, turkey, and chicken. He also began a stretching regimen in an effort to maintain his mobility. When he started, he was shocked to learn that he wasn't able to lift the toes on his right foot. What was more earth shattering to him was that his body awareness was so low, he hadn't even noticed!

Richard also began a quest of inner emotional work. He started meditating and visualizing himself in perfect health. He sought assistance from medical intuitives who helped him identify emotional blocks in his energy systems. As he journeyed through his past, Richard made efforts to contact people whom he had hurt to offer apologies and ask forgiveness. He looked at his life with a new level of awareness and acceptance and was able to make peace with his past. The power of self-forgiveness was at work in his life.

As Richard began taking good care of himself for the first time ever, his cognitive and physical awareness continued to increase. He became aware that if and when he had negative thoughts, his stress level would increase and exacerbate his symptoms. His body told him when he pushed beyond the boundaries of moderation, and now he listened.

The importance of self-love and self-care, have made a significant impact on Richard's disease process, but the benefits of this wake-up-call extend far beyond the physical. His relationship with his wife and family is more open and honest then ever before. He is more willing to be present in all of his personal and professional relationships. Instead of seeing the world as a competitive place, he now sees cooperation. Misery has transformed into gratitude. Richard would be the first person to tell you that PPMS has been his greatest teacher, instructing him on how to love himself. Now two years later, he can still walk a mile and the journey toward self-love continues.

Shortcuts

→ Check your self-love battery.

→ Forgiveness of self is the key to increasing self-love.

→ To love or be loved by another, we must first love ourselves.

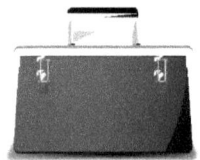

Tool Kit

→ Use self-love affirmations. "I love and accept my strengths and my weaknesses."

→ Use the grief process to help forgive yourself.

→ Practice self-compassion.

→ Accept all aspects of yourself.

→ Graciously accept compliments.

→ Make a self-appreciation list.

→ Write a love note to yourself.

→ Treat yourself to something special.

> "You yourself, as much as anybody in the entire universe deserve your love and affection."
>
> ~ Buddha

12
READY, SET, REVIEW

When you are about to take the trip of a lifetime, it is a good idea to review what you have packed before you leave. In this case we have packed a lot of information into a few short pages and thus into your brain. Let's review.

We have learned some important things about our vehicle or ourselves:

→ Commit to good maintenance by drinking more water, eating more fresh foods, and getting regular exercise. Also, get the appropriate quality and quantity of sleep.

→ Understand yourself to be an energetic being as well as a physical being and practice noticing the exchange of energy – emotional and otherwise – in your daily activities and interactions.

→ Cultivate relationships with people and frequent places that make you feel energized and positive. Actively create and refine a solid "A Team" of friends with whom to surround yourself.

→ Have a healthy understanding of your navigation system that consists of the subconscious, the conscious, and the ego.

→ Be mindful of the deeply rooted behavior patterns in your subconscious and work to stay in the conscious mind as much as possible in order to have free will over your decisions and emotional and behavioral processes.

→ Notice and experience the difference between your True Self and your ego.

→ Recognize that fear is a tool of the ego and understand that feelings of scarcity, anger, jealousy, and threat are the ego's way of controlling and attaching to details and/or outcomes.

→ Strive to align your life with your True Self.

→ Obey and practice the five *Rules of the Road*

♯1. I take *radical responsibility* by looking at myself instead of outward at life's circumstances. I will assume all people, events, and situations are in my life for my highest good even if I am unable to understand the point of it all in the current moment.

♯2. I will practice being *grateful* with the understanding that gratitude is the energy that attracts more for which to feel grateful.

♯3. I will practice *letting go of control* by focusing on controlling my own reactions vs. controlling the actions of others. I will take what comes my way and release attachment to the way I think things should be or how things will turn out.

♯4. I will practice *being in the current moment.* I will practice watching my thoughts to recognize if I am spending my mental energy in the past and/or present and immediately return my thoughts back to the present moment. Utilizing eye contact and my five senses will assist me in this quest.

♯5. I will practice *self-love* and continue to grow in my capacity to love others and myself.

Now we are packed, stacked, and ready to roll. Next, we will explore the steps that create the road trip of a lifetime.

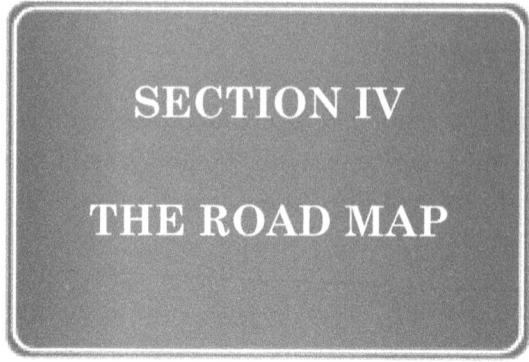

SECTION IV

THE ROAD MAP

Are you ready to begin a new life journey? Now that you have a better understanding of your vehicle, are actively taking the necessary steps to do good maintenance, and following the rules of the road, you are ready for *The Road Map*! Section III, *The Rules of the Road*, gives you the practical steps necessary to create a life full of abundance and meaning. This section contains the steps necessary to consciously co-create a new reality. These steps are based on the principles of the Law of Attraction, which literally means that like attracts like.

As we discussed in Chapter 4: *Electrical System – Hardwired or Hot-wired*, our entire universe, including you and your thoughts are made up of energy, which vibrates at a particular speed. The Law of Attraction demonstrates that our thoughts and emotions will resonate with other "like" frequencies in the field of possibility, creating reality into form. Simply put, your thoughts and emotions create your reality. James Allen states, "A man cannot directly choose his circumstances, but he can choose his thoughts, and so indirectly, yet surely shape his circumstances."

The Law of Attraction formulates what you perceive as your reality. This is nothing new. You already actively participate in the Law of Attraction, the same way you participate in gravity. You don't have to understand it for it to work. It is working right now. We are simply suggesting a more conscious way to conduct your journey because *Life's a Trip*. Once you understand *The Road Map* and you start actively and consciously participating in it, you will have the tools necessary to create the life you want.

"All that we are is the result of what we have thought. The mind is everything. What we think we become." So said, Buddha. The ideas in *The Road Map* have been taught throughout the millennia by many spiritual masters, and more recently, by other teachers such as James Allen, Neville, Jerry and Ester Hicks, Deepak Chopra, Wayne Dyer, Oprah, Panache Desai, Dr. Joe Dispenza, Joe Vitale and many, many more. Here we will synthesize this information into shortcut form to help get it into your otherwise preoccupied brain. So, buckle-up and pay attention…no texting while driving!

Chapter 13: Step 1 – Know What You Want

Chapter 14: Step 2 – Watch Your Thoughts

Chapter 15: Step 3 – Change Your Thoughts

Chapter 16: Step 4 – Feel

Chapter 17: Step 5 – Believe

Chapter 18: Step 6 – Perceive

Chapter 19: Step 7 – Participate

Chapter 20: Step 8 – Receive

13

STEP 1
KNOW WHAT YOU WANT

It sounds ludicrous to start out on a road trip and not know where you are going, doesn't it? In order to know where you are going, you first have to know what you want. Do you want sea, mountains, or big city? Will you visit people, or will you visit places? It makes sense to first know what you want before you decide which direction to head. Right? Unfortunately, many people follow a life plan that is expected of them but never stop to ask the very important question, "What do *I* want?" It is very common for people to let their life journey be determined by societal expectations, their religion, or even worse, their parents! Before we know it, we find ourselves traveling so far down the path that we assume it is too late to change course. Some find that their life doesn't resemble what they would have chosen for themselves at all! Knowing what you want out of your life is fundamental. It is the first step in the process of creating a more interesting, fulfilling life. World renowned author, Deepak Chopra states, "Being aware of what you want is such an obvious first step in the process of desiring that it is amazing how many people ignore it." Let's face it, if you don't know what you want, you're just plain lost.

Many areas in life require your time and attention: love, relationships, career paths, money, parenting, education, friends, spirituality, and self-development are just a few. To say you want to better your life just isn't enough. It is far too vast a statement to create the energy needed to attract what you are asking for. It is important to have clarity and be specific. Many people don't know what they want. Some can say what they want but deep down it's not really what they want at all. They may think they want it because it's expected of them, like getting married or choosing a specific career path because daddy paid for college. Some people feel trapped in their current circumstances. They just keep doing what they are doing without much thought at all. Others may not have any clue what they want. It is a good bet that at some point during your lifetime the answer to the question, *What do I want?*, didn't come easy. Here are some shortcuts to help you answer that question.

A simple way to identify what you DO want is by looking at what you DON'T want. It may be more of a challenge to identify what you want, but it's usually no problem at all to list the things you don't want. Let's start here. Pick an area of importance in your life and write down what you know you don't want. Make a fat list and be as specific as possible. Then write each item's opposite. Here are a few examples:

- I don't want a low paying job = I want $50,000 a year.
- I don't want to be sick = I want to be completely healthy.
- I don't want my child to sass mouth me = I want my child to speak to me in a respectful tone.

Once we reframe our statements into the positive, "I want," it is imperative to the process to let go of the negative statement, "I don't want." The Law of Attraction dictates this necessity. Louise Hay asks, "How often have you lamented about what you didn't want? Did it ever bring you what you really wanted? Fighting the negative is a total waste of time if you really want to make changes in your life. The more you dwell on what you don't want, the more of it you create."

Here's the classic story we hear from many of our single friends. Karen had a friend who wanted to be in a new relationship. She couldn't understand why she kept ending up with losers. Karen asked her to make a list of qualities she wanted in her new man. The list looked like this:

- I don't want a cheater or liar.
- I don't want someone who's ugly.
- I don't want to have to support his ass.
- I don't want someone who will put me down.
- I don't want to sit around watching movies every night.

Mid-list Karen couldn't take it anymore. She brought to her friend's attention that she was making a list of "don't wants." This list was a sure-fire way to bring her more of the same: cheating, ugly, broke, boring, insecure boyfriends. Exactly what she had been getting – but didn't want. Together, they crafted her original list into a new one, consisting of the same statements reframed into the positive. The list transformed to this:

- I want a partner I can trust.
- I want a partner who is attractive to me.
- I want a partner who is financially secure.
- I want a partner who treats me kindly and respectfully.
- I want a partner who enjoys adventure and travel.

She taped the list on her bathroom mirror, and every morning she would read it and smile. Meanwhile, she kept an open mind, met new people, went on countless dates, tried internet dating, and even looked twice at the UPS driver to make sure she wasn't missing her soulmate. A few months later, her new man showed up. She met him through a local internet site. Quickly she realized they had the same interests, frequented the same restaurants, and liked doing the same things. He also had the qualities she was looking for. He was handsome, called when he said he would, and was emotionally present in their relationship. Four years later, they are still together and blissfully happy. Karen's friend didn't stop there. She employed her list making talents to other areas of her life. She is now out of debt, and they are going to Hawaii for vacation, fulfilling one of her life's biggest dreams.

Compare that to Glenda. Her story is unbelievable – but true! Glenda is in her sixties and has been married for forty years. In her younger days she made a list of what she didn't want and shared it with her friends and family. She knew exactly what she didn't want: a guy who was ten years older or more, someone divorced, someone with children from another marriage, a Polish guy, and a guy named Lenny, because she never wanted anyone to call her Squiggy. (In case you don't know what that means, it is a reference to a 70s television show, *Laverne & Shirley*.) Funny list! Even after all those years of marriage she can still recite her list with a hint of bewilderment because she got exactly what she focused on. She married Lenny, a Polish divorced guy, who is more than eleven years older with two kids. Glenda cringed at our suggestion that "Squiggy" would be an adorable grandma name. No one calls her "Squiggy;" she had to draw the line somewhere.

If you are still struggling with not knowing what you want to do with your affection, your life, your career, or your time, here is another shortcut to help you identify what you want. Ask yourself these simple questions:

- What have I always liked to do?
- What brings me joy?
- What feels effortless and comes to me naturally?

These gifts of the True Self, as we discussed in Chapter 6: *The Key*, are themes that thread through an entire lifetime. People can change dramatically during their lives. However, their gifts and true nature remain consistent. For proof, one of Amity's childhood friends posted a scan of their fifth grade yearbook class picture on Facebook. In the upper corner of the page, she signed this poor guy's yearbook and wrote, "To a cute kid who needs to study more. Your Friend, Amity." For more than thirty years Amity has been giving out self-improvement advice, like it or not. Some things never change!

Spend some time looking back for themes that have been expressed through your whole life. Reacquaint yourself with these themes, and you will find your answers.

Another simple way to figure out what you want is to pay attention to when you feel good. You feel good when you are in harmony with your True Self. This harmony allows you to tap into the powerful force of creation and lets your natural gifts shine. It will point you in the direction of what you want out of life. Feeling good is different for everyone. Some people feel good and experience a hyperactive state, like they just drank a three-shot venti cappuccino. Other people feel good through contentment, which feels warm and fuzzy. Some even get chills when they connect to inspiration and creativity. Start paying attention to the cue your body gives you. It will be as unique as you are. Your body was designed to give you feedback, to keep you safe, to procreate, to physically perform and to do many other amazing things. Your body communicates to you through physical sensation and emotion. Pay attention; It is amazing what you can learn about yourself from simply listening to your physical body. Notice when you feel good.

It's OK if you have a mental block when it comes to knowing what you want. Don't give up the search. We benefited greatly from taking a Passion Test Workshop facilitated by Lori Anderson. *The Passion Test*, written by Janet and Chris Attwood, helps people identify their top five passions in life and live by them. It is a fun, easy way to get in touch with what you truly want. You can read the book, find a facilitator near you, or take the test online at http://www.thepassiontest.com.

Once you have clarified what you want, write it down. There is power in writing something down. Perhaps the power comes from taking an intangible idea and making it tangible by writing it out. Or maybe it is because, as humans, we have a history of taking the written word more seriously than the spoken word. Make a list of your goals, and again, make it specific. We like to use a $3.00 white board. Put it somewhere where you can see it on a daily basis like in your office or next to your bed. Review your list daily. This will help you train your thoughts to focus on what you really want. Author and motivational speaker Brian Tracy says, "Goals are the fuel in the furnace of achievement."

Elite athletes are great examples of people who know what they want. In an interview with *60 Minutes* in 2009, Michael Phelps and his coach, Bob Bowman, revealed a secret. Coach Bowman pulled out a list written an entire year prior to the 2008 Olympics in Beijing, where Michael broke a world record – eight gold medals in swimming. Written on the list were the swim times Michael hoped to achieve in Beijing that following year. Upon review of the list, it turns out that Michael Phelps hit six out of eight times exactly. The two races in which he did not meet his timed goal were the 100- and 200-meter butterfly, but he still won. In the 200-meter butterfly, he was off by nearly a second when his goggles filled with water. Needless to say, he still managed to win all eight gold medals. Phelps stated he was a little disappointed because he didn't achieve his goal of hitting all eight times but overall felt it turned out OK. Uh, yeah, we would agree! Making a list is powerful, and you don't have to be Michael Phelps to do it.

Another one of our favorite ways to record specific goals is to have an annual retreat. You can do this with your spouse, or with your friends, or even alone. We do this on our wedding anniversaries, imagining what we want our next year to look like. It is a sweet and fun way to connect with our husbands, and put some collective energy behind our goals. Some of the things we write down are family-oriented ambitions, but we also spend time discussing and scribing our individual intentions. It is a great way to continue growing together and individually in our marriages. Single people of the world – don't be discouraged! One of our friends does this kind of annual goal setting on her birthday during a silent retreat. You may also want to consider doing it with your A team of friends. Find the best and most powerful way that works for you.

Inspirational coach and author, Lori Anderson, encourages her clients to use vision boards in addition to, or instead of, intention lists. Vision boards are created with pictures usually cut out from magazines to represent the individual intentions. Hung prominently so the user can see it often, a vision board stimulates the creative side of our brain through visual perception, thus utilizing more of our faculties to cement our goals and intentions.

Lastly, as you contemplate what goals and intentions to put on your list, leave room for the unexpected. Shoot higher than what your head may tell you. Listen to your heart's deepest desires and expect to be surprised at the results of this new way of thinking. Deepak Chopra says, "What you intend for yourself determines what you get. Although it seems like a paradox, you must have a vision of the future to surprise you, for without visions, life dwindles into ritual and repetition. A future that merely repeats the present can never be surprising." Expect the best – or even better.

Karen's Story: 4Runner Miracle

My first experience with the practice of goal setting was well before I even heard the term "Law of Attraction." But looking back, it was one of my first steps in understanding how thoughts literally create your reality. Fourteen years ago, married with a small child, we were in desperate need of a new car for my husband. He was tired of driving an old beat up car with over 150,000 miles on it, and he really wanted a Toyota 4Runner. A brand new, black, fully loaded 4 Runner, to be exact. My husband's position at the time was in medical sales. He was doing well, but with a new wife, new child, and a new mortgage payment the extra expenses were a serious drain on the budget. However, that didn't deter him from wanting that new car and wanting it bad! He even went to the car dealership and looked at it, got the brochure, came home, and put a picture of that black 4 Runner up on the wall in his office. In order for us to obtain the finances to get that vehicle my husband figured out how many sales it would take. He put that number on the white board in his office beside the picture of the car and nicknamed it the "wall of profit."

Every day for one month he said to himself, "I will hit that number of sales." Now you must understand, my husband had been in his job for four years, and he knew what a realistic number was, and was not. He put up a CRAZY number. It was a number he had never accomplished before and an amount not many of his seasoned counterparts had even been able to hit. He was not deterred. He really wanted that new ride.

The picture and number stayed on the wall in his office, and I forgot about it. He did not. He knew he would make that number. He didn't quite know how, but he had faith and determination. He did his day-to-day duties to the best of his abilities with a knowing that it was going to happen. Leads came his way, doctors wanted to buy new equipment from him, and things were happening. Was it coincidence that it happened in the same month that he intended this outrageous forecast? It all lined up, and at the end of the month he called me in to his office to inform me that not only had he hit that number, but he had exceeded it by $100. We were blown away. Awesome! Ironically, he never put another number on the board for 10 years. We saw it happen without even knowing how it happened. We didn't yet comprehend that we helped make that happen by knowing what we wanted. What we did know clearly is what we wanted, and that specific focus got us the results: his beautiful, black, fully loaded, new 4Runner!

Shortcuts

→ Know what you don't want. It will help you figure out what you do want.

→ Figure out what you want by noticing what makes you feel good.

→ Look at your life's history for patterns. What have you always liked to do and been good at?

→ Define specifically what you want.

→ Write down what you want and put the list somewhere you can see it daily.

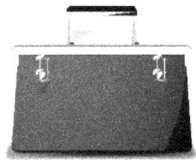 **Tool Kit**

→ Get a white board and write down your goals.

→ Annually set goals.

→ Take the Passion Test.

> "If you go to work on your goals, your goals will go to work on you. If you go to work on your plan, your plan will go to work on you. Whatever good things we build end up building us."
>
> ~ Jim Rohn

14

STEP 2
WATCH YOUR THOUGHTS

Philosopher James Allen said, "We cannot truly know ourselves unless we first understand how our minds work and create patterns of thought in our life. Understanding other people and things outside of ourselves becomes much simpler once we understand ourselves." In order to take control of the wheel and be the driver on this journey, you must become conscious of the inner workings of your own mind. The first and most important step in this process to develop a healthy habit of watching your own thoughts. Without this vital step you will merely remain a helpless passenger in your own car, subject to the whims of your runaway mind. Humans have between 12,000 and 60,000 thoughts in their heads per day. According to research, as many as 98% of our thoughts are exactly the same as we had the day before, which means, many of us unconsciously experience the same thought or thoughts hundreds of times over in a single day. Imagine the truckload of worthless, habitual thoughts that are holding you hostage on your journey.

Your thoughts are a result of the culmination of your past experiences influenced by your dynamic external environment and the complex internal environment of your body's chemistry. In other words, there is a lot going on in there to produce those mostly mindless, tens of thousands of thoughts per day. All of your past experiences have been processed and stored in your brain through the forming of neural networks. These millions of neurons are wired together and fire together in your brain. As a result, your brain has been hardwired into a system of thought patterns which function a particular and familiar way. It's like having a grid of well-traveled superhighways cemented between your ears, which produces the same old thoughts, the same old way, over and over again. It may be helpful to comprehend a bit more about the anatomy of our brains so this particular human derangement of habitual thought can be more fully understood. We will give you the anatomy of the brain – shortcut style.

Thoughts are conjured from three major areas in your brain: the neocortex, the limbic brain, and the cerebellum.

The neocortex is responsible for higher functions of the nervous system, including voluntary muscle activity and learning, language, memory and complex thought. It is the thinking part of the brain and constitutes about 85% of the human brain's total mass. It's that gooey, wrinkly grey matter that we picture when we think of a brain floating in a jar in a science lab.

The limbic brain is the chemical and emotional brain. It is located deep inside the skull and is the most evolved and highly functioning part of the brain. The limbic brain contains some very important structures: namely the hippocampus, hypothalamus, and amygdala.

The hippocampus plays a role in long- and short-term memory. It functions as a building block for forming, retaining, and recalling thoughts. Without a hippocampus, events could not be processed into memory. The hippocampus is also responsible for spatial memory and navigation.

Your hypothalamus is a gland at the heart of your endocrine and hormonal system, which responds to your thoughts. It releases chemicals related to the emotions attached to the thoughts. It is the reason a toxic thought could affect your emotional and physical state. In the presence of stressful thoughts, the hypothalamus releases hormones that can negatively affect your emotional and physical state and confuse your brain.

Your amygdala is responsible for your fight or flight response. Children who were raised in stressful environments, or people who live in perpetual states of fight or flight, are shown to have hyperactive amygdala function, which can lead to abnormal behavioral responses and emotional disturbance.

The last major area of the brain is called the cerebellum. It sits at the base of the brain and acts as a jumbo data processor. It helps control your body's autonomic functions, movements, and reflexes. The cerebellum stores, processes, and perpetuates skills, actions, attitudes, habits, emotional reactions, and many other memorized programed states of being. This is why the cerebellum is referred to as the seat of the subconscious. It's the wizard behind the curtain of your awareness.

This information doesn't quite qualify you to become a brain surgeon, but it should give you the foundation to understand how thoughts form and become part of our perpetual thought process. When you have a new experience that is processed and recorded by the neocortex, the limbic brain simultaneously assigns a highly specific chemical signature to the information. We experience that chemical reaction as emotion. These emotions and chemical imprints allow us to form long-term memories and neural pathways in our brains. The greater the chemical response produced by the limbic brain the more cemented that emotional memory becomes. Scan your personal history for the most glaring memories for a moment. You can bet the memories formed under high emotion are the most easily accessible and vivid in your mind. For example, we bet you could recall the exact moment you heard that the World Trade Center had been hit by a plane on 9/11. The emotional response provided by your limbic brain of fear, compassion, grief, worry, and anger cemented the details of that day into a neural pathway in your brain and created a memory. How each of us individually processed the events of that day determined what, and to what degree, that particular tragedy penetrated our subconscious minds and our attitudes and behaviors moving forward. For Amity, hurricane Katrina and its aftermath was enough of a personal shock to her system to seep into the recesses of her subconscious. It changed her response to perceived threats, initiated repetitive thought patterns related to weather events, and even altered her attitudes toward government and humans.

The brain and the body are so miraculously intelligent that there are many, many factors that influence the way our brains, thoughts, and emotional systems work. Hormones, childhood experiences, traumas, rewards, stressors, environments, and even our prenatal experience have all played a role in our brain development. The end result is that every single brain on the planet is different but formed in relatively the same way: information comes into the neocortex; the limbic system gives the thoughts a chemical and emotional imprint; and neural pathways are formed. Emotions, situations, and events in our lives cause our thoughts to travel down these neural pathways frequently until we solidify these pathways into familiar neural highways in our minds. Then, through repetition, these thoughts slip into our cerebellums and become habitual thought patterns that drive our behaviors from our subconscious into the reality of our lives. Our repetitive thought patterns become part of who we are and how we act. Our thoughts sink in and become our subconscious mind, which motivates 90% of behavior. The whole avalanche starts with these persistent repetitive thoughts. Scary! This process is so subtle and happens so naturally that most of us are completely unaware of the thoughts that inhabit our minds. Lao Tzu, who according to Chinese tradition lived in the sixth century BCE, was believed to have said, "Watch your thoughts; they become your words. Watch your words; they become your actions. Watch your actions; they become your habits. Watch your habits; they become your character. Watch your character; it becomes your destiny." The shortcut to finding out your individual destiny is to relentlessly watch your thoughts. Let's talk a little bit about how to do that.

Earlier in our discussion of *Rule of the Road #4*, we discussed watching your thoughts in order to stay in the present moment. In our Tool Kit we reviewed the method of wearing a bracelet or rubber band around your wrist to quickly and easily remind us to check in with our thoughts. Here are a few more simple suggestions to pack in your Tool Kit:

→ Place "check in" notes in strategic places around your house or work place. This strategy will call your attention to your thoughts regularly throughout the day.

→ Set a reminder alarm on your smart phone or watch.

→ Designate a specific location to check in, like every time you stop at a red light while driving. We do some of our most impressive daydreaming and repetitive thought patterns cruising the road.

→ Check into your thoughts during a specific task, like doing the dishes or showering. Challenge yourself to notice all of the random thoughts that go through your mind while you do menial tasks.

While you are practicing watching your thoughts, it is important to notice what kind of thoughts you are having. It's not just about quantity. It's also about quality. In Chapter 9,

Rule of The Road #4 – Be Present, we discussed whether your thoughts reside in past, future, or present time. It is also important to ascertain if the thoughts you catch yourself thinking are positive or negative. In an article by Jennifer Hawthorne titled *Change Your Thoughts, Change Your Mind,* she says that according to research, of those 12,000 and 60,000 thoughts per day, 98% of them are recurrent thoughts, and out of those, 80% are negative. Hawthorne states, "Negative thoughts are particularly draining. Thoughts contain words like "never," "should," and "can't," complaints, whining or thoughts that diminish our own or another's sense of self-worth deplete the body by producing corresponding chemicals that weaken the physiology." Remember our Ego loves conflict and drama, so if your mind is wandering, many of us are wandering our way into imaginary scenarios about what we or someone else "should" do or say in these ego-created mini dramas. Unless you are some sort of freak of nature with an unusually sunny disposition, chances are there are energy-depleting recurrent thoughts running through your head all day, and you aren't even conscious of it.

In *The Winner's Brain* authors Jeff Brown and Mark Penske quote advice for becoming more aware of what's going on in your mind from Harvard medical school neuroscientist and psychologist, Sara Lazar, "If you imagine your thoughts flowing like water in a stream, you can detach from them and focus on the emotional tone behind them. You'll start to see the patterns of emotions and actions. Recognizing those patterns is the first step to changing them."

Another way to start noticing your stream of thought is through stillness. Sit in a quiet place and attempt to empty your mind of any thought. Notice how long you can sit without a thought entering your stream of consciousness. Keep in mind that if you become aware that it's been 15 seconds since you had a thought – that is a thought in itself! It is very difficult.

As you sit in stillness attempting to empty your mind, imagine that your thoughts are helium-filled balloons, and your mind is the empty space of the sky. As thoughts emerge into your awareness, picture them as balloons floating into your conscious space. Just notice the thought balloons. Don't get into a conversation with these thoughts; After all it would be crazy to talk to balloons. Don't judge the quality of the thoughts either. Just notice and imagine the thought balloon floating away out of your awareness, and bring yourself gently back to the quiet empty space of the sky. With exercises like these, you can familiarize yourself with the nature of your thoughts and then begin the process of realizing that *you are not these thoughts*. You are much greater, much more aware, and much more powerful than these thoughts that run rampant inside your mind.

Keeping a journal is another really effective way to monitor your thoughts. Writing things down is a powerful tool to help you become more conscious of your thought patterns, and it creates a record for your review. In *Mindsight: the New Science of Personal Transformation*, Dr. Daniel J. Siegel explains that he keeps a journal of his daily activities, noting his shifts in mood, his mindful practice (or not) and his aerobic exercise. He states that this was another opportunity to develop his capacity to observe his internal and external experiences and to reflect on the workings of his mind.

As you become more proficient in watching your thoughts, you may also be able to recognize some of your self-talk. Self-talk refers to silent repetitious messages you say to yourself in your mind. Certain situations can trigger emotional responses which ignite habitual thought patterns and self-talk. When Amity's daughter was one year old she would sit for hours entertaining herself with various toys. When she fit something together, or discovered something new, she would say out loud to herself, "Good job!" This is a positive form of self-talk.

Unfortunately, as we get older, go through more crap, and assimilate other people's opinions of us, we tend to replace that positive self-talk with negative self-talk. Here are some examples we hear often:

→ I have no luck.

→ I will be single for the rest of my life.

→ I can't afford it.

→ I could never do that.

→ I don't have the experience.

→ She is so much prettier.

→ I'm not smart enough.

This list could go on forever. It takes the ability to watch your own thoughts and then a degree of honesty to accept the reality of what may be going through your head. At first, you will be able to pick up obvious thoughts and repetitive thought patterns. Then you will get to a deeper level of listening and be able to pick up penetrating thought patterns. The journey may surprise you. Start practicing! It's not that hard! You have thousands of opportunities a day. Watching your thoughts for negativity is like being able to see a warning light go off on your dashboard. Just like the warning light, a negative thought signals that something is not right. Without awareness, you are just mindlessly being held hostage by the repetitive thought patterns set up in your head, and you will find yourself riding around in the same old circles.

Amity's Story: Back to Work

As I began practicing watching my thoughts, I was amazed at some of the reoccurring thoughts that played out over and over in my head. One of my subconscious mind's favorites is to fantasize about getting back into the work force. My husband and I had decided years ago that in order to create the life we wanted it was time to give up my career and fully support the home front. We were about four years into our first small business venture and Kevin was branching out into new areas of business development. Leaving the work force was not an easy decision for me to make for many reasons. I loved my job and my perks. Although it required a lot of time on the road, I got to work with interesting people and visit amazing places all over the US. What made it the most difficult to quit my job was my mental programing. My parents raised me to highly value financial independence and always be able to provide for myself.

Over time I suppose I built a mental superhighway for this thought process. I had a lot of fear surrounding the idea of being financially dependent on my husband and the vulnerability that came along with that scenario. Despite my fears, letting go of my personal career aspirations was the best plan of action for our goals as a family. The decision for me to be a stay-at-home mom would allow my husband the flexibility he needed to respond to the growing responsibilities of our businesses. He could travel when necessary and at a moment's notice, without having to compete with the travel demands of my employment. This also gave us the ability and the time to provide our kids with extracurricular activities like gymnastics and soccer. Although the plan sounded ideal and was the envy of many of my working friends, it did not sit well with me and took many years for me to settle into my new role as homemaker.

During that time frame I would be going about my day and out of the blue I would take a left turn in my mind and jump on the superhighway of doomsday employment. What if the business failed? How many months could we survive on our savings? Would we have to borrow money from family members? Or worse, move in with my parents? Before I knew it, I would be perusing the want ads. Although this was one of my subconscious mind's favorite pastimes, it was absolutely TOXIC for what I was trying to achieve in my life.

Having "back to work" fantasies was simply a ridiculous waste of energy and time. I also recognized that my thoughts, which are energy, were aligning and attracting circumstances that would support more of what I was thinking about. Distractions in the form of low-pay employment were coming out of the woodwork. I was literally "roadblocking" my own plan for success. It drove my husband crazy!

I have been watching this particular thought process for many years now. At first I would look at the want ads a few times a week. As I became more disciplined, I scaled it back to a few times a month. Then, I would only do it when money got tight. It has been a long time since I have actually held the want ads in my hand. Canceling the paper subscription helped. I have come a long way from sneaking the paper into the bathroom when my husband wasn't looking but to this day I am continually amazed at how often I still catch myself trying to take the on-ramp to the Get-A-Job Highway. Just recently a friend of mine decided to re-enter the work force. Something about her situation yanked my emotional chain, and that old subliminal habit to fantasize about getting a job flared up. Luckily, I have practiced enough to catch myself flirting with those old behavior patterns and am now able to recognize them, interrupt them with conscious thought, and stop them before they turn into action. I have learned through experience that repetitive thought patterns can be identified and reprogrammed in the adult brain, and old behavior patterns can be avoided. This can be true for you too, but first you must start by watching your thoughts!

Shortcuts

→ Practice watching your thoughts and it will become habit.

→ Identify your particular repetitive thought narratives.

→ Distinguish the quality of your recurrent thoughts.

→ Recognize your self-talk.

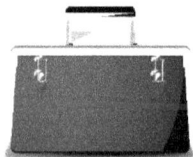

Tool Kit

→ Wear a bracelet, rubber band, or medallion as a reminder to check your thoughts.

→ Place notes in strategic places to remind you to check in.

→ Set a reminder alarm on your phone or watch.

→ Designate places to check in to your thoughts.

→ Watch your thoughts during specific menial daily tasks.

→ Keep a journal.

> "All that a man achieves and all that he fails to achieve is the direct result of his own thoughts. His suffering and his happiness are evolved from within. As he thinks, so he is; as he continues to think, so he remains."
>
> ~ James Allen

STEP 3
CHANGE YOUR THOUGHTS

Eckhart Tolle says, "Awareness is the greatest agent for change." We hope you have been getting your fair share of practicing this new awareness by watching your thoughts, as suggested in the last chapter. If so, it is safe to assume that you now know whether the majority of your recurrent thoughts are in the past or future, self-defeating or self-promoting, and toxic or life-enhancing. Chances are, if you are a novice at watching your thoughts, the majority of your thoughts are framed in the negative. Having negative thoughts is like heading toward a destination that we don't want to visit. It's like wanting to take a trip to paradise but having the GPS programmed to hell. Every time we take a turn, we are following directions given to us by our old programming. No wonder our lives continue to be laced with the same problems over and over again. Depressing? We think not!

The most important shortcut in this entire book is this: YOU CAN CHANGE THE WAY YOU THINK! It is a scientifically proven fact called neuroplasticity! With the emergence of MRI technology and the combined data collection by physicians who study the effects of stroke victims, the old belief that the brain and its function are set in stone in childhood has given way to the new understanding that the brain has an amazing capacity to form new neural pathways. MRI studies have shown that areas of the brain damaged by stroke remain damaged, despite the patient's ability to regain movement in the area of the body previously affected, which suggests that there are compensatory mechanisms built into our brains. This new knowledge has spawned decades of research into brain plasticity.

We now know that forming new neural pathways in the brain can affect body function, emotion, and behavior. Studies show that changing a negative thought into a positive thought actually changes the chemicals released in the brain, and over time the brain has the plasticity to change neurologically. Dr. Joe Dispenza, a leader in the field of leveraging neuroplasticity to produce positive change in life, says, "Neurons that fire together, wire together to form neural pathways." The opposite is also true. If you don't use it, you lose it. We want to lose the old way of thinking and develop new neural pathways around healthier, happier, more successful ways of thought. To do this we have to have the awareness to catch ourselves in the action of our old thought processes. Then we must STOP, and redirect our thoughts with conscious attention. In other words, we can use our free will to change our thoughts.

We did not begin this road trip with you to just go around in circles. Let's start changing our mental programing so we can enjoy some new scenery. It is easier than you think. All you need is awareness and determination to change. Keep mindful attention on your thoughts and the next time you catch yourself traveling down that old familiar superhighway in your mind, decide to build an exit ramp. Build that exit ramp one thought at a time. Do it over and over again, and you will find that the new exit ramp you built leads to a brand new superhighway of neural pathways. Except this time your new superhighway system will be paved by your conscious awareness instead of your history, your upbringing, your fears, your habits, and your subconscious. In *The Biology of Belief* the totally adorable Bruce Lipton states, "Endowed with the ability to be self-reflective, the self-conscious mind is extremely powerful. We can actively *choose* how to respond to most environmental signals and whether we even want to respond at all. The conscious mind's capacity to override the subconscious mind's preprogrammed behaviors is the foundation of free will." Amazing! By thinking new thoughts, you actually can change the way your brain is wired! You have the power to stop those hardwired patterns that have been established over the years and get hot-wired with a new way of thinking.

Don't give up, it is absolutely possible to change the way we think, rewire our brains, and reprogram our subconscious. Some people embrace change, others not so much. It is like smoking, some can quit cold turkey and some people need nicotine gum or the patch. If you are in need of a little roadside assistance to change, below are a few of the many, many ways in which you can begin to reprogram your thoughts and rewire your brain in order to create your new reality. "As the physically weak man can make himself strong by careful and patient training, so the man of weak thoughts can make them strong by exercising himself in right thinking," said James Allen.

The following list is a compilation of techniques that will help support you to change your thoughts and rewire your brain. This information is in no particular order. We have practiced, studied, and played with many of these methods over the past twenty years, blundering through life. Some have worked better for us than others, but that is probably more about our own personal evolution than the techniques themselves. We practiced many of these tools for a time and then moved on to something else. Other techniques we find ourselves going back to over and over again, depending on the magnitude of the situation we are dealing with. One thing is for certain, the more we learn and practice, the bigger our tool box gets, and the better and faster we know how to use it. New techniques are being developed all the time, and we plan on continuing to explore their applications and effectiveness. We hope you do too. We encourage you to play with this list of ideas. Find the one that resonates most with you, and start there. Your tool box will be as unique and individual as you are. Dig in, start practicing, and keep exploring!

1. Affirmations

Affirmations are ready-to-go replacement thoughts to be used after identifying a recurrent negative thought. Example: "You are driving me crazy and I am about to poke your eyes out!" You create a positive statement to replace the energy draining negativity. Example, "I have unlimited patience." Now use your replacement thought EVERY time you catch yourself going down that negative dead-end road. Over time this new thought pattern starts to feel natural and begins to sink into your unconscious. Louise Hay is a great resource for learning more about the power of affirmations.

2. Reframing

Most of us have been conditioned to talk about what we don't want. If you have children or if you think back to your own childhood experience, examples abound. "Don't chew with your mouth open. Don't run with a stick in your hand." Don't, I won't, and I can't are constants of our contemporary language, and you can probably identify plenty of "I don't want" statements that you've made. In Louise Hay's book *You Can Heal Your Life* she explains, "What you put your attention on grows. I don't want to be lonely. I don't want to be unhappy. I don't want to be sick. This list shows how we are culturally taught to fight the negative mentally – thinking that if we do so, the positive will automatically come to us. It doesn't work that way. How often have you lamented about what you didn't want? Did it ever bring you what you really wanted? Fighting the negative is a total waste of time if you really want to make changes in your life. The more you dwell on what you don't want the more of it you create." Instead of framing your words as what you don't want, make it a habit to reframe them as what you do want.

Make reframing fun. Ask your family and/or friends to participate and support you. In our homes it is a game we all participate in. The kids are involved and are encouraged to catch us telling them not to do something instead of what we want them to do. Of course this exercise expands far beyond the parent/child relationship. It exists in all of our interpersonal relationships and also exists in our own self-talk.

Reframing also involves taking something that is perceived to be negative and looking for the positive in it. An example would be: *I hurt myself so I am unable to participate at the gym this week.* [Instead of looking at the negative,] *I will get fat and lose interest in exercise,* look for the positive and focus on it: *I will have time to do that project around house or read the book I have been meaning to finish.* In *The Winner's Brain* Jeff Brown and Mark Fenske state that there is MRI evidence that the act of consciously putting a positive spin on things (reframing) actually changes brain activity patterns, specifically by engaging areas of the prefrontal cortex. This in turn dampens the response from the amygdala, which produces the flight or fight response. Practicing reframing will help you transform your thoughts to the positive and eventually make it a habit.

3. Labeling

This technique, described in *Mindsight: The New Science of Personal Transformation* by Psychiatrist Daniel Siegel at UCLA School of Medicine, involves identifying how you feel emotionally and then labeling those feelings. For example, catching yourself in the repetitive negative thought, *maybe I should move out,* you can then recognize and label that thought as "fear." For example, fear of abandonment can be translated into the desire to go buy running shoes and get the hell out! This labeling strategy is often all it takes to move your thought process from the fight or flight response of your primal brain to the higher reasoning centers of your brain, called the Neocortex which reduces stress chemicals from flooding your brain and keeps you in a more reasonable state to process information. Reasonable is cool.

4. Emotional Stress Release or Holding Your Bumps

The phrase "hold your bumps" makes a dirty mind wander, but *these* bumps are subtle protrusions about an inch above each eyebrow near the center of your forehead. Have you ever seen someone distressed grab hold of their forehead? That's the body's natural instinct to activate the frontal lobe to calm down and think more clearly, shifting out of the fight or flight response to relax. The key is to simply experience your stressful thoughts and feelings without judging them while gently holding your bumps for two to five minutes. Keep focusing on the stress until you feel a noticeable shift in your body and mind. You may notice your breath deepening, your heart rate dropping, and it will become increasingly difficult to solely focus on the distressing emotion or situation. Other random thoughts will begin popping into your head. As you allow the negativity to dissipate, you will be aware of new ways to think and respond.

This technique, Emotional Stress Release, was developed by John F. Thie, D.C. author of *Touch for Health*. It is one of the most effective things you can do for yourself (or with another person) before, during or after a stressful event. We like to say, "Hold your bumps." It is a simple, discrete and effective tool to use in stressful situations. Try it!

5. Snap Out Of It

This is the good ol' fashion technique of behavior modification. Put a rubber band around your wrist. Every time you catch yourself with the negative thought, snap the rubber band and then replace the unwanted thought with one of your ready-to-go affirmations or a scene that is more pleasing. We aren't sure how much faster the snap out of it technique will work than just plain ol' replacement thoughts, but the idea is to snap the brain out of its ruminating habitual thought process with a physical sensation to assist in creating a new neuropathway for the pleasant thought. Amity swears by this one. And if she could, she'd have us all outfitted with custom-fit shock collars! It works, but don't hurt yourself.

6. HeartMath® Coherence

A technique developed by HeartMath researchers involves focused attention on the heart to consciously activate a positive emotion such as love, gratitude, or appreciation. HeartMath researchers have amassed data to prove that igniting these emotions, and feeling them in your heart center, shifts the heartbeat into a more coherent electrical and magnetic pattern. This "coherence" immediately activates a cascade of biochemical events that positively affects our neurology and physical bodies. Check out the research at the HeartMath Institute for more mind-blowing information.

7. Ho'oponopono

An ancient Hawaiian technique, described in Joe Vitale's book *Zero Limits* is used to practice forgiveness and reconciliation. Stripped down for shortcut purposes, it is basically a mantra: *I love you, I am sorry, please forgive me, thank you.* It is applied to everything and everyone, even if you can barely stomach the thought of using those words, given whatever unpleasant circumstance you may be dealing with.

The power of the words and the feelings attached to the intention of the phrase work to shift the negative energy associated with the unpleasant circumstance. Sound like hocus-pocus? We thought so, until we tried it! It really works, and we both had a lot of success with this method, especially when applied toward our family members.

8. Exercise

We have discussed the importance of exercise in the "Know Your Vehicle" section of this book, but there is another equally important effect exercise has on your brain. In *The Winner's Brain* Mark and Jeff Penske affirm, "Exercise has such a positive, generalized effect on your brain, it almost makes the benefits to the heart, lungs, and muscles seem incidental. Recent neuro-imaging and cognitive psychological studies have documented how a regular exercise program can increase attentional focus, improve learning and memory, reduce impulsivity, enhance mood, lower stress, and increase the volume of important structures in the brain."

The researchers expand on that by saying it doesn't make a difference whether you are a young person who regularly jogs or a "golden-ager who takes a daily stroll." Get off your butt and exercise!

9. Repetition or Mantra

A mantra is the repetition of a sound, word, or phrase that helps you achieve transformation. Traditionally, a mantra is given to you by a spiritual leader or teacher, but any word or phrase that helps you focus and feel good will do. Many people use the name of their deity and repeat it over and over again. "Jesus, Jesus, Jesus…" or you may want to use a favorite affirmation like, "I am calm and loving, I am calm and loving, I am calm and loving." The idea is to use the repeating mantra as a focal point for your attention. This will help you avoid distraction and the voice of your own ego. The key to transformation is to use your mantra often.

10. Meditation

Meditation is the practice of concentrated focus or attention for the purpose of increasing awareness of the present moment, reducing stress, promoting relaxation, and enhancing personal and spiritual growth. Some common methods used to facilitate the meditation process are focusing upon a particular sound or object, bringing full attention to one's breath or movement, or using deliberate visualization. The medical community is now studying what practitioners have known for a millennium; meditation has the power to change the way you think and even change the way your brain is wired. Here is proof. Psychologists studying the effects of a meditation technique known as "mindfulness" found that meditation-trained participants showed a significant improvement in their critical cognitive skills and performed significantly higher in cognitive tests than a control group. These results were attained after only four days of training, and participants only meditated for twenty minutes each day. "In the behavioral test results, what we are seeing is something that is somewhat comparable to results that have been documented after far more extensive training," reports Fadel Zeidan, a post-doctoral researcher at Wake Forest University School of Medicine and a former doctoral student at the University of North Carolina at Charlotte, where the research was conducted. "Simply stated, the profound improvements that we found after just four days of meditation training are really surprising," Zeidan noted. "It goes to show that the mind is, in fact, easily changeable and highly influenced, especially by meditation."

Other research looks at the effects of meditation on brain connectivity. Writing in the Proceedings of the National Academy of Science, researchers in China and at the University of Oregon describe experiments on 45 students. Some of those students were taught a meditation technique known as integrative body-mind training (IBMT). The researchers used brain-imaging techniques to examine fibers connecting brain regions before and after training. Students trained in the IBMT approach for 11 hours or more appeared to develop new fibers in a part of the brain that helps a person regulate behavior. Control subjects did not form the new fibers.

There are many types and methods of meditation. We encourage you to experiment and see what works best for you. The easiest way to start is to set aside five minutes in the morning and sit quietly, eyes closed, with your spine erect. Concentrate on your breath. Notice its temperature, rate, depth, and rhythm. Single-mindedly focus on the breath. If other thoughts pop into your awareness, notice them without judgment or mental conversation, and let them go. Return your focus to the breath. Many people complain that they can't stop their wandering thoughts and feel as if they aren't meditating the right way. Hogwash. That is exactly what meditation feels like in the beginning. It's like learning to dance if you have no rhythm. It's uncomfortable at first and you think you aren't doing it correctly. You might even hate it and want to quit, but if you stick to it, it will get better. Soon you will set your soul free. As you continue to practice meditation, the mental chatter or noise in your head will begin to dissipate. Your ability to focus will increase in clarity and duration. After you start to improve, you may even find moments or stretches of time where there will be complete silence and absence of thought. This is where the magic happens, so go get your "Om" on! (Om is a mystical Sanskrit sound used in meditation.) It is a powerful tool for transformation.

11. Prayer

Prayer is a word that means a lot of different things to a lot of different people. So for the sake of staying on the same page let's discuss it. In general, prayer is an active discussion with God or some other holy representative of God. It provides us with some time in our day to reflect on what is important to us, our needs, etc. Most people were taught to pray as kids before bedtime. As children or adolescents our prayers probably resembled a Wish List: "Dear God, I love my Mommy, please help me grow tall and get that Atari play station. Also, if it's not too much to ask, the next time little Johnny makes fun of me, can you make sure that he trips into a mud puddle? Thanks." Unfortunately, many adults still pray like that, which we would describe as a private holy moment of narcissism. Take stock and look at your prayers. Do they consist only of what you want, what you need, and what you desire? Do they include elements of service to others, requests for being a better you, and – most importantly – gratitude? We would suggest that no prayer is a bad prayer, but like Boone's Farm is to Mondovi Private Reserve, there are varying degrees of quality. If you would like to challenge yourself, read Hay House author, Carolyn Myss. She delivers a good asskicking in the quality of prayer department.

There is little argument that prayer is a positive influence regardless of your level of narcissism. In fact, there have been over a thousand studies on how prayer improves health. People who pray get sick less often. Studies from Harvard show that prayer initiates a relaxation response that translates into promoting healing and boosting your immune system. In *Positive Energy: 10 Extraordinary Prescriptions for Transforming Fatigue, Stress, and Fear into Vibrance, Strength and Love,* author Judith Orloff states, "The relaxation response during prayer has been shown to reduce stress, so you are more optimistic. Your link to a higher power lends purpose and meaning that makes life worthwhile." She also suggests that energetically, "Prayer, as an expression of goodness and love, opens your heart, activating healing vibes throughout the body. It tips the energy balance from negative to positive by instilling hope, well-being, and compassion." Other prayer experiments have shown to decrease crime in New York City and increase fertility rates in women when strangers prayed for their success without their knowledge. If prayer can accomplish all this, then there is no doubt that regularly practicing prayer can help you change your thoughts to the positive and help re-wire your brain.

Here is a simple prayer to help you focus on the positive.

Dear God:

Please untie the knots that are in my mind, my heart and my life. Remove the have nots, the can nots and the do nots that I have in my mind. Erase the will nots, may nots, might nots that may find a home in my heart. Release me from the could nots, would nots and should nots that obstruct my life. And most of all, Dear God, I ask that you remove from my mind, my heart and my life all of the 'am nots' that I have allowed to hold me back. Especially the thought that I am not good enough. Amen. ~ Father Ronnie Knott

12. Visualization

Visualization is the act of creating vivid pictures in your mind. Visualization is important because it activates the powers of your subconscious mind. Seeing yourself already achieving your goal makes your brain believe that you've already achieved it. There are many visualization techniques, but the key is to see yourself in first person, as if the event is happening through your eyes, as opposed to watching it happen to you. Add sound, smell, and especially emotion to your visualizations to increase the realism and power.

At the University of Chicago a study was conducted by Dr. Blaslotto to determine the effects of visualization on sports performance. He gathered a group of basketball players and set out to test how visualization training would impact a player's free throw performance. He randomly assigned the athletes to one of three groups, and he took their free throw percentage before starting the experiment. The first group went to the gym for one hour a day and practiced free throws. The second group went to the gym for an hour a day, but instead of touching a basketball, they would lie on the ground and visualize themselves making successful free throws. The third group was the control, and they did nothing. After 30 days, the three groups were retested. As expected, the third group, who did nothing, did not show any improvement. The second group, who had physically practiced without visualization, improved their free throw percentage by 24%. The first group who did not physically make a single free throw actually improved their free throw percentage by 23%! One percentage point lower than those who practiced everyday for one hour! Many great athletes regularly use visualization techniques to enhance their performance.

A recent study showed dramatic benefits of visualization for surgery with patients who listened to a pre-op surgical guided imagery relaxation tape before having major bowel surgery. The patients had less pain and anxiety, used less medication (185 vs. 326 mg of opioid), and had quicker recovery of bowel function (58 hours vs. 92 hours) than patients who did not listen to the guided imagery. Another study involved surgery where patients were awake but given IV pain medication. Three groups were used: a control group, a group with someone sitting next to the patient giving them attention, and a group with someone sitting next to the patient suggesting relaxation imagery. All groups could have as much pain medication as they wanted. The relaxation group had significantly less pain, anxiety, medication use, time in the operating room, and significantly fewer complications. Only one relaxation patient became unstable after surgery versus 12 patients in the control group.

Visualization doesn't just work in sports and health care; it also works in the arena of life. As you can see, visualization has scientifically proven results. This is a simple and powerful tool anyone can use to improve their life.

13. Thought Field Therapy (TFT) / Emotional Freedom Techniques (EFT)

TFT/EFT is used to manipulate the body's energy by tapping on acupuncture points and meridian lines – the body's energetic pathways. The tapping technique is designed to relieve undesirable states like fear, anxiety, and stress. It has also been used to treat phobias, addictions, and post-traumatic stress. Some critics say that tapping can serve as a distraction and make it appear to alleviate the root distress versus having a real impact on the body's energetic system. However, many thousands of people have used EFT and TFT successfully and ultimately changed the way they process and perceive information. This technique was widely used in the aftermath of hurricane Katrina. Over 20 clinical trials published in peer-reviewed journals have shown EFT to be effective for phobias, anxiety, depression, post-traumatic stress disorder, pain, and other problems. It is also used for physical symptoms, to improve relationships, enhance performance, and increase abundance. An estimated 10 million people use EFT and TFT worldwide. Cheryl Richardson, author of *The Art of Extreme Self Care*, is a big proponent of the tapping technique and claims that it helped her overcome her fear of flying. There are many videos on the internet of this simple, easy to learn technique.

14. Yoga

In the minds of many westerners, yoga is the practice of postures, related exercises, and breathing designed to promote physical and spiritual wellbeing. However, yoga is much, much more than most people assume. There are many different styles of yoga, and there are many different ways to practice or live yoga. The beauty of yoga is it can be whatever you want or need it to be. If you want to practice yoga for the physical benefits of lengthening and strengthening your muscles, aligning your skeletal system and promoting good health, then go for it. Or, if you want to practice yoga for the spiritual benefits and meditative benefits, then go for that too. Yoga is also good for the mind by helping to balance the hemispheres in the brain. Typically, the last pose in yoga practice, called *savasana*, is a time for integration of the mind, body, and spirit – just like meditation. It is thought that through the physical practice of yoga, the body can prepare for meditation more effectively by first releasing stored physical energy, which will help quiet the mind during meditation. Yoga can be practiced by anyone of any age and any health status. It can be very transformational if you are open to it.

Amity started practicing yoga by default. After having two kids, and being fatter than ever, she decided to return to the gym to reclaim her body. Her first body pump class was a rude awakening to just how far she had let herself go, so she looked for something a bit less strenuous. Aerobics, Zumba, and all the other group exercise classes left her feeling like she would stroke out. Out of necessity, she resorted to a beginner yoga class. She hated it. Her mind raced through the entire hour. She thought she would crawl out of her skin because of the slow pace of the class, but she was able to make it through without the risk of pulmonary explosion. The instructor encouraged the new people in the class to stick with it for at least six classes before they formed an opinion of yoga.

Reluctantly, Amity continued. After the fifth class she felt different. She noticed the strength in her core body return, and after sitting on the floor she no longer rolled around like a beetle to get back to her feet. The best 'side effect' she noticed was how calm and peaceful she felt after that fifth class. It was almost as if she had taken a Xanax and drunk a beer. She was hooked. Over the next year she shed 20 pounds, only doing yoga three times a week.

15. Proclamations of the Soul

Proclamations are spiritual declarations of Truth. They are like affirmations on steroids. In *Proclamations of the Soul* Rich Work explains that proclamations of the soul "assist in transmuting and removing those distorted or disharmonic energies that have been created and interfere with your free-will choice and the ability to manifest your desires." Amity's husband, Kevin – an all American, sports-loving, regular type of guy – swears that by using one of the proclamations in Rich Work's book he was able to heal a twenty-year-old knee injury. He used the proclamation and focused prayer energy toward his knee and has been pain-free for over five years.

16. Hypnosis

Hypnosis is a guided state of deep relaxation in which you have heightened focus, concentration, and inner awareness. When under hypnosis, you usually feel calm and relaxed, and you can concentrate intensely on a specific thought, memory, feeling, or sensation while blocking out distractions. Under hypnosis you're more open than usual to suggestions, and this can be used to modify your perceptions, behavior, habitual thought processes, and emotions. Many people have a false belief that while hypnotized someone else has control over you. However, your free will remains intact, and you don't lose control over your behavior. We have both experienced hypnosis with Dr. Bryan Weiss and can attest to this. The only thing strange we experienced was our sense of time during the session. An hour of time passed in what felt to be fifteen minutes, but other than that, it was very relaxing.

17. Acupuncture

Traditional Chinese theory explains acupuncture as a technique for balancing the flow of energy or life force believed to flow through pathways (meridians) in your body. Energy flows through our body via a network of "roads" like a highway system. Stress, anger, or any intense emotion acts like a traffic jam, blocking the free flow of energy in the body. By inserting very fine needles into specific points along these meridians, acupuncture practitioners assist in unblocking your energy flow. Acupuncture points serve as the on and off ramps to the energy highway and can help energy flow smoothly. Acupuncture not only helps alleviate the *symptoms* of stress and anxiety but can alleviate stress and anxiety itself.

From a Western perspective, acupuncture works to alleviate stress by releasing endorphins into the brain, where they alleviate pain. In addition, acupuncture improves circulation of blood throughout the body, which oxygenates the tissues and cycles out cortisol and other waste chemicals. The use of needles is misleading. The needles are so fine that you can barely feel them being inserted into the skin. Acupuncture treatment is actually very calming. It decreases heart rate, lowers blood pressure, and relaxes the muscles. While you are working on reprogramming your thoughts, keeping your body's energy in balance can expedite the process.

18. Subliminal Audios / Sleep Meditation CDs

This is a great technique for shortcut fans because you can do it while you sleep! These audio recordings aim to reprogram your subconscious mind while you sleep. Subliminal audios distract the conscious mind with words or music while inaudible tracks work on the subconscious. You can use these anytime during the day or night. Meditation CDs are also nice because they can lull you to sleep and put you in a deep relaxed state while giving you positive suggestions. These CDs are readily available on a variety of topics. Karen thought these were a little weird at first, but she recommends giving it a full six to eight weeks to decide if they are right for you.

19. PSYCH-K®

PSYCH-K is a technique used to change subconscious beliefs by increasing "cross-talk" between the two hemispheres of the brain, thereby achieving a more "whole-brained" state. When the right and left hemispheres of the brain are in simultaneous communication, the brain has the potential to re-script long standing behavior patterns.

20. Brain Gym®

Brain Gym integrates three brain dimensions for successful learning and performance. It uses simple movements to coordinate the brain/body/senses and to reduce stress, which makes learning easy and enjoyable. It is used in the classroom to improve focus, organization, communication, and attitude. It can also be applied to achieve goals in sports, careers, relationships, etc. For more information and to find classes or consultants for a personal session visit braingym.org.

21. Aroma therapy

Your sense of smell is a pleasant and easy way to initiate some change in your thought processes. In *Whiff! The Revolution of Scent Communication in the Information Age*, the authors declare, "In the last two decades, researchers around the world have conducted studies that focus on the influence of aromas on mood. We are now certifying what the ancient

Egyptians knew: aromas can assist and benefit us in maintaining a positive outlook on life, especially in times of stress and worry." Science is confirming many of the benefits of scent as a catalyst for mental and emotional wellbeing that have long been practiced by aromatherapists.

A study conducted at Yale University in 1983 showed that eight major factors of mood are affected by fragrance. "Fragrances can have a beneficial effect on irritation, stress, depression, and apathy, and can further enhance the positive factors like happiness, sensuality, relaxation, and stimulation."

Two examples of scents that have been studied and used in aromatherapy are jasmine and violet. Jasmine stimulates alertness, improves focus and hand-eye coordination and enhances athletic performance. Violet enhances learning speed by 17% and is known to improve concentration while studying.

Some popular essential oils are handy to have in your Tool Kit.

→ Lavender calms, relaxes and balances by triggering alpha waves in the posterior part of the brain.

→ Orange connects with your childlike joy. The up-lifting oil can improve mood and inspire play.

→ Peppermint stimulates alertness and mental concentration.

→ Rose has one of the highest frequencies of any essential oil. It opens us to receive and give love, especially self-love. The pure essential oil is the most effective. Rose floral water is an option.

Experts suggest using only pure, organic, high-qualtiy, therapeutic essential oils Synthetic fragrance oils don't have the same effect. Kayse Williams' Sacred Alchemy blends reduce emotional stress and anxiety and support emotional rebalancing. Her Clearing Series, based on the Chinese Law of Five Elements, removes energy blocks of sympathy, grief, fear, anger, and joy in meridian energy flow. Inhaling the aroma of therapeutic grade essential oils affects the emotional limbic center of the brain in seconds, lightening your mood and brightening your energy. Check out her website: http://www.sacred-alchemy.com. Aromatherapy is a fun and easy way to assist you in making deep shifts happen gently.

22. Rewrite Your Story

We all have stories that we tell about our lives. If after learning to watch your thoughts, you have discovered that you have a story that is less than attractive, one in which you play the role of victim, or a story that is just plain ol' boring and depressing, try rewriting it. Literally. Instead of being the victim in your story, rewrite the details so you become the hero who overcomes adversity. Then craft a happy ending. Make up your happy ending if you have to. The happier the better! This will force your brain, in a conscious way, to explore new possibilities and form new connections through creativity.

Byron Katie, author of *Loving What Is* and many other self transformational books, has a system called "The Work" that asks a series of simple questions to help you reframe your perceptions of reality and rewrite your story. She challenges you to honestly answer whether your belief systems are actually true and then provides a mental pathway out of your perceived experience. This helps you to see your life from a healthier and more realistic perspective.

23. Just Breathe

Believe it or not, a slow, deep, deliberate breath can significantly help you change your thoughts. Not only will it help oxygenate your brain, it will also promote relaxation and help you think more clearly. It has also been scientifically proven to affect the heart, the brain, digestion, and the immune system. In India, breath work (called pranayama) is a regular part of yoga practice and has been practiced for thousands of years. Pranayama literally means control of the life force.

Michael Singer, author of *The Untethered Soul,* in an interview with Oprah on her Super Soul Sunday show describes how he uses the breath to deliberately create space between his true self and the energy of his thoughts. He details taking a deep breath to initiate a relaxation response in his shoulders and body which allows him to slip back into that place where he becomes the observer of his thoughts. He describes it as "falling behind" the energy of the thoughts. As he holds his center with the breath, he says he can feel the energy of the thought rush out in front of him and then dissipate. You can do this too; it just takes some practice. It feels good. Take a breath.

As you can see, there are many ways to approach changing your thoughts. So no excuses! The list provided in this chapter could provide you a lifetime of experimentation if you put your mind to it. We are sure there are plenty of methods out there to try and many more on the way. The point should be quite clear; if you can recognize a negative thought, you can consciously choose to change it. Change the way you think and the way you think will change. Your brain will produce chemicals related to your positive mindset, and every cell in your body will benefit, making it much more likely that you will achieve your desires. Put your energy into being aware and this will get easier – we promise. But you have to participate. Reading just isn't enough. You actually have to DO something. We have tidied it up and broken it down into small little nuggets for you to try. Get busy changing your thoughts. This is how you make your road trip awesome!

Karen's Story: It's Me, Not You

I knew it wasn't good. I wasn't happy. My husband wasn't happy. Everything I did to try and make it work, didn't work. I tried different ways to say it. I sugar coated it. I didn't even know what I was trying to fix. But it had to be him. It couldn't be me. Nothing was wrong with me.

I put all my energy into him. He was broken. So I would fix him. He drank often, not crazy drinking but frequently at home. He drank outside on our porch while he smoked. Smoking was not allowed in the house. I would tend to the children, and he would have "his time" outside coming down from his workday, workweek, or whatever stress he wanted to relieve. After a few years of this, it started becoming a problem. It was his "drinking" that was a problem. I would mention it to him. He would drink less and try to be more present, and it would get better for a few weeks. About every three months the same situation would reoccur. He would be the problem. He wasn't giving me what I needed. I felt alone. It was his drinking. I felt myself struggling for his time and attention. It started to feel like the alcohol was "his girlfriend," and I felt competitive and jealous. I would count his drinks. I would check the wine bottle in the morning to see how much he drank. Then I would punish him for "going over" our agreed upon limit. When he drank in excess our intimacy declined. I didn't want to be around him. He would rather be with "her." It was upsetting and insane.

Against my better judgment, I gave him an ultimatum. I knew it was wrong, but I couldn't help it. "Stop drinking or I am gone." I couldn't take it anymore. I felt as if I was sharing a relationship with his alcohol. It wasn't as if he went to bars, strip clubs or out with the guys. He did none of that, but he still chose "her" outside on the porch a few times a week instead of doing what I thought he needed to be doing with his family.

The hostile exchanges continued until he said he would quit. I still watched, expecting the drinking to continue. He didn't drink, at least not at home. Perhaps he drank while away on business, but I never knew it for sure. He had yielded to the pressure and was making changes. After three months of his no drinking plan, I didn't feel any better. I still wondered and I was still paranoid. Sure, I felt like I'd won a battle against his girlfriend (the bottle of wine), but I still felt bad and I wasn't happy. I was on the edge expecting him to drink. When he came home from work meetings, I would give him a kiss and a secret sniff to investigate. I was still focused on him. During the three months he quit, I encouraged him to go to AA. In fact, I even researched it for him, so he would know when and where to go. He never went. He said he didn't need or want to go. He could quit if he wanted and he was proving it.

While researching AA, I came across Al-Anon meetings. So I decided I would go. Initially I went in an attempt to lead by example, not necessarily because I thought it would be of benefit to me. I would tell him I was going so that hopefully he would go to AA meetings.

When I went to my first meeting, I had no idea what to expect. There were moms, dads, sons, daughters and grandparents from all walks of life in attendance. Their common bond was that they each cared about someone whose drinking affected them negatively, and they were there to learn how to deal with it. I was told they conducted this meeting just like an AA meeting. You introduced yourself, told them why you were there, and listened to other people's stories. I didn't say a word at that first meeting but sat there and cried my eyes out listening to other people struggle with the same issue I had. Our partners had the problem, and it was ruining our lives.

This was where I learned my first lesson. I cannot control others. I cannot do the work for them. It was not MY problem. It was his problem. I was looking at it completely wrong. Why was I taking on his shit? I wasn't the drinker, why did I feel like I had a problem? I had a classic case of codependency but didn't know it. What I soon learned was how to not take on his stuff. It came with a lot of bumps and bruises and wasn't easy to master.

The key to that radical self-discovery was to have a change in perception. I needed to change my thoughts about it. It was his deal not mine. If my needs weren't being met, it was my job to communicate that to him. The alcohol was not creating our problem. In our case the problem was him not being aware of what I craved – his time and attention. He wasn't aware of how I felt. All he ever heard from me was nagging and bitching and controlling thoughts about his drinking. So I changed the way I looked at his drinking and what I was not getting in the relationship. I learned, after a few Al-Anon meetings and multiple phone conversations with Amity daily for weeks, that I could not change him, even though I desperately wanted to.

After awhile he started having a drink now and then. He couldn't help but look over his shoulder as I tried to change how I felt about his drinking. "It was

HIS deal, not mine." This time instead of going into the same cycle, I really tried to let him know what I needed from him as my husband and partner and the father of our children. And he gave it to me. It was hard not to count his drinks or give him a nasty look when he went for another beer, but I practiced. I told myself it was HIS deal. If drinking produced outcomes that were not favorable for him – like dragging the next day because he had a hangover, a DUI, or no action in the bedroom – then that was HIS deal. I had a tendency to save him before he felt any consequences. Now his consequences would be his own.

In retrospect, I delayed his and my happiness. I was too focused on his drinking to realize that my happiness was not tied to his. He could not affect me unless I let him. It was very liberating to not have to worry about him or his drinking or his consequences. He was not a child. He was a grown man. He knew what to do and how to do it. He didn't need a mother. He needed a wife. I realized all this once I started focusing on me and how I was causing my unhappiness by trying to change other people. I understand now that I can only change myself and how I view things.

It was amazing how fast the change came once I got it. When I really backed off and stopped counting and measuring, he took control really fast. In retrospect, it makes perfect sense. Before, he had never had to control his drinking because I was controlling it for him. In my mind I was trying to help, but in reality I was hurting him.

Don't get me wrong, I realize that many who struggle with an alcoholic partner don't have someone who is able to deliver like my husband was able to do in this situation. His ability to show up and meet my needs made a big difference, but the process of changing myself was no small task. The feeling I had to control his drinking was very strong, and it took me multiple meetings and reminding myself hundreds of times, "This is his deal." It was a big challenge to learn to verbalize what I really needed from him. The drinking was a detail of my problem — it was not the cause. The lack of communicating my needs was the cause of my problem. My husband still drinks today, but now I have made it clear that it is his responsibility and the consequences will be his own. I continue to focus on my needs and communicating them in a respectful manner. That is all I can do. He may or may not keep his drinking in check. If he does, great for us. If not, it is his deal, and my responsibility to myself is to get my needs met. Time will tell.

I still catch myself analyzing the wine bottle, but now I am able to remind myself that this is his deal, not mine, BEFORE I have any negative emotions. Each time is as an opportunity to remind myself not to take on his problems as my own. My challenge is to stop trying to change other people. I only wish I had understood sooner that what I needed to change was myself and how I viewed things. This lesson was my beginning. For that I am grateful. In *Excuses Begone*, Wayne Dyer shares this poignant H. Jackson Brown quote, "Never underestimate your power to change yourself. Never overestimate your power to change others."

Shortcuts

→ You can change your thoughts.

→ Changing your thoughts will change your life.

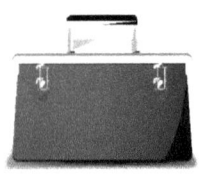

Tool Kit

→ Affirmations

→ Reframing

→ Labeling

→ Emotional Stress Release (ESR)

→ Snap Out of It

→ HeartMath® Coherence

→ Ho'oponopono

→ Exercise

→ Repetition or Mantra

→ Meditation

→ Prayer

→ Visualization

→ TFT / EFT

→ Yoga

→ Proclamations of the Soul

→ Hypnosis

→ Acupuncture

→ Subliminal Audios / Sleep Meditation CDs

→ PSYCH-K®

→ Brain Gym®

→ Aroma Therapy

→ Rewrite Your Story

→ Just Breathe

> "Whatever is true, whatever is noble, whatever is right, whatever is pure, whatever is lovely, whatever is admirable – if anything is excellent or praiseworthy – think about such things."
>
> ~ Philippians 4:8 (NIV)

STEP 4
FEEL

Thoughts + Feelings = Beliefs.

Feelings, or emotions, are the way the physical body experiences the thoughts we think. *Feeling it* is like engaging the turbo boosters on your vehicle. What you feel is the turbo charge behind your thoughts. Changing your thoughts or "positive thinking" is only a short-term solution. In order to create real change, we also need congruence between our thoughts and our feelings. If you are forcing yourself to think one way but in reality you feel another way, you are sending out mixed signals. In this case, your brain is sending out one signal and your body is broadcasting a completely different and more powerful signal. In Chapter 4: *Electrical System – Hardwired or Hot-wired*, we discussed the research being done by the Institute of HeartMath, which reveals that the heart's electromagnetic field is approximately five thousand times greater in strength than the field produced by the brain. Joe Dispenza, author of the incredible book *Breaking the Habit of Being Yourself* describes your thoughts as being electric signals sent into the quantum reality of the universe, which organizes events and circumstances in the field of possibility where reality is born. Then the much more powerful electromagnetic force of your heart (or *feelings*) magnetically pulls the organized quantum reality back to you to form your experienced reality. This describes the mechanics behind the theory of how reality is organized and formed out of the field of pure potential. In the field of pure potential, anything is possible, and anything we can think can actually happen. Bring it!

It is absolutely imperative that we learn to *feel* the way we choose to think! With feelings that are five thousand times greater in strength then our thoughts, it is easy to understand how emotion magnifies your energy. The higher the emotion the stronger the energy you emit. The stronger the energy the faster it will match up with like energy to produce your reality. Here is an example that illustrates this point. Imagine an emotional intensity scale of 1 to 10. You are working on creating more abundance in your life. You catch poverty mentality thoughts, and you are replacing them with thoughts of abundance. You meditate and pray about it. You picture yourself abundant, and when you do this, you muster about a 2 on the scale of emotional intensity – but you are working on it. Three weeks go by and you are doing pretty well staying on track. Then on the fourth week, your dreaded bills come in. You can feel your anxiety rising. Sprinkle in some resentment and shame for living beyond your means. You struggle to maintain a positive thinking pattern, and you feel a knot in the pit of your stomach. Then out of the blue, BAMMM, you get hit with an expense that you were not expecting. Just for fun let's say it is a $200 electronic traffic ticket that someone else in your family got while driving your car, and nobody bothered to tell you about it. Now you won't be able to afford to get your hair done and color those horrible roots growing in on your head, or get your brakes fixed on your car, which you so desperately need to do. Do what now? You lose your mind and your cool, and you have a full-fledged fit of 10 on your scale of 1 to 10! In this case it is a fit of negativity, so it is really a negative ten or −10. Let us do the math for you: a positive 2 plus a negative 10 equals a negative 8. Get it? Now what are you *really* attracting? Don't fool yourself. Just because you are having positive thoughts doesn't mean you are having positive feelings. The good news is that it is absolutely possible to create feelings that match your thoughts. It just takes awareness and practice.

Negative feelings and emotions are destructive. Positive feelings are empowering. Here are a few of our favorite shortcuts to avoid a full on fit:

→ Breathe. Really breeeeeatthhhhe. Take a big deep breath. This will oxygenate your brain and help you think more clearly instead of going into fight or flight. It will also bring your attention to your body, which can redirect the mind. A good deep breath will give you a pause and allow you to feel a little bit of space between you and whatever is pissing you off.

→ Our next favorite comes from Eckhart Tolle's book *A New Earth*. He suggests that in the heat of the moment you repeat to yourself, "This too shall pass, this too shall pass." We know for a fact that this statement is true. It always passes, sooner or later.

→ In Miriam Williamson's book *Return to Love,* she suggests that when you feel worked-up ask yourself, "Do I want to be right or happy?" This is one of our favorite shortcuts. Not only has it helped us defuse many potentially ugly situations, but it has helped us learn to keep our mouths shut when it is appropriate to do so – a lesson we continue to work on!

Creating or Enhancing Positive Emotion:

→ Smile. Yes, smile more! It makes you feel happy. Call centers and customer service departments believe in smiling so much that many of them require mirrors on the desks of all their employees so they can see themselves smiling while they talk on the phone. It works. Their customers can hear their smiles. Studies show that even an artificially induced smile brings about happier emotions. You can even smile when you're pissed. After you stop feeling like a crazy person, it feels kind of good…well, at least better. And if you do it in front of people while you are losing your cool, it is weirdly intimidating and can serve as a sweet warning signal.

→ Share your positive emotions and encourage people to share their positive feelings with you. When you share your goods, you are offering your positive energy to someone else. Energy frequencies tend to match up. You literally have the ability to lift someone's spirits. In Bruce Lipton's book *Biology of Belief* there are some cool graphs of how energies join together and even compound when they are matched together. Have you ever wanted to bail on plans to go somewhere because you had a bad day or were tired, but you just couldn't get out of it and had to go? Then you got to where you were going and everyone there was having such a good time you ended up swinging from the chandeliers? That happens to us often. It's possible because our energy and the energy of others have the ability to impact how we feel.

→ Another great way to increase positive emotion is to do something kind for someone else. In *The Power of Now* Eckhart Tolle tells the story of helping a man in despair. During a phone conversation the man was expressing that he was having trouble wanting to live. Eckhart asked him if he could think of anything helpful he could do for someone else. After some contemplation the man said he had noticed that a neighbor had a mess in front of her door and perhaps could use some help cleaning it up. Eckhart asked him to put down the phone and go do it while he waited. When the man returned to the phone his whole attitude and outlook on life had changed. Helping others is a great way to feel good. Gretchen Rubin, author of *The Happiness Project*, states, "Although we presume that we act because of the way we feel, in fact we often feel the way we act."

→ Visualization and expansion is another technique that can be used to manufacture and enhance good feelings. We discussed the power of visualization in Chapter 15: *Change Your Thoughts*, but it can also be used to intentionally manufacture feelings and emotion. You can do this by simply setting aside time, finding a quiet place, closing your eyes, and beginning to picture yourself doing, or being, or creating whatever it is that you want. Use vivid and descriptive pictures in your mind as if you are acting in a movie in your own future. Be the actor in your visualization and use your other senses to get into your part by also smelling, touching, and hearing the environment you are visualizing. Once you are really into it, you will start to feel the positive emotion being produced in your body. That positive emotion is what you are after! It has the power to affect your brain, your body, and your future reality. So hold on to it. With your imagination, gather up that positive feeling and ball it up in your heart. Give the feeling a color and a temperature. Steep in it. Then breathe into it, drawing a breath in through your nose, down into your chest. With every breath visualize and feel that emotion growing larger throughout your whole body. Feel it in every cell and then imagine it growing beyond the boundaries of your physical body into the space around you. Expand it as far as you can imagine, until it feels as if that positive feeling is one with the entire universe. If this sounds like a foreign language to you, let's illustrate this technique using the example of abundance. Remember when those damn bills showed up in your mailbox and you felt knots in your stomach? This time, because you are developing a new sense of awesome conscious awareness, you caught yourself getting uncomfortable. Instead of taking a ride on the crazy train, you instead decided to take some deep, deliberate breaths. You open the bills and check the balances while you consciously insist on remaining calm. Then you put the bills down and go sit outside or in your favorite place where you relax and begin your visualization. You imagine you are walking into the gas station. Smell the faint scent of drip coffee and the disgusting hot dogs. Feel yourself approach the counter and briefly admire all the choices of gum and mints. Smile at the clerk then reach into your pocket and feel the dollars between your fingers and request your 100 million dollar lottery ticket! Go ahead and wink at the clerk just for fun. Then fast forward a few days. You pull out your ticket – feel it, look at the numbers, notice where you are sitting, and feel yourself there. Start checking the numbers. The first one matches, you are a bit surprised. The second one matches, and you quickly look ahead to the third. It matches too. Now your heart is racing, and you are having a hot flash. You check the remaining numbers, and they seem to be a match. You start going blind from shock, and you check and recheck the numbers. You have won! All the excitement, relief and anticipation to go shopping and share your extreme wealth rushes into your body. Now hold that feeling as long as you can. When you are finished, go back to paying your bills. Then if you need to, go win the lottery in your head again!

OK. Back to reality. Does that mean that in the future you are guaranteed to win the multi-million dollar lottery? NO, EINSTEIN! Technically speaking, according to our Google search and depending on the type of lottery you play, you do actually have *ONE* chance in about 13,983,816 to 176,000,000 to win. Realistically, you have a better chance of becoming president or being crushed by a vending machine but that is not the point! The point is that you are creating a coherence of energy between your mind and your body, between your thoughts and your feelings, which is sending out energy into the field of infinite possibilities. That energy can then match up with like energy and be magnetically drawn back to you because you *FEEL IT*. Now in our current example, when that energy matches up with abundance and returns to you, it will probably not be in the form of the winning lottery ticket. The universe and the field of pure potential are filled with countless possibilities of abundance. Maybe you will get an opportunity for a better paying job, get some inheritance, or partner up with someone with financial resources. Be open to surprises. You may not be able to imagine how it will come. The less you try to control the details, the easier the opportunities will flow (See Rule of the Road #3). Ester Hicks, who writes extensively on The Law of Attraction, says, "Whatever it is you are feeling is a perfect reflection of what you are in the process of becoming." How you feel about something and how much you feel about something will definitely impact the quality of your life's trip.

Amity's Story: Big Girl Dreams

My second-grade daughter had big dreams. She set her heart on a complete room makeover so she could ditch her "little girl room" and transition into something more sophisticated. In order to prepare for this big transition she relentlessly watched kid room makeover shows on HGTV and thumbed through all the furniture advertisements that came in the mail. One afternoon we were running errands and happened to be close to a Room To Go kids store. She was bent on having a look, for the sake of research, of course. We wound our way around the maze of furnishings and then it happened...she fell in love. Love at first sight with a bunk bed. Now this was no ordinary bunk bed. It was the kind that was a full bed on top with a workstation below. It had all the bells and whistles and was decorated with colorful locker doors. She was convinced that the bed would even encourage her to study because it made school look fun. I was convinced that it would NOT be fun to make the bed everyday but I resisted my temptation to squash her dream. As much as I wanted to help my sweet baby girl get the room of her dreams, it just wasn't in the cards financially. The bed cost $1,000 – money that we did not have. We discussed that financial fact and made a plan.

I considered going the route most often traveled by well-meaning parents, which included her raising money herself to pay for the bed by doing dishes, folding the laundry, and picking up dog poop. But this plan had flaws. She was too young to babysit or cut grass, which left us with limited options for her to work for money. And who was I kidding? At that time I didn't have any extra to pay her anyway. Even if I turned her out to the neighborhood to try to make the money on the open market, she would surely have outgrown the bunk bed fantasy altogether. Instead, we decided to test the Law of Attraction Theory!

She knew exactly what she wanted – the bunk bed. We printed a picture of it and put it on the bathroom mirror. Then every night, when I put her to bed, we imagined that she was being tucked into that bunk bed. She visualized herself climbing up the cool steel ladder and felt herself as if she was suspended five feet above the ground in bed. We talked about how beautiful her new bed was and how comfy the mattress felt. As she drifted off to sleep she would feel thankful in her heart that she was able to get the bed of her dreams. She really got into it. She FELT IT! We did this for a week or so, and then I did what moms do best – I forgot about it. Totally.

Life raged on: soccer practice here, acting lessons there. We were riding in the car to one of our various activities, invariably eating dinner from behind our seat belts when the phone rang. It was PawPaw. He had called to talk about his adventures taking care of the affairs of his elderly stepmother. This was a conversation we had regularly so I was half listening as I wrestled with a ketchup packet for one of the kids. Paw went on to say that as he was going through old paperwork he had come across an old Gerber Life Insurance policy that his mother opened for him when he was a baby, back in the 1940's. He said it wasn't worth much, but he wanted to split it with my brother, and me. He said I'd be receiving a check in the mail for about $1,000. WooooHoooo! Pay some bills, new make-up and clothes and maybe even a massage for Mommy! I couldn't wait to get my hands on some extra fundage! It had been a very long time since I'd had any extra to treat myself. I couldn't wait!

After I hung up with my generous dad, I shared the good news with the girls. Heck, I might even take them to the movies to celebrate. But then, from way back in the third-row seat, I heard the voice of my sweet, enthusiastic, and tremendously grateful seven year old, "MOM, I'M FINALLY GETTING MY BUNK BED!"

And she did!

For the record, making that bed is a bitch!

Shortcut

→ Use feeling to enhance the positive and defuse the negative.

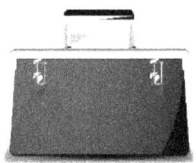

Tool Kit

→ Breathe.

→ This too shall pass.

→ Do I want to be right or happy?

→ Smile.

→ Share your goods.

→ Do something nice.

→ Imagery.

> "Just as your car runs more smoothly and requires less energy to go faster and farther when the wheels are in perfect alignment, you perform better when your thoughts, feelings, emotions, goals, and values are in balance."
>
> ~ Brian Tracy

17

STEP 5
BELIEVE

If you think it and you can feel it, you just might be able to believe it! Just when you think you have it all figured out, we are here to tell you that changing your thoughts is only part of the road trip. There needs to be congruence between your thoughts, feelings, and beliefs in order to create real change. Positive thinking just isn't enough. That's why there are so many haters out there telling us that positive thinking just doesn't work. The truth is, it can work but not without the interaction of your feelings, and your beliefs. When all three are working together it is like having the mind (thoughts), the body (feelings), and the subconscious (belief systems) in perfect concert to create the map of your life.

Beliefs are filters. All of our experiences are filtered through our belief systems. Just like when your car needs an oil change, and the filter is dirty, it would be plain stupid to change the oil and not change the filter too. The same is true for your thoughts. If you start thinking new thoughts but those thoughts are filtered through a polluted belief system they will not have the same impact for changing your life.

Remember that pesky, all too powerful, subconscious mind? It is filled with thoughts that have been generated so many times that they have become your beliefs. You don't have to have any conscious awareness to think these repetitive thoughts; they are on autopilot and have become your belief system. Your belief systems drive your thoughts, and your thoughts reinforce your belief systems. Belief is a powerful tool. We need it for the endurance and time it takes to create real change. To believe something is to know it as truth. When we believe something, we hold it in our minds as being true even when we are not consciously thinking about it. With belief comes a deeper knowing and thinking pattern that can penetrate the subconscious. It is not enough just to change our thoughts, we also need to change our core beliefs.

Go back to the analogy of thoughts being energy. Every time you have a consciously positive thought, with the intent to create a better life for yourself, you send out a wave of energy with a specific frequency. This energy signature matches up with like energy to help synthesize events, circumstances, people and opportunities to support you. However, if your subconscious is still programmed for repetitive negativity, related to a belief system that no longer serves you, you will be sending out a higher number of negative thoughts, with a lower energy signal. The positive thoughts from your conscious mind can't compete with the number of negative thoughts generated from your subconscious! Remember, these lower frequency thoughts also seek like energy patterns and are continuing to co-create the life that your are mindfully attempting to change.

In *The Biology of Belief,* Bruce Lipton says, "Your beliefs act like filters on a camera, changing how you see the world. And your biology adapts to those beliefs. When we truly recognize that our beliefs are that powerful we hold the key to freedom." So how does one go about changing their beliefs? First, you need to challenge your existing belief patterns. Dr. Wayne Dyer has a simple method we heard him share at a Hay House "I Can Do It" event in San Francisco. During his lecture Wayne asked the audience to use a questioning method to decide if their current belief system is accurate. He said, "Ask yourself, *Is that true? Has it ever happened before?* If it happened once before, then that is evidence that it can happen again." Money was the topic in his example. He asked the audience, by a show of hands, how many people had unexpectedly received money sometime over the course of their lifetime. In an audience of about 3,000, 90% raised their hands. The money showed up in the form of bonuses, inheritances, gifts, refunds, and more. The point was, if it could happen to 90% of the people in the audience, why couldn't it happen to you? It gave us a rational way to change our belief systems.

Go ahead, challenge your belief systems, whatever the topic. Run around like we did asking, "Is that true? Has it happened before…ever?" We came to the conclusion that most of our beliefs were not even our own. We hijacked them from our parents, our friends, and our society. Some of our belief systems were so imbedded in us that they were even hard to detect. Many of our constructs came from religious beliefs, prejudices, and role expectations. This may be the case for you too. Now that you have developed the habit of watching your thoughts, you can start to challenge some of those repetitive thoughts and beliefs. If you are trying to identify some of your own belief systems, you can bet that they will occasionally show up in your speech.

Here is an example from an interaction I had with a friend. In conversation, my friend Julie condescendingly referred to the people who lived in an affluent neighborhood nearby as *"those people."* It struck me as funny since we didn't know many people from that area and the ones we had met seemed to me to be perfectly nice and normal. I was compelled to pay closer attention to her opinion about money. Soon I noticed a consistent theme. Money = bad, dirty, and greedy. But why? Are all affluent people bad? Of course not. Did she even know one rich person who was dirty or greedy? Probably not. And even if she did have direct experience with someone who fit the bill, does that mean it should be applied to all people? No! There's no telling how this negative belief system has impacted her life, but I'd bet you a million dollars that it has put a damper on her prosperity.

This is just a small example of an ingrained belief system that can live in your head. Try challenging some of these beliefs and consciously decide if they serve you or if they attract negativity into your life. If so, it is time to let them go. Amity once held a belief that all men were cheaters. She formed this belief system in the typical fashion, through hardcore experience. One boyfriend after another would prove to be unfaithful. Instead of assuming these young handsome men were just learning lessons in their youth like many people do, she decided to go for a much more pessimistic alternative: all men are pigs! And thus reinforced her beliefs with reality, one heartbreak at a time. Finally, that belief system was undeniably challenged. She was dating a seemingly wonderful guy. He was handsome, fun, and a hard worker. All cylinders were firing and things were physically heating up, but he was holding back. There had to be a reason for his resistance. Amity's mind panicked with all the deal breakers she could imagine. She was falling for him hard, and all the signs were suggesting that he felt the same too. Why was he holding back? Finally the day came when he fessed up. He didn't want the relationship to go any further until she knew the truth about him. Her heart stopped as she prepared for the worst while he delivered the news. "I was married," he muttered. For an instant she thought she heard "I'm married," and panicked. Her voice trembled as she asked for clarification. "You *are* married or you *were* married?" A hot flash came over her, relieved that he was divorced. Never in Amity's wildest imagination could she fathom how this wonderful man could ever be married and then divorced at the ripe old age of 25. It just didn't compute in the polluted belief system she had established. She couldn't hold back the tears as he shared his story about marrying his college sweetheart, working three jobs to put her through grad school, then her leaving him for her study partner, a man he had befriended and welcomed in his home. It shattered Amity's former belief system – where all men were cheaters and all women were victims – and provided a clean filter for her to work with. This new awareness and experience helped Amity break the pattern of her belief system. She stopped attracting cheaters, and infidelity has not been an issue in her life ever since.

As we challenge our beliefs throughout our journey, we discover that our beliefs do not define us as much as we expect. They are just beliefs, true or not, images floating in our head that we can choose to buy into or not. Nothing bad will happen if you let your negative, erroneous, and unproductive beliefs go. You won't implode. You will still be the same old person, just a little less delusional. We have come to the conclusion, as we hope you do, that it's just as practical to believe something positive, uplifting, and proactive. It might make this trip something to write home about.

James Allen, in his book *As a Man Thinketh*, addresses the idea of belief by stating, "He who cherishes a beautiful vision, a lofty idea in his heart, will one day realize it. Columbus cherished a vision of another world, and he discovered it." In 1492 Christopher Columbus set sail from Spain, believing against most others, that you could get to the East by going west. It took him seven years to convince the Spanish king and queen that he could do it. The voyage was supposed to last only a few days based on maps of that time. After more than sixty days at sea, the sailors aboard the vessel were fearful of starvation and filled with dread. They lacked the courage to sail onward into the unknown. On October 10th, scared and angry, the sailors aboard his ship threatened mutiny if he would not turn around. He believed land was close. He could not give up. Exhausted from persuading his sailors to stay on course when a course wasn't available, Columbus promised them that if they did not see land in three days, they would return to Europe. Two days later, at dawn, land was spotted. Shazam! Thank you, Mr. Christopher Columbus.

The thoughts we think are driven by our belief systems, and our belief systems drive our thoughts. Just like one big giant habitual recording being played on a loop setting: thoughts, emotion, beliefs, thoughts, emotions, over and over again. Cleaning your belief filters, so your thoughts are in congruence with your core beliefs, is a necessary part of creating the life you want. Belief will help cement your positive attractor thoughts into your subconscious mind and help you stay the course on your journey. New thoughts, new feelings, new beliefs = new thoughts, new emotions, new life.

Amity's Story: We Will Win

In the spring of 2005 my husband Kevin was invited to attend South by Southwest in Austin, Texas, by the Music Commissioner of Louisiana. Kevin was knee deep into a new venture called Hot Local Music (HLM), a technology business to help local musicians and venues manage and promote their music. The Commissioner had offered us some space at his booth promoting Louisiana music during the convention. HLM had all the latest and greatest technology utilizing the web and mobile phone platforms. We were low on cash but rich with a vision of leveling the playing field for local artists by providing them with big label technology. HLM was a bit before its time and had two major problems: first, back then local musicians and venues were NOT on the cutting edge of technology; second most of them were broke with little or no money to pay for our service. At any rate, we were determined to make our debut at South by Southwest, one way or another.

I had quit my pharmaceutical job about a year earlier and for the first time in our marriage things were tight financially. We were adjusting to the expense of a second child and lack of income from my "retirement." We scraped together all the cash we had, rented a cheap hotel, and carpooled our HLM team to Austin, TX. We arrived in the evening and checked into our hotel. It was a far cry from the hotels we used to stay in when we were selling drugs in the pharmaceutical business. Unfortunately for us, it appeared that there were a few people loitering around the parking lot in that same line of work, but they were selling the non-prescription kind. I checked my pride and braced for the worst.

As we made our way to our rooms I was thinking *What is that smell?* and *What is with all the barking?* Then it dawned on me. People actually lived in this hotel! They were cooking dinner and feeding their pets! Nice! To make matters worse, we could only afford one pass to the conference. We created a makeshift schedule of who would use the pass and when. The rest of the time was spent trying to act like we belonged in the scene, while passing out marketing materials and talking up HLM.

On our last morning there I happened into a meeting room at one of the host hotels. It was Apple's demo room for their Prologic music recording software. They were having a raffle for prizes. The rules were only one entry per person, and you had to be present to win. The drawing was that evening. I am usually not the kind of person who enters drawings, but one of the prizes was a Brian Moore guitar. My husband, an avid musician, would love to have a new guitar. I hurried out of the room to collect the rest of our crew and forced them to participate in the demo by entering the drawing on Kevin's behalf. When I filled out my entry, I folded it in half and drew a big smiley face on the back. I dropped it into the box and I just knew in my heart, I BELIEVED, that we would win that guitar.

The hours dragged on, and everyone was getting restless to leave and head home. Kevin was tirelessly working the floor in the convention while we gathered in the lobby and sat around, tired and bored. The drawing was about two hours away when talk broke out about retreating to our hotel. I had a fit. My tirade went something like this, "We have scraped our last dollars together to be here. Kevin has worked his ass off at this convention. The least we can do is not bail on him because we are bored. He has sold every guitar (three of them) and every amplifier he had to help make ends meet so we could be here. WE ARE ALL STAYING SO KEVIN CAN WIN THAT GUITAR!!!!! Reluctantly, they stayed. I was pissed! They probably were too.

We filed into the Apple room about ten minutes before the drawing. Kevin had joined us and added his name to the drawing. The room was curiously empty, and Kevin played with the software like a kid in a candy store. A few more people straggled in as the drawing began. The first prize awarded was the Prologic software valued at about $1,100. The emcee called the name "Dave Johnson." We were all shocked. Dave was our IT guy! Score! Next prize up was an additional software package that enhances the Prologic software by giving the user the ability to record hundreds of additional instruments. It was worth about

$300. "Paula Casentini" was called over the microphone. Paula is the wife of one of HLM's executives! Score again! A few more names were called and a few more prizes given. Then it was time for the grand finale – the Brian Moore guitar worth about $1,800. The man called a name, but the guy was not present. He called another name, not present. My heart was beating so fast. Kevin turned and winked at me and gave me a big smile. Then the room filled with the sound, "Kevin Carriere!" We all went bonkers. Kevin had won the guitar! I had chills running up and down my spine. I just knew he would win that guitar. I BELIEVED it!

That trip cost us about $300 in hotel costs, $350 for the South by Southwest pass, $200 in gas, and we had brought most of our food. We spent less than $1,000 to get there on a wing and a prayer and left with $3,200 in prizes and one very happy husband!

 **Shortcuts**

→ Beliefs are filters for your thoughts.

→ It is not enough just to change our thoughts, we also need to change our beliefs.

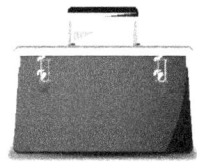 **Tool Kit**

→ Challenge your beliefs by asking yourself, "Is this true?"

→ Examine the beliefs of your family and friends. Do you accept these as truth?

→ Choose to believe in the positive and something uplifting.

> "It's the repetition of affirmations that leads to belief. And once that belief becomes a deep conviction, things begin to happen."
>
> ~ Muhammad Ali

18

STEP 6
PERCEIVE

So far on our trip we know where we want to go and, along the way, we are monitoring our dashboards for warning lights (negative thoughts). We know how to change those negative thoughts into productive affirmations and infuse them with lots of feeling. We are practicing this consistently and passionately enough to create new belief systems. Now the magic starts to happen. All the energy you have put out into the field of possibility will begin to organize and start to show up for you. It's time to pay attention! Keep your windshield clean and all of your mirrors free of obstacles. Remain alert and watch for signs, or green lights, as we like to call them. It may be something as simple as a friend making a recommendation, one that you may not pay any particular attention to, but days later you hear that same recommendation from a completely different source. Two green lights, pay attention! These signs may also present themselves as helpful opportunities or important people to get you further down the road. These simple signs are encouraging reminders that you are, in fact, manifesting what you have set your mind and heart to accomplish. Pay attention! Perceive it!

The key to being able to *perceive it*, and even notice all the green lights is to remain open to the possibilities. Most of us go about our day with a mission in mind. Our egos run the show, and we have an idea of what we need to do, what to expect, and how it is going to happen. This is a perception killer. In our efforts to remain focused, we shut ourselves off to the infinite possibilities and opportunities that are all around us. All you Control Freaks, beware – this can be your downfall. If you have it in your head that your plan will go down just as you have designed it, details included, you are taking your road trip with a hell of a blind spot. Revisit *Rule of The Road #3* in Chapter: *Let Go of Control*. Rest assured, a universe that can unfold into the wondrous world we live in needs little help from you to synthesize the millions of potential synchronicities to get you from point A to point B.

The opportunities that often cross your path are not always obvious. Expect surprises and practice anticipation. Expect things to move in the right direction, but expect them not to happen the way you have imagined. Live your life as if every moment has the potential to deliver something unexpected and wonderful. An open mind and an open heart are required to remain open to life's possibilities. Just like having a dirty windshield will cut down on your vision, having a closed heart and a closed mind will do the same. When you are closed, you resist the natural flow of life. Don't listen to the advice of others and revert back to your favorite childhood word *no*. The worst thing about being in a closed state is that it is far too easy to miss life's little signs nudging you in the direction of fulfillment.

Make an effort to remain open. There is a definite energy shift in the body between feeling open and being closed. When you are in an open state of being, you are willing. You say *yes* easily, and change flows naturally. You feel lighter in your body, and little things roll right off your back. When you are in an open state, you are in harmony with the current moment and much more likely to see subtle signs and threads of synchronicity in daily events.

For example, Amity was having a dental problem. It was not an emergency; she just had some questions and a desire for a second opinion. She was traveling at the time and for whatever reason, her flight was cancelled, and she became stuck in the Houston airport for six hours. The other passengers were livid. Amity, however, was practicing her shortcuts and made the mental decision to accept the change in plans and enjoy the day. She remembered specifically thinking, *I wonder what adventure I will have today?* While standing in line to be rescheduled to a different flight, a terribly annoying lady in front of Amity was in need of a phone. Recognizing her own discomfort and resistance to this woman, Amity decided to change her thoughts and be helpful. She offered up her cell phone, and the lady relaxed and eventually resolved her flight issues so the rest of the line could make some progress. About an hour later the annoying lady spotted Amity having lunch in the terminal and invited herself to join. *Great, see what I get for being helpful!* raced through Amity's head as she faked her willingness to share her table. After about five minutes of small talk, they got around to discussing why they were flying through Houston. As fate would have it, the annoying woman was on her way to a dental convention! Second opinion accomplished!

Another perception killer is the tendency to deny your own intuition. If you pay attention, we bet you will find that many times a day you will have the natural urge to do or say something out of the ordinary. Unfortunately for most of us as soon as this natural urge happens, a little voice pops in our head that says, *Don't say that, you might disturb that person,* or *Don't do that, you don't have the time.* We have thoroughly conditioned ourselves to completely ignore our own divine intuition. Intuition can serve you greatly in leading you in the right direction on your journey. Cultivate your intuition. The best way to do this is by listening. As soon as you hear those thoughts in your head, try to shut them down, and consciously push the override button. Force yourself to act on that urge. Go ahead, strike up that conversation with the person sitting next to you. How else are you going to find out who or what fate has put in your path today? Follow your intuition. It just might lead you to that perfect person or perfect situation to assist you on your path.

Karen's Story: MOJO

While researching material for this book, I came across an article that recommended some motivational books. I picked them up from my local library and brought them home to review. After looking at the titles, I found that some of them referred to sales techniques, so I shared one with my husband entitled "MOJO: How to get it, How to keep it, How to get it back if you lose it." He felt like the content was relevant to his work so he started to read it. During the next few weeks, he began to apply some of the techniques and philosophies he learned in the book. He was feeling good and seeing the results in his work. Around the house he would make comments like "getting my mojo on" or he would text me, "feeling my mojo today." I replied by texting back, "Your customers want More Joe," making a play on his name Joe.

For the next three weeks, we played with this saying during our daily routine. After a long workweek that was peppered with a lot of positive thoughts and feelings producing great results, he was winding down from his week enjoying a drink on the porch. He found himself wondering how simple thoughts and feelings could produce such dramatic sales results. He began to wonder if he was just fooling himself. Maybe his great week was a coincidence. His gaze wandered across the patio where a small white ball caught his eye. A few minutes later Joe came running in and said, "Are you playing some kind of joke on me?" Totally confused by his question, I said, "What are you talking about?"

In his hand he held a golf ball. "What's that?" I questioned. Joe loves to golf and at the time we lived on the 5th hole of a public golf course. He hadn't been golfing recently, and rarely in the five years of living there had any golf balls hit our screened in patio area. As a matter of fact, no golf balls had ever made it through the screen onto the porch. "Look at the ball," Joe said. At first glance, it looked like a regular old golf ball. But when I looked closer, written on the ball was the word "MOJO!" We looked at each other in disbelief. He said, "Did you put this on the deck?" I said, "No!! Where did you find it?" He said, "Right outside on the porch in front of the pool!" I had been out at the pool with the kids all afternoon for hours and had never seen a golf ball. Joe showed me the exact spot where he had found it, which was four feet from the main entrance to the pool. I have no idea how we did not see it there. Even freakier, the ball had "MOJO #3" written on it. The very title of the book he had been reading the last three weeks! He was LIVING mojo and there it was! We know that "Life's a Trip," but being surprised by this simple yet powerful act still puts goose bumps on our arms. Finding that MOJO ball blew us away. We talked about it in disbelief all night.

Joe must have been inspired because the next day he woke up bright and early and went to play golf with a friend. Again, he came home with a bizarre look of disbelief on his face. "You are NOT going to believe this!" he said. He went on to tell me that after striking his Titleist 1 ball off the first tee, which was a straight shot right down the middle, he and his friend could not find it. They drove to the spot it dropped and circled and circled. How could it be lost, it was right down the middle? After a vigorous search they returned to the area where they thought the ball originally dropped. There they spotted a ball. Joe picked it up and turned it over. Written on the ball was MOJO #4! He was totally freaked out! He picked it up and put it in his pocket so he could show me and not risk losing it. After hearing the story, I was skeptical. Was he sure he didn't hit that ball? How is that possible? Did he take the ball from the day before? He showed me both MOJO balls. He said he is 100% confident he put a Titleist ball down to hit; he even lined up his club with the linear guideline on the ball and double-checked the name on his ball. He said in his whole life and all the years golfing he has never heard of, or even seen a MOJO golf ball. To find two golf balls at the point in his life where he is reading about and acting out mojo was CRAZY. Both MOJO balls are currently displayed in his office as a constant reminder that what you put your attention on is what will show up in your life, crazy or not. Watch for the signs and perceive it!

Shortcut

→ Remain alert and open to all the signs, opportunities, and support that life offers.

 **Tool Kit**

→ Ask, "What adventure does life have in store for me today?"

→ Expect surprises and practice anticipation.

→ Follow your intuition.

> "What you intend for yourself determines what you get. Although it seems like a paradox, you must have a vision of the future to surprise you, for without visions, life dwindles into ritual and repetition. A future that merely repeats the present can never be surprising."
>
> ~ Deepak Chopra

19

STEP 7
PARTICIPATE

You can't expect your vehicle to drive itself – participation is a requirement. Just thinking about your life's trip isn't going to cut it; you actually have to *be* the driver and DO SOMETHING!!! At this point in your journey you know where you want to go, relentlessly watch your thoughts, correct your thoughts, feel what you want, believe you can create it, and remain alert watching for the signs that point you in the right direction. However, what happens when one of those signs, opportunities, or requirements to participate shows up? It is time to play ball and TAKE ACTION! Thinking about what you want and doing something about it are two different things. You have to start *doing it* and let action toward your goal become habit. When you combine action and participation with your intentions, you will move from thinking and feeling into doing and being. When intentions are married to participation, you are *BEING* what you want to create. You get to *BE* the driver of your life!

Action is simply defined as the process of doing something. Physicists define action as:

$$S[\mathbf{q}(t)] = \int_{t_1}^{t_2} L[\mathbf{q}(t), \dot{\mathbf{q}}(t), t] dt$$

Which leads us to this obvious conclusion: *WTF?*

We wanted to put this definition in to simply remind you (and ourselves), that most of us really don't know squat. Don't take it personally. It's OK not to be a know-it-all. Besides, it is impossible to know everything. We are just making the point that we should be humble in our assumptions and remain open to other information and opinions – it's just good manners for being human.

As important and fundamental as these two definitions are, we prefer to think of action in terms of energy in motion. Action is the physical manifestation of thought into form. Einstein proved that all matter is made up of energy, and quantum physicists are studying how the energy of thought influences the quantum field of pure potentiality. Action, therefore, is the bridge between possibility and reality. The more action we put behind our intentions, the more energy is committed to making the most of our journey! So why is it so hard to actually get off our butts and do something?

Action and participation require an open mind, an open heart, and some good old-fashioned guts. In the previous chapter, we discussed staying open and following our intuition. You may be perceiving and exploring opportunities on your journey, but the difference between perception and participation is ACTION. It sounds so simple, right? Perhaps not.

There are many things that can get in the way of turning thought into action. The greatest obstacle is fear. Participation is going to require you to get out of your comfort zone. You have heard the old cliché, "You can't do the same things and expect different results!" The more you get accustomed to getting out of your comfort zone, the more comfortable you will become being uncomfortable. It's that simple. It is amazing to what lengths people will go to avoid feeling any discomfort. In fact, most of us are so emotionally numb or hypersensitive to emotional pain that we would rather suffer physically. Let's go run a million miles or kill ourselves in the gym before we face our problems, or God forbid, try something new, right? Plan to do something out of your comfort zone at least once a month. This doesn't have to be something spectacular like singing karaoke or jumping out of an airplane, although we hear both are pretty thrilling. It can be something simple like forcing yourself to strike up a conversation with a stranger in the Starbucks line. If you really want to have fun with this, challenge yourself to give a stranger a compliment, sing out loud while you shop, or bust out a dance move when no one is expecting it, or even better, call someone out of the blue and tell them why they are important to you. OK, we are getting carried away, but you get the point. Get used to being uncomfortable. If you feel frozen, it may be useful to psych yourself up by putting on the count, "one, two, three, GO!" and just do it! Learn to let the feeling of discomfort pass through you instead of holding on to it in your mind and body. It's just a feeling. Like all feelings, they come and go. Let it pass you by like the wind. Practice. We have to be willing to take action instead of making excuses in order to avoid pain.

Yes, people, we actually have to dig deep, stop the excuses, and do something! Do something that propels us toward making the most of our journey. Action is making an investment in what you want to create. Action creates momentum and is proof that your intentions and your thoughts match up. It is the difference between magical thinking and the reality of manifesting what you want out of life. It is the difference between saying you want something and actually being willing to do something about it.

Another way you can participate and take action is through a daily practice of silence, prayer, meditation, or any other regular contemplative activity. We have touched upon the many ways this kind of daily practice positively affects the body and the mind, but in spiritual terms, communing with yourself or a higher power (or both) opens new possibilities for guidance in your life. Making this a priority will put you in alignment with the Universe and your highest good and give you the time and space needed to cultivate your co-creation. If you think you are the kind of person who can't afford to sit in silence for 20 minutes a day, then you are exactly the person who can't afford not to.

Add the energy of action toward your life goals and pursuits. Refer back to your "Know What You Want" list and ask yourself, "Is there any action I can take right now to help me attain my goals?" The answer may be something as simple as a phone call, an internet search, asking someone for help, or whatever it may be to put some energy behind what you want to create in your life. Remember, there is always some tangible action you can take, even if it is just to take five minutes to go envision yourself with your goal attained. Review your plan and progress once a week. Write it down and post it on your mirror so you can see it and remind yourself that action adds to the energy of creation. Also, use your powers of perception to act spontaneously when the opportunity arises. Be ready and willing to act. Whenever you make an action that moves you toward the life of your dreams, the reward is inherent. The action itself will make you feel good. It will build your self-esteem and reaffirm your commitment to improving your life. Participation is an act of self-love.

Amity's Story: All Talk No Action

Recently I went on a girls' trip with some friends I have known for many, many years. We are all in the same stage of life: busy with kids, careers, husbands and everything else that keeps us from seeing each other, with the exception of the once- or twice-a-decade getaway. In an effort to accommodate everyone's discretionary income levels, we decided to stay at our friend Bernadette's house, the only household devoid of children. Unfortunately, it was not devoid of animals! Bernadette was going through another big transition in her life. After two divorces and a ten-year relationship with a younger man, she was single again.

After we arrived and brought in our suitcases, we settled in on the couch to catch up and have a glass of wine. While we were talking, a cat jumped up on my lap, then another cat jumped up on the chair across the room; then another one darted across the floor. "How many cats do you have, Bernadette?" I asked. She replied with a laugh, "You will have to count them." That was a game that didn't sound fun to me! Maybe she was lonely, but she definitely wasn't alone! It turns out there were six cats and two dogs. Disturbing.

As we caught up on each other's lives, Bernadette told us that she wanted to move back to her hometown of Cleveland, Ohio, so she could be closer to her parents and siblings for support. Although she had lived in New York for 20 years, she didn't have many girlfriends, and her social network had been decimated by her recent breakup. We all agreed that since she was going through a major transition anyway, why not go big and move home.

Throughout the weekend, the girls and I would throw out suggestions or ask questions regarding Bernadette's moving plan. The first thing I noticed were the water stains on the ceiling in a few of the rooms, and I asked if she had had them checked out by a professional. She told us that they had appeared after a big storm in the area but didn't have a plan to get them fixed. My next question, "Can't you file it under your homeowners insurance and get it repaired?" She said that she had filed it but her insurance company only gave her eight hundred dollars, which was not enough to cover the cost of repairs. I didn't want to embarrass her by asking what she had done with the money, but I was sure the money was long gone. The other gals chimed in and offered possible do-it-yourself solutions, but Bernadette said that she would never be able to match the drywall finish. It just so happened that our friend Kristy's husband was in the construction business and she knew exactly how to do that particular dry wall finish, but it fell on deaf ears. The things we were pointing out were the big jobs, but there were plenty of other easier fixes to getting the house ready to sell. A few cans of paint would easily cover the hideously outdated wallpaper, and we offered to knock it out that weekend. That was the last thing Bernadette wanted to do with her girlfriends in town even though we assured her that we wouldn't mind a bit. Even easier, a good garage sale could have cleared out a ton of personal items, otherwise known as "buyer turn-offs" – but she wasn't having it.

The weekend continued and so did the dialogue about the potential move. I will list a few highlights just for fun: A for Action and E for the Excuses that followed.

A = When are you going to put the house on the market?

E = The market is bad, so I may wait awhile. I need to fix the ceilings and paint. I also want to make sure I have a job in Cleveland first.

A = Have you looked for a job in Cleveland?

E = There is only one company in Cleveland that is in my line of business. I am worried about the pay cut I might have to take moving back to Ohio. I might not be able to get a house as nice as this.

A = Have you considered downsizing to a condo? It seems like a four-bedroom house with a yard is a lot for one person to keep up with.

E = Well, I need someplace to keep my animals. I don't think a condo would be good enough.

A = How are you going to show your home with all the cats and dogs (and smell of pets)?

E = I don't know, I can't get rid of them.

E = I don't have enough money. I need my parents to help me out so I can get home to Cleveland.

A = Bet feeding all those animals is expensive!?!

It went on and on like that. It was becoming painfully clear Bernadette just wanted to fantasize about moving and not actually do it. It was time to quit making suggestions and move into allowing – allowing someone the space to live in their own crazy world and respecting their process. As you can see, there ain't a lot of action happening toward getting Bernadette back to Ohio!

Shortcuts

→ Get off your butt and do something! Take action!

→ Participation requires an open mind, an open heart, and some good old-fashioned guts.

→ Action fuels momentum, producing energy for attaining your goals.

→ Action is the physical manifestation of thought into form.

Tool Kit

→ Get out of your comfort zone.

→ Let the fear of action pass through you.

→ Count 1,2,3. Just do it!

→ Do one tangible thing a day toward your goals.

→ Review your action plan regularly.

"Remember, people will judge you by your actions, not your intentions. You may have a heart of gold — but so does a hard-boiled egg."

~ Author Unknown

20

STEP 8
RECEIVE

There is one last important step in The Road Map. You can completely master Steps 1 through 7 and not reap the rewards of your efforts unless you are able to *receive* what you have asked for. It sounds bizarre, doesn't it? Of course, we would gladly receive the abundance, the love, the whatever it is that we want, right? Maybe not! What if becoming wealthy alienated you from friends and family because your money made them uncomfortable or envious? What if, in order to have the relationship you've been longing for, you were required to move across the country and leave your hometown? There are consequences involved with receiving what we have asked for. Some of these consequences are acceptable to us and some are not. Some consequences are foreseeable, and some seem to come out of nowhere and slap us upside the head. Regardless, it is important to challenge our belief systems and consciously rid the limiting beliefs from our mental process. Receiving requires us to let go of any fear related to getting what we are so desperately trying to cultivate in our lives.

We have a friend who says he is looking for the perfect partner. He can describe all the attributes he wants in a woman. He uses the Rules of the Road, and he follows the steps in The Road Map. We have watched the "perfect match" show up for him at least five times over a two-year period. Each time one of these beautiful, smart, sexy ladies shows up, she is too short, too fat, laughs funny, wears hats, snores, whatever. If he can't find any particular physical flaws, then he swears the timing isn't right. He is too busy or something else is in dire need of his attention. See, our friend is great at manifesting the perfect women, but *receiving* the love from one of these perfect matches, not so much!

"Asking is the beginning of receiving. Make sure you don't go to the ocean with a teaspoon. At least take a bucket so the kids won't laugh at you." ~ Jim Rohn

What is it that would make us bring a teaspoon instead of a bucket? Or better yet, who would pack a tiny suitcase for a huge road trip? World-renowned self-help guru Louise Hay would suggest that a lack of self-love is the core issue that keeps us from realizing our amazing potential in receiving all that we ask for. In her book *You Can Heal Your Life,* she suggests that there are many ways in which lack of self-love shows up in our lives, "People criticize themselves because they have learned to believe they are not good enough. We mistreat our bodies with food, alcohol, and drugs. We choose to believe we are unlovable. We procrastinate on things that would benefit us. And we attract mates who belittle us."

When someone gives you a compliment, do you simply accept it graciously or do you minimize yourself? We used to do this all the time! For example, when someone said, "I like your outfit," our old-self response would be, "This old thing? I got it at Goodwill for five bucks." Not only was this a subtle way of disrespecting ourselves, it also reinforced our poverty mentality! Double yuck! Now we respond with a simple, "Thank you – you made my day!" Double win! We feel good, and they feel good for offering the compliment.

Does any of this sound familiar? Dig deep. It is crucial to the success of your Road Trip to seek the ways in which you can improve upon loving yourself. By watching your thoughts, you will discover the ways you silently criticize yourself.

Perhaps you punish yourself, blame yourself, or torture yourself with guilt. We all have our subtle, or not so subtle, ways to hate on ourselves. We just choose not to recognize it, or we dismiss it as a necessary evil to keep our lives on track. Well, we call "bull shit!" Your best chance at improving your life is through loving yourself.

It takes courage to recognize the ways you belittle, blame, disrespect, and minimize yourself. How do we stop this vicious cycle of self-hate and feeling of unworthiness? It's your obligation to use replacement thoughts and affirmations to correct it. If you need a refresher in this area, go back to Chapter 15: Step 3 – *Change Your Thoughts*. If you mistreat your body with food, alcohol, or drugs, fess up and get real about what you are really doing to your body and spirit. If you think you can't do it alone, get help. Do it because you want to love and respect yourself, not because your wife, your mom, your boyfriend, or anyone else said you should. If you believe you are unlovable, then use loving affirmations to change the way you see yourself. If you procrastinate, lovingly discipline yourself. If your family or your mate belittles you, learn how to effectively and safely stick up for yourself. Again, if you need a refresher, refer back to Chapter 11: Rule #5 - *Love Yourself*.

Here is the shocking truth, so listen up! Others will not love and respect you until you learn to love and respect yourself! If you are one of those people who wonder why other people take you for granted (like we used to be), let us save you the dead-end road and give you the answer. It's because *you* take *yourself* for granted! Learning to love and respect yourself is the most important thing you can do. It is perhaps our highest calling. Once you practice loving and respecting yourself, you will be amazed at how others will find it easy to love and respect you. And if they can't or won't respect you, you will be amazed at how unacceptable that shit will be, and you will let them mosey on down the road without you!

Dr. Wayne Dyer reminds us, "You are always a valuable, worthwhile human being – not because anybody says so, not because you're successful, not because you make a lot of money – but because you decide to believe it and for no other reason."

Without a foundation of self-love we are inclined to sabotage our greatest good. When we sabotage ourselves, we prevent ourselves from *receiving* what we have manifested. On a deep level we don't believe we are worth it, so we screw it up. Carolyn Myss, author of *Sacred Contracts*, expands on Carl Jung's description of psychological patterns called archetypes. Myss suggests that we all share the common archetype of the Saboteur. Myss explains, "The Saboteur exposes fears and issues related to low self-esteem that cause you to make choices that block your own empowerment and success or allow others to sabotage you. When you learn to recognize such a pattern, instead of ignoring it or denying its presence, it becomes your friend and helper."

Everyone has a Saboteur to some extent or another. It requires a lot of honesty to recognize this pattern in ourselves. Perhaps you can look into your past to seek examples of how you may have sabotaged yourself. If you are really courageous, perhaps you can identify how you are presently sabotaging yourself. Once you learn to recognize your Saboteur and tame the beast, you can use your *Road Map* and get on with not only manifesting but also *receiving* whatever it is that contributes to your amazing journey!

Receiving is the most critical part of making the most of your journey. Practice receiving every day. Receive compliments. Receive help. Receive knowledge. Receive guidance. Receive affection. Receive attention. Receive kindness. Let the Universe know you are willing to receive by demonstrating it. Why? Because you know you are worth it!

Hayle's Story: Our Favorite Saboteur

One of our best friends from college is a professional Saboteur. Hayle is the kind of girl everyone loves to party with. She is gregarious and a ton of fun. She laughs hard and loud, and she wears her big pure heart on her sleeve. Hayle is also very intuitive. She is so honest that it tends to get her in trouble. The best thing about Hayle is that she is always willing to put other people's needs in front of her own. Unfortunately, her best attribute is also her worst because she slaughters herself in the process. Here are a few of the ways Hayle has painfully sabotaged herself throughout our years of friendship.

After graduating from college we moved to Atlanta, Georgia, to start our nursing careers. We loved Atlanta. In the 90s it was like living in a college town but everyone had jobs instead of classes. The weather was great and our futures were bright. We made it our business to try to convince the rest of our friends to move there too. Hayle finally took the bait and moved in with us in our two-bedroom apartment. It was an emotional move for her because her entire dysfunctional, co-dependent family lived in New York and none of them had ever left the clan. Hayle's family dysfunction was not due to anyone's negligence, it was purely circumstantial. They tragically lost their mother when Hayle was 10, her sister was 12, and her baby brother was only 6 months old. Her parents were in the process of divorce when her mother was hit and killed instantly in a head-on auto accident. As young adults, her siblings relied heavily on each other and expected that she'd be at all family functions, holiday celebrations, and birthday parties. There was no encouragement offered to support her decision to move. In fact, they were not afraid to share their disappointment and lack of approval. The guilt weighed heavily on Hayle's mind and heart.

The other major factor that made it difficult for Hayle to move away was her relationship with her boyfriend at the time. They had split up and got back together too many times, and she thought moving away might seal the deal. He was a nice enough guy on the surface. He was attracted to her big personality and wild ways, but once they dated for a while he didn't find that so attractive anymore. Instead of just dumping her and finding somebody new, he apparently decided that crushing her spirit and changing her personality would be better. Despite all the emotional baggage, Hayle made up her mind to be strong and go for it. She ended the relationship and moved to Hotlanta!

In the early 90s the nursing job market was ridiculously tight. Many of our fellow graduates were having a hard time finding work. We had secured jobs in private doctors' offices and used our connections and charm to get her hired. It was great for a month or two, but Hayle continued to feel conflicted about being far from home. She felt guilty for leaving and worried constantly about what her family was thinking about her decisions. Supportive and loving friends surrounded her, but she could not get comfortable in her new environment. Hayle's Saboteur started to rear its ugly head.

First, Hayle wrecked her car. It was a pretty nasty fender bender. She was hit by a pickup truck carrying a bunch of construction workers in the back. Before she could get out of her car, they scattered and left the truck totally abandoned in the middle of the street. Her car was in working condition, but cosmetically it was marred. Afraid that her insurance premiums would go up and lacking insurance from the missing driver, she decided to live with the damage. With no money to fix it, she sucked it up and drove a beater. Luckily she was not hurt.

Next, Hayle started getting warnings at work. She was distracted and frazzled and had a hard time keeping her focus. Her body was at work but her head was with her family in New York wondering and worrying and feeling out of control about what was happening there. One weekend she took a ride on the back of a motorcycle and burned her leg on the exhaust pipe. A few weeks later her burn became infected. The doctor she worked for pulled her into his office and explained to her that he could not afford to have her caring for his patients when she could not adequately take care of herself.

Hayle was very emotionally fragile and starting to spiral out of control. We were concerned and planned an intervention. Amity pleaded with her to calm down and take care of herself. She tried every rationalization she could think of, including not being able to take another "death" call. It was like talking to a brick wall. Hayle's Saboteur was in full force, and she could not hear or see any of what we were trying to say. The Saboteur wouldn't allow it.

Then came the final straw — she totaled her car. It was smashed up so badly that when we saw it, it took our breath away. It was a miracle she wasn't hurt or killed. We attributed her survival to her body being as hard as her head. Hayle cracked; she couldn't take anymore. Her ex-boyfriend gave her an offer she couldn't refuse. He would come pick up her car and get her a new one if she would come home and move in with him. She did.

Being back home in her familiar surroundings made Hayle feel safe. She felt secure with her family, her new car, and her boyfriend. For a little while she tricked herself into believing that the dysfunction was a small price to pay for the security and comfort she felt being at home. As usual, her unhealthy reality returned. Living with the ex eventually disintegrated. Hayle broke up with him again but thought it better to stay in New York close to her family.

Her Saboteur was not yet satisfied. A few months later, after a drunk-dial and a moment of weakness, she was pregnant. She came to visit us in Atlanta to clear her head and make some decisions. She decided to stay in her hometown, but she was not going to get back with the ex despite being pregnant with his child. She knew that if they couldn't make it work that many times before, the stress of a child certainly wouldn't fix things. A few weeks later, he was diagnosed with a rare and aggressive form of cancer. He proposed to her from his hospital bed. She said yes. Who could blame her? You just can't make this stuff up!

At Hayle's wedding the groom's sister was sitting at the head table with Amity, and she empathetically said, "I hear that you aren't a big fan of my brother and Hayle getting married." Amity replied, "I just wish she would have married someone who loves her at least as much as I do." And with that, eight long years of marriage commenced.

After Hayle's second child was born, Amity and her husband Kevin went to their house to visit. Sometime during their brief stay, while they were enjoying a meal and sharing stories, Hayle confused or exaggerated some minor detail for the sake of a funny conversation. Her husband, unimpressed by the inaccuracy in her story, told her to "Shut the F up!" She paused for a moment, obviously embarrassed, but said nothing to defend herself against the verbal abuse. For a brief moment, Amity's husband seriously considered delivering a beat-down in the man's own living room. They left the next day with a promise from Kevin never to return until they were divorced. Time ticked slowly.

Hayle tried and tried to make her marriage work. We would see her on girls' trips every once in a while. After a few days of being out of her environment, glimpses of her true personality would resurface and shine through. We actually renamed her old fun personality Juanita. We loved it when Juanita would come out and play. One particular trip, we saw her over a weekend in Michigan at Karen's house. It was the worst we had ever seen her. She was extremely thin and discombobulated. Neither of us wanted to drive in the car with her because she was so obviously on the edge. She was driving around in her car with the music blaring, cigarette in one hand, coffee in the other. She rolled through stop signs and couldn't pay attention to directions. It was scary to watch her desperately trying to overcompensate for her fragility. In her defense, Hayle was trying to do everything right. She was seeing a counselor and trying to stay in touch with her emotions, but in reality she was an inch away from a straightjacket and a padded room. Before she left we tried once again to intervene, to tell her how much we cared about her, and to plead with her to take care of herself first. If she could only love herself a fraction of how much we loved her, she would be so much better off. It was an ugly weekend and at one point she even threatened to leave. Somehow the strength of our friendship prevailed, and she did her best to listen. It was heartbreaking but we knew we couldn't do the work for her. It was her road to travel. We gave her one of our sets of the Clearing Series aromatherapy oils from Sacred Alchemy and crossed our fingers.

Finally, and we say FINALLY, a few years after that Michigan trip, she decided to get divorced. A few more years later, after a long emotional battle, she actually accomplished it. Then she began to pick up the pieces of her shattered self to reclaim her life. The worst of the sabotage was over.

Since then, Hayle has made a lot of progress. She has even changed careers and started her own successful business. She is better and better at recognizing when she is setting herself up for sabotage. She is learning to draw healthy boundaries so she can protect herself from family and friends who try to suck her in. She is listening to her intuition and loving and respecting herself more. Each year we see her becoming more aware of her patterns and making better choices for herself and her life. No longer her nemesis, her Saboteur is now her ally, warning her of danger. Best of all, she reintegrated with Juanita. Hayle is back to being that fun loving, belly-laughing friend we fell in love with in the first place!

Shortcuts

→ In order to *receive*, you have to KNOW that you are worthy.

→ Examine your deep-seated belief systems and let go of fear.

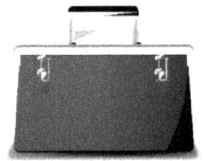
Tool Kit

→ Practice self-love.

→ Utilize affirmations to fortify your self-worth.

→ Overcome your Saboteur.

→ Demonstrate your willingness to receive daily.

> "No matter how qualified or deserving we are, we will never reach a better life until we can imagine it for ourselves and allow ourselves to have it."
>
> ~ Richard Bach 1936

SECTION V

ROADSIDE ASSISTANCE

We are traveling down the home stretch of our journey together. You understand and appreciate your very unique vehicle, you know and practice the golden Rules of the Road, and you are following the Road Map to consciously create your trip. In Section V, we will discuss what to do when breakdowns, detours, and unscheduled stops interrupt your journey. Inevitably, things won't always go as planned, so we will explore strategies to help you get back on track. Then we will give you a front row seat for two of our most amazing tales from the trenches, where you can see *Life is a Trip* in action.

Chapter 21: Breakdowns, Detours & Unscheduled Stops

Chapter 22: Grand Tales from the Trenches

Chapter 23: Happy Trails

21

UNSCHEDULED STOPS, BREAKDOWNS & DETOURS

Congratulations, you have come a long way, Baby! What could go wrong? Well, we all know shift happens, right? Breakdowns, detours, and occasional unscheduled stops are part of most any journey. These inevitable and troublesome "perceived problems" are really just opportunities in ugly packaging. As we utilize Rule of the Road #1, Take Radical Responsibility, we will come to understand that each of these breakdowns, detours, and unscheduled stops are meaningful gifts to warn us, to guide us, or to deepen our understanding of our journey and ourselves. If we are barreling down the road with blinders on, these bumps in the road come as dangerous obstacles. They can blindside us if we are driving too fast and not paying attention. What happens when you hit a minor obstacle in the road if you are going at a high rate of speed? It can throw you into chaos. As we become conscious observers and conscious participants in our lives, these inevitable unexpected obstacles are much easier to identify and navigate.

UNSCHEDULED STOPS

Unscheduled stops are things that happen to you, or other people in your life, that affect you by requiring your time and attention but don't change the course of your life's journey. They have the potential to throw a wrench in your schedule, but they usually don't last too long. Dealing with these stops may feel uncomfortable, but they don't destabilize us or force us to change direction. We call them unscheduled stops because of their unpredictable and unexpected nature. Here is a list of some of life's unscheduled stops.

Hormones

We hate to admit it, but hormones are another form of unscheduled stop. Being nurses, we understand that most people are uninformed about the intricacies of how our bodies work, especially when it comes to the subject of endocrinology and how hormones affect us. The statistics say that 60% of women are affected by PMS (premenstrual syndrome). We say if you have a period, you may not have a "syndrome" but you are definitely affected. Undoubtedly, you and your cycle have the potential to affect others. Pay attention.

Here is a very basic lesson about what happens hormonally in a women's body during a normal monthly cycle. The period starts. Then the ovaries begin maturing eggs for the next two weeks. During this two-week period, called the follicular phase, the estrogen level increases. Estrogen peaks during ovulation when the egg is released from the ovary. During ovulation, when the estrogen level is at its highest point, most women feel great. It is also at this point in your cycle that you are the most motivated to "get it on." This is Nature's way of perpetuating the species and attempting to turn that egg into an embryo. After ovulation, estrogen levels fall and progesterone levels rise. Progesterone helps thicken the lining of the uterus to prepare for embryo implantation. This stage of the cycle, called the luteal phase, lasts another two weeks. If there is no pregnancy, then the progesterone levels fall, the period starts, and the cycle begins all over again.

Some research has been conducted to demonstrate how these hormone levels affect women in the real world. One such study demonstrates that women have higher test scores during the follicular phase of their cycles than they do in the luteal phase of their cycles. This suggests that an estrogen-infused brain is sharper, academically speaking, in the first two weeks of a woman's cycle.

A team of researchers, conducting another study, swabbed the inside of women's cheeks to check their hormonal levels. They took full body pictures of the women as they entered a nightclub. The study concluded that women who were close to ovulation wore less clothing. Another study published in the *Personality and Social Psychology Bulletin* supports this finding. They also concluded that while a woman is ovulating, she is more likely to wear revealing clothes than when she is not ovulating. This suggests that when women's estrogen levels are at their highest, they feel more confident and are willing to show more skin to attract the opposite sex. There are other studies that prove that women smell better and have more attractive voices and lap dancers make more money during the follicular phase and ovulation.

Dr. Christiane Northrup, whom we consider to be the Queen Mother of the OBGYN world, says in her work *Wisdom of the Menstrual Cycle,* "It has been shown experimentally that the right hemisphere of the brain — the part associated with intuitive knowing — becomes more active premenstrually, while the left hemisphere becomes less active. Interestingly enough, communication between the two hemispheres may be increased as well. The premenstrual phase is therefore a time when we have greater access to our magic — our ability to recognize and transform the more difficult and painful areas of our lives."

Once you understand the menstrual cycle and how it affects you, you can use that information to your benefit. We try to do most of our creative work during the first two weeks of our cycle and then do more reflection and personal growth work in the last two weeks. If you have the luxury of scheduling your work this way, give it a try. You may find that it helps you be more productive and in the flow with your natural monthly rhythms.

As we have become increasingly diligent in watching our thoughts over the past years, we are amazed and humbled by each of our body's hormonal ability to sway our perception and thoughts. During the first two weeks of our cycle, we feel like rock stars, we even look skinnier in the mirror! In the last two weeks, we are quicker to snap and more apt to tear up at sappy movies or commercials. The aggravating tendencies of our family members seem to be intensified, and the repetitive negative thoughts begin to resurface. Just when we are convinced that everyone else in our life is annoying, we check the calendar! Sure enough, it is us, about to start our periods.

We highly recommend charting your cycles on a calendar. Make a note on your phone on the first day of your period. Then count 28 days ahead and notate "period?" Whenever you have a particular strong emotional response to something, get in the habit of pulling out your calendar and checking the date. If it's within a week or so of your projected start date, use extra caution, reserve judgment, and feed the Evil Twin. "Feed the Evil Twin" is our catch phrase for "Slow down, shut your mouth, take good care of yourself, avoid alcohol and caffeine, and wait a week or two to reassess before reacting."

Becoming more aware of our hormonal patterns and how we are specifically and intimately affected by them enables us to gain more control over our lives. We can avoid the alternative of being held hostage by our hormonal fluctuations. Instead, we can learn to utilize our cycles to our benefit. Dr. Northrup says, "Premenstrually, we are quite naturally more in tune with what is most meaningful in our lives. We're more apt to cry — but our tears are always related to something that holds meaning for us. Years of personal and clinical experience have taught me that the painful or uncomfortable issues that arise premenstrually are always real and must be addressed." We have monthly unscheduled stops, which are always opportunities for growth. Who could ask for more?

Menstrual cycle regularity occurs from approximately the teenage years through the 40s. In case you are wondering, taking hormones for birth control, such as the pill, overrides this natural cycle in order to prevent ovulation. In perimenopause, the stage before menopause, the hormonal fluctuations can be significant for some women as the ovaries begin to lose their hormone generating capabilities. Menopause is a hormonal animal of its own. Again, do not underestimate the effect hormones may have on your mood, your emotions, your repetitive thought patterns, and your perceptions.

Don't think that men are not subject to hormonal fluctuation and emotional and mental cycles. They are. It just may not be as obvious as bleeding from your private parts. Psychotherapist Jed Diamond has been studying Irritable Male Syndrome (IMS) for 40 years with clinical research, including survey responses from over 10,000 men. IMS is defined as a state of hypersensitivity, frustration, anxiety, and anger that occurs in males and is associated with biochemical changes, hormonal fluctuations, stress, and loss of male identity. Again, it is important for all of us to consciously seek out our own unique patterns and decide if we want to make our bodies work for us, or not.

Lastly, a word to the wise. However tempting it may be for a person to patronize a woman for PMS, accuse someone of being crazy in menopause, or diagnose a loved one with IMS, it is not at all helpful. During a time of heightened sensitivity and risk of emotional outbursts, we would highly discourage it! An extra dose of love and tolerance is what a crazed PMSer, IMSer, or menopauser needs most.

Acute Illness or Injury

An acute illness or injury, like the flu or breaking a bone, can also serve as an unscheduled stop. Something as simple as catching a cold can throw you off your game, disrupt your flow, and make you feel as if you have fallen behind. An illness or accident of a friend or family member can also be considered an unscheduled stop because people we care about require our help, our time, and our attention. During times like these we are required to make room in our normal daily routine to take care of others or ourselves. Acceptance of the reality of these needs will enable us to confront the challenges with grace. An illness or injury can serve you by redirecting your focus and teaching you many lessons. Making room in your life for these unscheduled stops can fill your life with a sense of service and purpose and ultimately be very rewarding.

Other People's Breakdowns

Occasionally, other people's breakdowns may cause an unscheduled stop in your life. Your support may be required to a greater or lesser degree depending on the situation. Other people's circumstances, which are beyond your control, can periodically consume you. Sometimes it is appropriate and necessary to lend ourselves when people we care about are in crisis. Hopefully, with healthy boundaries, and a commitment to a well-balanced life, other people's dramas will not prevent you from traveling your own path.

In some cases, other people's drama has the ability to lead us astray. This can be particularly challenging for those of us who have empathy in overdrive. Empathy is the ability to put yourself in someone else's shoes in order to understand how another person may be feeling, acting, or behaving. Like all things, empathy can be a great strength or a great weakness depending on how it is used. Some people are so empathetic that they physically feel the emotional pain of others. We have a friend who is a massage therapist. When she first began working in the field, her empathy for others was so high and out of balance that she would "catch" whatever her clients would have. If she worked on someone with knee pain, she would get knee pain. If she worked with someone who was grief-stricken, she would be sick to her stomach for days. It took many years for her to learn how to set appropriate boundaries on her gift of empathy. Now she knows how to help others and protect herself at the same time. If you would like to learn more about empathy, how to increase or decrease your skill to a comfortable level of empowerment, check out the book by Karla McLaren *The Art of Empathy*. We consider it a must read!

Children's Needs

The needs of children rank high on the list of possible unscheduled stops that demand our attention. Pregnancy can be one of these, requiring us to change some of our ways for at least the next nine months. Eating right, taking vitamins, and avoiding alcohol, cigarettes, and drugs are all healthy requirements for an optimal pregnancy. Once those little buggers are in the world and in our house, the unscheduled stops will only continue and increase. Kids grow up fast and their needs change as rapidly as they do. We only have one shot at raising them individually and collectively. Putting your life on hold for the needs of your kids, or any kid, is usually well worth the effort. Having a healthy balance between the needs of your kids and your own is also important. Your children will learn how to manage their own needs by the example you set.

Death of a Friend or Family Member

Another example of an unscheduled stop is the death of a friend or family member. We are not talking about the death of someone who is intricately involved in your daily life, just someone whose funeral you need to attend. Or perhaps your presence is required to support the loved ones of the deceased. If you have the means and make the time to show up for people during their difficult times, it can make a huge impact on the lives of others. Acknowledging these types of unscheduled stops also helps you to grieve and heal from loss. Our friend Michelle always makes it a point to show up for funerals. I am sure she has more fun things to do with her time, but if one of her friends loses someone they care about, she shows up. Michelle drove three hours to show up for the funeral of Amity's mother-in-law and was a completely unexpected guest. The relief to see a friend's face showing love and support can provide comfort beyond measure. You can be that kind of cherished friend too. Honor the unscheduled stops in life.

Celebrations

Big celebrations are a fun form of unscheduled stops. Weddings, graduations, the birth of a baby, and other fun things can consume your attention and take you off your normal beaten path. Planning for these celebrations takes time and energy. It also may provide the opportunity for family interactions that may add or detract from your quality of life. Remember, if you are willing to be present and show up emotionally, these celebrations can be opportunities for growth. Celebrations can also plant beautiful memories along the path of your journey like wildflowers along the highway in spring.

Despite the nature of any of these varied and unique unscheduled stops, they present us with the opportunity to redirect our energy, reprioritize and deal with life as it is dealt to us. These "stops" require work, and there is inevitably something to be learned. The good news about unscheduled stops is that they don't change the course of your journey. They are just minor bumps in the road to deal with when they show up. Inevitably, they will happen. The next time you experience one of these unscheduled stops, accept it, incorporate it into your life to the best of your ability, and emotionally show up. If you do these things, "this too shall pass" and you can get back on track and head on down the road.

DETOURS

Unattended or unresolved unscheduled stops and other unforeseen events can become detours in our lives. Detours are more earthshaking than plain old unscheduled stops. They force us to take a new path in our lives. The destination may stay the same, but the route you thought would get you there suddenly becomes a different road. Detours can send you off into uncharted territory, change your direction, and feel very scary. Detours often come as complete surprises – and they always represent change in one's life. They can lead to breakdowns if you fail to make the curve.

Divorce

Divorce is a good example of a detour. No one gets married without picturing their partner along for the entire ride. Unfortunately, or fortunately for some, that just doesn't pan out. Divorce will change the course of your life whether it's messy or amicable, whether you want the split or not. This kind of detour is a painful and consuming process, but it undoubtedly opens up an immense opportunity to evaluate, change, and reinvent your life.

Relocation

Relocation is another example of one of life's detours.

Moving to a different place changes the familiar path that you are on. Relocation may be a choice or it may be a requirement, but it will always put a spin on your journey.

Job Change

Changing jobs or career paths also can feel like a detour. Getting fired from your job is an abrupt example and has the power to lead you in a direction you may never have expected. How one handles a situation such as this will determine whether this detour will lead to better opportunities or not. Even job changes that are planned and thoroughly thought out can represent major detours in life. There is always risk and uncertainty involved. With that comes the opportunity for improvement and reward.

Tragedy

A natural disaster, fire, or other tragedy will also change your course. These unexpected events leave people with no choice but to change. The shock that usually accompanies these happenings adds an extra element of chaos, which can spiral a person toward breakdown. Hurricane Katrina was a perfect example of this kind of detour. Every person that Amity knew or was acquainted with was forced off their usual path. The people that were on the cusp of change in their lives were thrown over the edge. Deaths, births, divorces, relocations, relapses, and struggles were all part of the deal. Mental and emotional flexibility combined with the availability and access to resources made the difference in how long it would take for people to recover, if ever.

Serious Illness

A serious illness or diagnosis can also cause a detour in someone's life. If it is serious enough, it may have the ability to restructure your trip completely. Take Richard for example, the diagnosis of his progressive degenerative neuromuscular disease meant that he had to completely change his diet, his exercise regimen, and his activity level. This led to lifestyle choices, job changes, and a whole lot of uncertainty. Health challenges, permanent or temporary, may force a detour in life's journey.

Substance Abuse

Let's face it – it's easy to get your hands on all kinds of substances that can alter your state of consciousness. If you don't have a personal dealer, look no further than your family doctor. For most doctors, a minor surgical procedure, a bit of anxiety, or a few sleepless nights are all you need to get a stash of legal, but potentially addictive, prescription drugs. Recreational prescription drug use is a big and growing problem. The Center for Disease Control says that drug overdose rates have more than tripled since 1990. In 2010 overdosing was the leading cause of injury or death for people between the ages of 25 and 64, exceeding car accidents. The CDC calls the prescription drug abuse problem an epidemic.

The temptation to escape our own personal hell for a little bit by taking a pill is a shortcut that many are too willing to take. There is no personal development; there is no expansion of consciousness when you are using drugs to escape reality. Although we are big fans of shortcuts, this is NOT a shortcut we would recommend.

Sometimes medication is necessary. But, before you resort to a medical solution, find out if your pain, anxiety, or sleeplessness is your body's natural warning system. Ask your doctor if there are any non-medicinal alternatives to dealing with your issues. If you listen to the warning signs your body is sending you, and you are willing to make changes, you may avoid the risks and side affects inherent in prescription drugs.

Alcohol Abuse

Alcohol is another crutch widely accepted in our society. Do you drink socially? If so, do you binge drink? Do you have just one drink a day but have to have it? People handle alcohol consumption differently depending on many factors including age, sex, weight, tolerance, and genetic disposition. It is up to you to identify and assess your alcohol consumption. Healthy drinking habits are personal boundaries that each of us needs to figure out and set for ourselves. Eckhart Tolle in *A New Earth* says, "When you drink alcohol or take certain drugs, you may also feel more relaxed, more carefree, and perhaps more alive for a while. You may start singing and dancing, which since ancient times are expressions of the joy of life. Because you are less burdened by your mind, you can glimpse the joy of Being. Perhaps this is the reason alcohol is also called 'spirit.' But there is a high price to pay: unconsciousness. Instead of rising above thought, you've fallen below it. A few more drinks, and you will have regressed to the vegetable realm."

Do you use alcohol to numb your life, loosen up, or escape from reality? Is it a problem in your work, relationships, or health? Be honest with yourself, or ask someone who knows you very well and is willing to tell you the truth. If your alcohol consumption is a problem, it will cause problems in your life, with your relationships, with your work, and with your health. You can choose to deal with the symptoms of the problem, the conflict the alcohol causes, or you can choose to deal with the root of the problem, the alcohol consumption. Your choice!

Technology Overload

We grew up in households where we were told that too much TV would melt the brains out of our heads. Who could have imagined that we would now be managing TV, gaming devices, cell phones, laptops, iPads, iPods, texting, tweeting, e-books and the like. Managing all that technology takes energy, and it can be a problem. The shear magnitude of information coming at us on a daily basis can be emotionally draining. We need to learn how to better manage our technology intake so it can work for us, not against us. It takes discipline to check emails, read the news, return phone calls, and search the internet only at certain intervals during the day instead of sitting in front of the computer all day like a trash receptacle. As we continue to integrate more and more technology into our daily lives, it just increases the importance of our need for silence. The more technology you use, the more your need to commune with nature and/or have a regular meditation practice. The balance for each of us is different, but it is imperative that we be able to calm our minds and connect with our inner selves. We need to run our technology instead of letting our technology run us.

Overworking

Working hard is an American tradition. It is a virtue but it can also be a curse. Overworking for many people is a socially accepted excuse not to be present in their emotional lives. It is a hard disguise to fault because of the many financial and professional rewards it provides, but it can be costly to your True Self and those you care about. Again, the balance for each of us is different. But balance is required. Be honest with yourself about how much energy is spent on work. If you have no energy left for yourself, your marriage, your kids, or your physical and spiritual life, than you are not balancing your energy and you are allowing your work life to take you on a detour.

Negative People

Another thing that can take us off track is our relationships with negative people. Your best defense against negative people is inner peace – to know your center so certainly that you can defend yourself against the negativity of others. If you have not yet mastered this, then beware of whom you hang around. The old cliché "Birds of a feather flock together" is true. It means you become who you hang around. Consider this, in a study done at Harvard Medical School, researchers found that a person's chance of becoming obese increased by 37% if their spouse became obese, 40% if an adult sibling became obese, and 57% if it was a close friend. If those you hang around can affect the size of your ass in the physical realm, just imagine how negativity can do a mind-job on you in the mental realm. Seek people who lift you up. Develop what we call an "A Team." An A Team consists of like-minded people who are committed to remaining positive. They are the people you can go to for advice and consolation, and they will support you in your effort to make the most of your journey. People on your A Team are committed to pulling you back on track if you happen to take a negativity detour.

The sooner we recognize the detours in our lives, the sooner we can redirect our course to whatever degree is necessary. Accepting the realities of our detours and consciously dealing with the details will help us to find our road again and minimize our suffering. We can get on with the journey and onto our intended path.

BREAKDOWNS

Breakdowns can come in many forms. They can be physical, emotional, and/or psychological. These are the extreme events or circumstances in life that render us compromised. Breakdowns can happen in an instant, but more likely they are a result of neglect. Disregard for your needs and an unwillingness to deal with the emotional components of unscheduled stops and detours can lead you into a breakdown. Breakdowns require the help and support of others. The worst mistake you can make is to think you can get out of one alone.

Here are a few examples of possible breakdowns:

Life Threatening Illness or Injury

There is nothing like fighting for survival. A life threatening illness or accident can consume your life completely. All energies and life forces are directed to continuing to live. Even in the most extreme cases of physical breakdown, there always exists an opportunity for emotional and spiritual transformation. If you are one of the lucky ones who makes it back from this kind of breakdown, you most certainly will have a different outlook on life.

Grief

Another form of breakdown is grief. Grief has the ability to be just as incapacitating as an illness. Grief can even slow the perception of time. There is a strange paradox with grief. While grieving, time feels like it is the enemy because it passes so slowly, yet it's the passage of time that actually eventually helps to heal the wounds. There are many personal lessons to learn through grief. Again, these lessons can be transformational.

Disregard for Self Care

Excessive work, stress, lack of sleep, no exercise, and poor diet can lead you into a physical and mental breakdown. The body can only take so much. This is a recipe for killing yourself slowly. Youth may be an antidote for some of these behaviors, but with age, a person's body will not continue to hold up and repair itself. Ensure that you are monitoring stress, staying active, sleeping the proper amount, and eating well.

Suicidal Thoughts and Tendencies

Suicidal thoughts and tendencies are very taboo in our culture. Because of this, we would bet they are a lot more common than people think. Any threat of self-harm should be taken seriously and addressed immediately. In most cases, the threat of suicide is a serious cry for help. In *The Art of Empathy* Karla McLaren argues that the edge of suicide is a natural but misunderstood emotional response to a situation that is no longer tolerable. The confusion comes into play by mistaking the urge to end the intolerable thing by ending ourselves when, in fact, ending the intolerable situation is what is called for. McLaren suggests that this suicidal urge is in fact a natural survival instinct that can serve us well if we can unravel the confusion.

Psychological Breakdown

The brain and the mind are complex. A very delicate balance of structural and chemical combinations inside our head holds our psychological health together. Substance abuse, illness, medications, injury, and many other factors can influence the balance of our psychological state. If you are feeling like you are close to breakdown, pull off the road and get to the shop. Ask for help. Breakdowns should be addressed immediately. Ask for help from friends, family, or a heath care provider.

During our journey there are many things that can take us off track from the life we are trying to live and create. Sometimes you can just feel it. It feels like you are just "off," or not in the flow of life. Obstacles keep popping up in your path. Wouldn't it be great if every time we started to veer off, a voice would pop in and warn us like it does with GPS or Map Quest?

Well, believe it or not, you do come with a warning system. Most of us have not been taught how to listen to it. This warning system is your emotions! If you feel bad and are experiencing a negative emotion, *that* is the warning signal that something is off track and needs to be addressed. Pay attention! This is your cue to go back to the basics. Do whatever it is that makes you feel good again. Once you feel good, you will recharge your life battery and get back on track.

As you continue to practice your newfound techniques, we hope that you will continue to get better at watching your thoughts and recognizing what your emotions are trying to tell you. All of us have certain individual tendencies because of our upbringing, our family values, our genetic disposition, our communities, and our education. It is up to each of us to recognize these patterns in ourselves, make corrections, and stay our course. It's not the cards you're dealt – it's how you play the hand. Remember, all breakdowns, detours, unscheduled stops, and things that take you off track are in your path for a reason. Embrace them, accept them, and learn from them. Get back to the basics of the Rules of the Road and The Road Map. Carry on.

Amity's Story: Hurricane Katrina

When I look back on my life, I can pinpoint a few major breakdowns, detours, and unscheduled stops. Besides the death of my boyfriend at age 22, the next most significant and life-defining event outside of my control was Hurricane Katrina. Being a Midwestern girl by birth, the extent of my understanding of bad weather amounted to a tornado. For those of you who are unfamiliar with the drill, a tornado meant seek shelter and hope to hell you were not in its direct path. Getting hit amounted to a crapshoot, but the odds were good that it wouldn't be you.

During my years in Louisiana, the threat of hurricanes provided the weather drama. In the first seven years we lived there, I think we evacuated at least six times. Before August 29, 2005, all of our evacuations were kind of the same. Big news hype, hardware store runs, packing and planning for a three-day mini-vacation consumed the days prior to knowing whether or not an official evacuation would be called. In the instances when we were asked to evacuate, we returned home to no damage. Sometimes we wouldn't even have had a drop of rain. Evacuations were no big deal, especially to us because my husband's parents lived only two hours north but safely away from the coast. It was a good excuse for us to visit family with extra time off from work and school.

As Katrina blew in, the preparations felt the same. I filled gumbo pots with water and put them in the freezer, moved my frozen pots to the fridge, filled the bathtubs with extra water just in case, and secured the house. We packed up the car with three days worth of clothes, the kids, and the dog and we were off. It was beautiful outside when we pulled out of our driveway to face the 130-mile, eight-hour, bumper-to-bumper drive to the country. Naively, I guessed we would be back in a few days.

At my in-law's house it was the same evacuation crew – our family and Kevin's sister's family, who came in from the Garden District in New Orleans. We settled in for some good Cajun food and non-stop news coverage.

The storm came and went. We felt a sigh of relief when we saw the reporters giving good reports from the French Quarter. It appeared we had dodged a bullet. New Orleans had been spared. In my mind I was already formulating our return plan and preparing for the yard clean up.

Hours passed. I was outside playing with the kids in the backyard and went back into the house to fetch my camera. When I went inside and saw the look on my brother-in-law's face, I knew something was very wrong. Everyone was huddled around the TV in disbelief. The levees had broken. The nightmare began.

I had totally underestimated the magnitude of a hurricane's devastation. The largest tornado I had ever imagined suddenly became dwarfed a thousand times. The reports of damage and chaos continued to worsen. My sister-in-law feverishly kept account of the fires that were burning in the Garden District to see if any of her friends and family homes were at risk.

A dark change was upon us. It affected everyone we knew in Louisiana and thousands more. It felt so big and overwhelming. There were no right answers, just more questions combined with confusion and a sense of helplessness mixed with mounting fear.

A few days later, we got word from Kevin's sister's in-laws that they needed a place to stay. All ten of them, plus two dogs! Many people in Louisiana don't have family or friends outside of their communities, and hotels were booked solid for miles. At this point, my immediate family needed to make some decisions. My parents were another six hours north, and we could go there to make more room for the arrival of all the others. My husband, however, was reluctant to go. He wanted to be able to be close enough to get home to assess the damage, empty the fridge, and check on some friends who had stayed behind. It was a struggle to make a decision – any decision. Our minds were burdened and fatigued. I did not want to be separated from my husband. There was no cell phone communication, no gas, no water or electricity back at our home. I was terrified he would go back and something would happen to him and I wouldn't know it. The fear was in every cell of my body painfully reminding me of losing the last man I loved. Unfortunately, the practical decision to separate was obvious. I needed to get my children to my parents' house in Arkansas where there was room for us and where things were more stable.

The drive to Arkansas was surreal. The highway going north was eerily vacant. In the southbound lanes heading toward us was an unrelenting line of military vehicles. For hours they filed past us. It looked like they were going to war. I wanted to celebrate but the response was so late. Atrocities were happening, people were dying. Again, I felt sick as the magnitude of it all settled again in the pit of my stomach.

In Arkansas I was a wreck. I worried constantly about Kevin and the people I hadn't heard from yet. I couldn't sleep or eat. I tried to force myself to enjoy my parent's beautiful place on Lake Hamilton but I couldn't help getting nauseated when ever we went for a boat ride, thinking about all of those poor people stranded in the flood. The sight of water made my skin crawl.

On a side note, I had been really working, reading and practicing my self-development or inner peace or consciousness expansion — or whatever you want to call it. I obviously had more work to do. The separation from Kevin yanked me at such a deep level I was surprised by my own fear. Sometimes you just don't know there is more work to do, or where the work is, until you are challenged. I was definitely being challenged.

In some aspects, I was doing OK. Other people at the time were suffering terrible anxiety over the loss of their stuff. I heard many people cry over the loss of their family pictures in particular. This potential loss of stuff did not phase me in the slightest. I remember thinking, "It would suck to lose all those pictures but it's not like I sit around looking at them very often anyway!" If my house was destroyed, I was content moving on and never looking back. I felt no attachment to my stuff at all. Not knowing what condition my stuff was in did not bother me. All I cared about was the safety of my loved ones.

In Arkansas I went about the business of getting my kids into a routine. I knew they needed it for a sense of normalcy and to get away from my anxious energy. I needed it because the anxiety was exhausting, and I needed time away from them so I could cry and let my emotion out.

As the federal and state agencies were failing to respond to the magnitude of the disaster, there was one system that excelled. The public school system was on top of their game. The week after the levees broke I walked my daughter into the public elementary school near my mom's house. When we arrived we were greeted by the office staff who came out to have a look at us. "We were told that we might start seeing refugees today." "Refugees?" I thought. The word felt harsher than I expected. My stomach sank as the magnitude of the disaster penetrated me a little deeper. The school was totally prepared to receive us. They immediately gave Camille a brand new backpack stuffed full of donated supplies and invited her to her new classroom, where she was placed with a teacher who was originally from Louisiana. They never asked me for identification, or required anything of us. They just received her with open arms. It was difficult to withhold the emotion as the gratitude welled inside me. I was so grateful for living in a country where this kind of education system exists and so appreciative of their kindness and genuine concern for us. Camille rode the bus home that very day and was dropped off at her grandparent's driveway. She had made new friends and had a light in her eyes that gave me a glimpse of normalcy and hope.

My sense of calm was short-lived as information started making its way from our neighborhood to the internet and finally to us. The first-hand accounts from the six or so people who rode out the storm were reporting that at least 50% of the homes in my neighborhood were heavily damaged, and there were no passable points of entry to get in or out, except on foot. Pictures were uploaded showing some of the damage and storm debris. It was almost unrecognizable. I could feel myself holding my breath as each picture uploaded. I was obsessed about staying online in hopes that there would be specific information about my house. Every time the phone rang my heart would race from dread. I was a wreck!

Meanwhile Kevin was making a plan to check on our property and, most importantly, empty the fridge before everything rotted and filled the house with the smell of death. The authorities were saying no one could come into the area and they had imposed martial law, which meant authorities could commandeer your vehicle if they saw fit. We were also reading unofficial reports of armed carjackings, looting, and generator thefts as people were becoming increasingly desperate. It was not a place any wife would want her husband to venture to, but there was no stopping him. I assumed he would go with his father and a few other well-armed and well-equipped men – that turned out not to be the case. Luckily, I didn't find out until later that he went alone with a 75-pound chainsaw, an extra supply of gas, and a couple of guns. He called to let me know he was heading in and that he would call me later that day when he could get phone service. I didn't hear from him for 48 very, very long hours.

All my years of self-improvement, yoga, meditation, and deep breathing could not help me find my center. I felt like I was cracking up. Every nerve cell in my body felt like it was vibrating, and I couldn't make it stop. Then a miracle happened. A huge box showed up on the front porch. Karen and my girlfriends in Atlanta put out a mayday call for help, asking their friends to donate cute clothes for their "refugee" friend who left with only three days packed. I was so touched by their effort and so relieved I didn't need to spend any of my much needed resources on clothes. As I dug through the pile I found a pill bottle at the bottom. In the bottle was a note from Karen, which read, "In case of emergency take one of these. I love you." Hallelujah, it was Xanax!

As you know, I don't condone the use of anti-anxiety medication unless it is absolutely necessary. This happened to be one of those times of necessity.

Xanax can be addictive and I tend to be very leery of medication like that, but the relief it provided me was a godsend, especially during the two days I couldn't reach Kevin.

It turned out that Kevin made it back to Mandeville and used the chainsaw to cut a path into the neighborhood. Apparently the sound of the machinery brought out the survivors. Soon he had a healthy to-do list that consisted of cutting trees out of neighbors' living rooms and the like. First, he was determined to go see if our house was in one piece, so he made his way on foot the few blocks it took to traverse all the fallen and broken pines. Later, he told me that he could barely tell what street he was on because everything looked so different from when we had left the week earlier. When he came around the corner to see our house, his body was literally shaking with anticipation. All five of the homes that surrounded us were hit by 30-foot pine trees to some extent or another, but ours appeared to be untouched!

Kevin wielded that heavy chain saw for hours helping neighbors. He shored up some holes in homes of people we knew to prevent further damage of their property and did as much as one guy with a chainsaw could. By nightfall he was exhausted and decided to sleep in his own bed.

Meanwhile I was getting word that people were dying from injuries they were sustaining in the clean up. One teenager was killed in front of his father by a falling branch. Others needed immediate medical attention for cuts, wounds and various accidents, but in a disaster area there is no phone service to call for help and 911 response. The hospitals were barely functioning if you were lucky enough to be able to get to one. It was scary. Very, very destabilizing and scary. Kevin had no cell service and couldn't call to reassure me.

The next day, after seeing how devastating the hurricane had been, Kevin decided to check on the salon we owned and then travel north a bit to make sure one of our friends who has a handicapped child was able to evacuate. Last we had heard they hadn't left. It turns out that they did ride out the terrifying storm, hiding in the bathtub for hours. They were able to get out a few days later. Along the road north Kevin came upon people who were completely oblivious to how dire the situation was. They had no electricity, no access to the news, and were completely unaware that all hell was breaking out just fifty miles away in New Orleans. Along with sound advice to get out of town, he gave the remaining contents of our meat freezer to help sustain those who wanted to stay.

Finally, late the next night, I received the call from Kevin I had been praying for! I was filled with mixed emotions. I was so furious that he hadn't called sooner. I was immensely relieved he was OK. I never felt such intense conflicting emotions of love, hate, fury, and relief all at the same time. He must have thought I was a lunatic. At that point, he would have been correct! I learned that my house was still standing and that our salon was undamaged. I was grateful beyond measure.

Reunited in Arkansas, Kevin and I awaited word of when to return home. Authorities continued to say that our town was inaccessible, but then we caught a break. The police department's electricity was restored, and our subdivision just happened to be the only one on the same grid. Kevin was going back in, but this time there was no way he was going to leave without me. The kids stayed in Arkansas with my wonderful parents. I was so grateful that they were financially sound and in good enough health to help us out in such an important way.

I wept in disbelief as we turned down the street toward our house. Along the way I could see straight through the living rooms of some of my neighbors homes, which had been sliced in half by the huge pines. Some never returned. The debris in my yard was mind-boggling. Pine needles, branches, sticks and trash reached me mid-thigh. As we began cleaning up, I wondered if I had made the right decision to return. It took two hours to clear a three-foot circle around my feet. Kevin would attempt to call out words of encouragement. He would say, "Just don't look up! Only focus on what is right in front of you and keep going, Baby!" Load after load we hauled to the edge of the street in the back of a pickup truck. After the first day, my hands were raw and every muscle in my body ached. I broke down and cried like a big ol' baby. If the truth be told, I actually threatened to kill myself by slitting my wrists with a pine cone.

The next morning I formulated a new plan that would keep me out of the yard. I convinced Kevin that I should go to the salon and start the clean up there. Hell, why not just open the place — we had to start making some money! I found a large piece of plywood and spray painted the word "OPEN," propped it out front, and opened the doors. Minutes later the salon was full of armed officers and National Guardsmen. After proving my identity and convincing them of my plan to stay out of the yard, I was permitted to stay at my own risk. The chaos in New Orleans was about 35 miles to the south, and we were separated by Lake

Ponchartrain. To the good fortune of the residents of our town, the bridge was damaged in the storm and closed. This forced all evacuations west and east of New Orleans instead of north through the heart of Mandeville, causing less disruption to our safe community.

At the salon, I had no electricity and no hot water, but a few people started to show up, customers I couldn't recognize because they had grown beards and hadn't showered in days. Some people had cash and others had nothing. I turned no one away. For months after, people were still dropping by to pay for the free haircut I gave them. The National Guard and the Sheriff's office continued to check on me, and I continued to cut hair without clippers or air-conditioning. I heard stories that broke my heart. I watched big tough guys cry in the shampoo bowl. One of my customers couldn't locate his elderly mother. He had set her up with a generator and supplies in Lakeview before the storm, one of the hardest hit areas in the city. She was in her 80s and never in her life had she evacuated. She was refused to leave, so her only son agreed to let her stay. He frantically searched the shelters in Little Rock and Houston. I saw the hope in his eyes when he saw her name on CNN and thought they had a lead on her in Chicago. Six months later they found her. Her body was in her house trapped between the sheet rock and the wall. Her son was devastated.

At the end of each day I would return home with a wad of cash to give to Kevin, my yard guy, but with a heavy heart from all the stories of loss and tragedy I would hear. Weekly I would make a pilgrimage to the nearest grocery store to stock up on food and alcohol. Alcohol was hard to come by because they had stopped the sale of alcohol in all the affected disaster areas to help restore order. During my first venture out, I was escorted by some volunteer firefighter friends. Our journey took eight hours, and we had to go almost all the way to Baton Rouge before we could find a stocked grocery store that was open. Under normal conditions Baton Rouge was only fifty minutes away. When we returned, Kevin was livid because I couldn't call to let him know where I was and that I was OK. Turn about is fair play, I suppose. My friends calmed him down by giving him some military MREs (Meals Ready to Eat), which at the time seemed like a fair trade for his wife!

Domestic chores are not my strong suit; however, I was so glad to have power and hot water at my house, my nesting instincts kicked in. I cooked and froze casseroles for days. Once we were sufficiently stocked, we sent out a message to our entire phone list. Text messaging was just beginning to work and we wanted to let people know that they could come for a meal and a hot shower. For weeks people would show up, clean up, and sleep in the air-conditioning if they wanted to. We laughed, we cried, we ate like kings, and we drank like fish. We continued the clean up, searched for missing employees, and trudged forward.

Financially, we took a serious blow. Ford Motor Company and our mortgage company gave us a much appreciated 90-day grace period. Our landlord for the business, who was from the area, did not. We blew through our savings to keep up with our lease and our mounting debt. Mandeville was still considered a disaster area, so there were few customers in town. My husband's other business was decimated by the storm. We got to the point where we started paying one of our business credit cards late. Before we knew it that credit card company shared our late pay information with our other credit card companies. Overnight our interest rates skyrocketed from 9.9% to 29.9%. Our monthly payments increased. Our debt started to rise. Our credit score tanked! Luckily, those practices are now illegal, but those laws went into effect to late too help us. Meanwhile, we had applied for a loan from the Small Business Administration. We felt confident that we could get a loan from them because we were already an established customer. The SBA had initially loaned us money to open the salon and we had paid off that 7-year debt in only 3 1/2 years. Surprise! We were denied because our credit score was too low.

Luckily, one of the products used in my husband's other business was spun-off from the mobile technology industry, and he landed an account that kept us from going bankrupt. Armed with that two-year contract, we decided to stay and slog it out with our employees.

Katrina and its aftermath was a maze of unscheduled stops, detours, and even a few breakdowns, but we made it out. We studied the Law of Attraction and we looked for reasons to feel good. We dealt with our unscheduled stops. We consciously co-created our new reality. We navigated our detours and found our way back on the path. For us, the path had lost its luster. We ultimately decided to forge a new one that felt even better and led us to Austin, Texas, where we are still living happily ever after.

Shortcuts

→ Recognize the ways in which you are enticed off track and seek to correct them.

→ Shift happens. Roll with it.

→ When you are walking through hell, don't stop and set up camp.

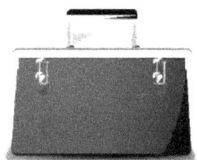
Tool Kit

→ Read *Life's a Trip: Shortcuts to Making the Most of Your Journey*.

→ Apply the Rules of the Road.

→ Use steps in the Road Map to stay centered and grounded.

"A bend in the road is not the end in the road unless you fail to make the turn."

~ Unknown Author

22
TALES FROM THE TRENCHES

During our personal journeys we have experienced some incredible happenings. The more we open our minds and the more consistently we follow the Road Map and live by the Rules of the Road, the more miraculous and wondrous the adventure becomes. We saved the most amazing stories for last in hopes that they will inspire you to ponder the possibilities of making the most of your journey and to set off on your own personal Road Trip toward whatever it is that you want to create.

Amity's Story: Anniversary Gift

When my husband proposed marriage to me, we had known each other little over a year, but he knew me well enough to do the "ring thing" right! He set the diamond on a simple gold band for the proposal with a promise that I could have it set or designed the way I wanted it. Designing things, to his chagrin, was a hobby of mine. I always had grand ideas about how I wanted something to look or how a project would turn out just right. Unfortunately, my designs usually cost too much money and never quite turned out the way I envisioned (Rule #1 Take Radical Responsibility). My new, shiny wedding ring was no exception.

I set off to design the perfect ring. I wanted the diamond set low to avoid getting the setting snagged on the rubber gloves I changed countless times a day at my nursing job. At the time, jewelry styles were just beginning to change from gold to silver so I couldn't decide between the two. As a default, I used both, which turned out to be a good lesson that sometimes not deciding is actually a bad decision. I met with the jeweler countless times and in the end I got an expensive but not so perfect ring. In fact, Kevin's favorite word for it was "hodgepodge." I didn't care (Rule #3 Let Go of Control). I got to design it and I loved it. I was in love (Rule #2 Be Grateful).

In my designer brain, I had imagined that my ring would be accompanied by a wedding band with diamonds all the way around (Step 1 Know What You Want). Unfortunately, I had blown the budget on the custom engagement ring design so I would have to go without the band. I informed Kevin that I was content to live without it until our five-year anniversary. I imagine he heard my grand plan much like the way Charlie Brown hears Snoopy in the cartoon. Kevin could care less about jewelry, with the slight exception of his desire to be able to provide what I hoped for.

We were happily married with kids and a new business as we approached our five-year anniversary. At the time, one of my friends worked at a beautiful jewelry store in St. Louis. I told her my five-year wedding band wish. She promptly replied that I did not need a wedding band. What I really needed was a redesign on my engagement ring. She was so right! This time under threat from Kevin to keep my design talents to a minimum, I stuck to the program and found an existing setting that would be new and improved. I loved it! Again, there was no room in the budget for a wedding band. Again, I bumped my wedding band plan, diamonds all the way around, to our ten-year anniversary. I informed

Kevin. His eyes rolled around the back of his head. Regardless, I knew someday I would get that wedding band (Step 5 Believe). I could just picture the band filling the long space between my knuckles, sparkling in the light, reflecting our future prosperity (Step 4 Feel).

Nine years of happy marriage was flying by. Karen called with a proposition I could not refuse. A Disney Cruise in May 2009. We were planning a year in advance, so I told her to pull the trigger and we would be there (Step 7 Participate). I paid little attention to the date, which happened to be two weeks past our ten-year anniversary and smack dab in the middle of Kevin's fortieth birthday. As the year passed many of our friends celebrated their 40th birthdays in style. Karen took her husband to NYC. Other friends went to Vegas. My poor husband was destined to turn 40 with Mickey Mouse, a horrifying fact that provided his work buddies with endless joke fodder at the office.

A few weeks before our ten-year anniversary, Kevin said, "We are going on a cruise in a couple of weeks, and we are knee deep in a new business again. The budget is tight. Here are your options for celebrating our 10-year anniversary. 1. We can go out for a great meal in New Orleans. 2. We can go for an overnight getaway in Biloxi, Mississippi. 3. I can get you a small gift. You choose."

For a fleeting moment the wedding band with the diamonds all the way around flashed through my mind (Step 2 Watch Your Thoughts). In an instant, I felt with total clarity that a ring had no real meaning or value. It was only a ring (Rule #3 Let Go of Control). What really had value was the relationship my husband and I had built over the last decade (Step 3 Change Your Thoughts). Now busy with kids, crazy travel schedules, work, and everything else, the most important thing was enjoying and maintaining that connection that has kept us best friends throughout those years. "I will take option #2, the night away with my husband," I announced.

We went to Biloxi and checked into our room at the Beau Rivage. To our surprise we were upgraded to a suite. It was huge and beautiful. It took everything we had not to call our friends and invite them to come enjoy it with us (Rule #2 Be Grateful). We tried to go to one of the dance clubs in the casino, but the music was too loud – a stark reminder that we were about to enter our forties. We weren't in the mood or financial position to gamble, so we spent most of the evening at the coffee shop, sharing dessert, enjoying each other's company and laughing our butts off. It was perfect (Rule #4 Be Present).

A few weeks later we were on the cruise. As it turns out, being with your family, friends, and Mickey Mouse is actually the perfect place to turn 40! We had a blast (Rule #2 Be Grateful, #3 Let Go of Control, and #4 Be Present). The kids wanted to be in the Kids Club the majority of the time, and a large portion of the ship, including the spa, was dedicated to adults only. One of the stops on the cruise was to Disney's Private Island. The island had an adult-only beach, so we signed up for a yoga class and sent the kids to Kids Camp to dig for treasure. After a few hours of complete paradise we started to feel guilty about being away from the children, so we headed back to the family beach to regroup. The kids were having a blast and continued their treasure hunt while we had a few drinks in our lounge chairs. It was hot and the beach was crowded. We started baking in the afternoon sun and the kids started to go on meltdown. I began noticing that the blissful thoughts I had in my head were turning sour (Step 2 Watch Your Thoughts). I consciously relaxed, brought my attention to my breath and deliberately attempted to think loving thoughts toward my self. "I love myself even though I'm hot and cranky. My agitation is an invitation to change scenery. I am OK. I can choose to be loving" (Step 3 Change Your Thoughts and Rule #5 Love Yourself).

It was time to go back to the boat. We started the process of gathering up all the stuff, our five kids, and husbands. At the time it seemed an insurmountable task. My youngest daughter Addison, who was four at the time and stubborn as an ox, was doing her best to pack up. She had a towel over her shoulder, goggles around her neck, no shoes to be found, and a plastic cup full of little seashells. "Dump the shells," I told her. She was not having it. Addie had worked hard all day to gather those shells, and she was not about to dump them. "The shells belong to the beach," I said as I raised my voice and gave her a stern look. "This is my treasure!" she yelled. At that point I snapped and grabbed the edge of the cup, and we did a little tug-o-war between us while water sloshed over the rim. As we teetered on the edge of making a scene, a glimpse of light caught my eye from the bottom of the cup (Step 6 Perceive). Interested, I gained my composure and convinced her to let me investigate. I dug my pointer finger around the shells, and from the bottom of the cup I pulled a silver wedding band with what appeared to be diamonds all the way around (Step 8 Receive)!

Addison had dug it up from about a foot down in the sand. It was caked with dirt and sand. I wasn't even sure if it was real. We checked the beach to make sure no one had lost a ring, but we were quite sure by its condition that it had been buried for quite some time. When I returned home I took it to the jewelry store to clean it up and see if it was of any value. Sure enough, it was real. It was an antique wedding band with small diamonds all the way around. The metal was worn on the inside as if it had been worn by someone for a lifetime. It fit me perfectly and goes beautifully with my engagement ring (Rule #2 Be Grateful). After some serious coaxing and a promise from me that I would include her as the hero of the story every time I tell someone about my wedding band, Addison agreed to give me her treasure for Mother's Day. I got my wedding band, diamonds all the way around, delivered by the Universe, on my tenth year of marriage, right on schedule (Step 8 Receive).

For me, that little miracle reinforced that I was on the right path. I was doing my best to consciously live by the Rules of the Road. I had intended that ring. I let go of my expectation to have it when I didn't get what I wanted. Not for one moment did I feel bad when I thought about my ring. I felt excitement for when I would get it in the future. In the meantime, I focused on what was really important and felt genuine gratitude in my heart for what I already had, including a solid relationship with my spouse. I was open to the wonder and miracles in life. And my perfect ring showed up, right on time.

Karen's Story: Austin or Bust

In 2009 I was ready for change. I hung a sign on my bathroom mirror for everyone in my house to see. It said, "I am in a healthy loving relationship with someone who cherishes and respects me. I live in Austin, Texas near my best friend where my family and I have a support system. I am present in my relationship with my children. I enjoy travel and I am abundant." I was getting good at creating the things I wanted in life. A vacation here, a bonus there, were all great, but I was ready to make real changes in my life. Change that would alter my family's future in a major positive way. Go big or go home!

We had been living in Florida for seven years. I was grateful for our beautiful home (Rule #2 Be Grateful). Although I loved the house, I knew that I didn't want to call Florida home for the rest of my life. My family was aware of my desire to leave the Sunshine State. We all agreed that if we were going to move, it should be before any of the kids entered high school. I fantasized about moving back to Georgia, the Carolinas or somewhere in the Southeast where trees were a rich forest green and hills were abundant.

The same year we were contemplating our future location, Amity and her family moved to Austin, Texas. I flew to the Lone Star State to help my best friend organize her home a month after she arrived. I was surprised to find rolling hills, lakes and an abundance of trees. It was not the Texas I envisioned, which was one of flat lands and tumbleweeds rolling across the highway. She knew my desire to leave Florida and did her best sales job to convince me that Austin was the place for us. We explored the area by going to various restaurants with views of the amazing Texas sunsets, the picturesque lakes, and plenty of fantastic live music. I was hooked! I knew this was our next destination. I was thrilled! My excitement showed, and after a few more trips to Texas with my husband in the coming months, he was sold.

I placed our intention to move to Austin, Texas, in my mind (Step 1 Know What You Want), and we wrote it on the white board in my husband's office. We hung a picture of Lake Austin on the wall to be sure we visualized our future many times a day. The plan was for my husband to use his skills as a successful sales rep, combined with the power of thought, to manifest more sales and more income. More income was a necessity because we needed to pay down the mortgage on our home, which had become severely upside down in a housing market that hit rock bottom. In a nutshell, we bought the home for $600,000 and it was worth $340,000. We were $240,000 in the hole. We couldn't just sell the house and move. We needed to make up the difference or wait until the housing market recovered, if ever. That large number did not deter us from knowing a move to Austin was happening. Waiting on an economic recovery in Florida was also not an option. We didn't know exactly how we would do it, but we knew moving to Austin was happening. My husband was the main provider and we rationalized that his income needed to increase for this to happen. The master plan consisted of him selling a ton of product, and if he met his projected goals, he thought we could be in Texas within the next two years. I was on board with that plan, but reminded myself to keep the vision clear and let the details take care of themselves (Rule #3 Let go of Control).

My husband started putting his projected sales number on the wall in his office. I would check in with him a few times a week to encourage him to watch his thoughts to make sure his words were matching the projected goal (Step 2 Watch Your Thoughts). January came and went and his sales numbers were declining. WTH? I noticed my mind constantly replaying the current situation. I recognized the barrage of negative thoughts filling my mind. *What if he didn't sell enough? What if we couldn't move? Maybe he can't do it.* I tried to catch those thoughts. When I did, I'd make sure to look for the positives that were happening with our finances in order to bring me back in alignment with gratitude. We were still able to live very comfortably, my husband was a great salesman, and we were fortunate to have the opportunity to make a lot of money (Step 3 Change Your Thoughts and Rule #2 Be Grateful).

To help keep our thoughts on track we visualized living in Austin. We framed a picture of a house from the neighborhood we liked in Austin and hung it up on the wall in his office next to the picture of Lake Austin. We sat and looked at the picture of what we believed looked like our future home, and imagined what it would feel like being in Austin with our friends in our new life (Step 4 Feel). I kept my focus on moving to Austin despite the continued decline in his sales numbers. I realized that as much as I tried, I couldn't control his thinking, only mine (Rule #3 Let Go of Control).

The months continued to slip by. In May, things were not looking good. We were making a lot less per month than we had in years. We decided I needed to go back to work to help pay the monthly bills. That same month I was reading the newspaper and noticed an article about a government-sponsored bank program to help those affected by the housing crash. It stated the banks could write off a portion of home mortgages if you qualified for the program and were willing to go through a short sale process. This might allow us to cut our losses and get out from under the house at a discounted rate. I showed my husband the article with a curious excitement (Step 6 Perceive). He was not impressed and gave me a stonewall response. He insisted it was just a slow season and he could sell more to get the funds to pay down the house. He acknowledged that his thoughts were consumed with worst-case scenarios and committed to refocusing his thoughts (Step 3 Change Your Thoughts).

Two months later, friends of ours in the neighborhood were transferred out of state. They did a short sale on their home and knew the process. I was able to talk in depth to them about their situation and experience. I went to my husband and shared my new-found information. I asked him to consider this, "What if we could pay a lot less than $240,000 and get out of our current home for an amount close to $50,000 by filing for a short sale?" Again, my husband's response was a big, fat negative. My husband's ego was attached to the idea of excellent credit, living on the golf course, and caring about what everyone would think. He didn't like the negative stigma that he thought was attached to people who did a short sale. I felt deflated after our conversation, knowing that our current financial situation was deteriorating along with our options to move. I stepped up the hours at work and was now working close to full time. His income was half of what it was six months earlier. The tension and frustration was growing between us. I could see he was caught up in what was going wrong at his job as his agitation and withdrawal increased.

I remained committed to the plan despite the lack of progress. I felt that a move to Austin was happening (Step 4 Feel). I decided to focus on what I could control, which was my thoughts, and let him have his own experience (Rule #3 Let Go of Control). Two months passed, it was September. While reading the Sunday newspaper, an article jumped off the pages at me. The banks were now writing off BOTH first and second mortgage balances when you went through the short sale process. I vividly recall running into my husband's office waving the newspaper in my hand ready to read him the article. I felt like I had won the lotto. I knew this was it. This was the answer. I felt it in every bone in my body. I went to my husband and said, "This keeps showing up. We really need to consider it!" (Step 6 Perceive). He read the article and was not moved like I had hoped. He looked me in the eyes and said, "No way." A screaming argument ensued. I knew in my heart this is what needed to be done. I felt it in every cell of my body and trying to convince him was not easy (Step 4 Feel).

His ego was strong and attached to "keeping up with the Joneses." A short sale, in his mind, meant we couldn't pay our bills. He was more concerned about what people would say than our commitment to our future plan. I was pissed! With no budging in sight, I stated, "If you don't do this, we are over." I am not proud of the threat, but it was not an empty threat. I just had a knowing that this needed to be done. I was never so sure of anything in my life (Step 5 Believe). I also knew that if something keeps presenting itself, you need to pay attention

(Step 6 Perceive). This was the third "sign" that we needed to do a short sale. The first was the initial newspaper article, the second was our friends sharing their short sale experience with us, and then this second article showed up. It was crystal clear to me. Finally, reluctantly, he agreed. I told him to get out of my way! I knew this was happening, and it was going to be simple and easy. I was going to drive this truck myself and get us to Austin, with or without him (Rule #1 Take Radical Responsibility).

The following week I contacted a realtor (Step 7 Participate). She showed up and informed us that the market was slow. For sale signs were littering the neighborhood. No houses were moving in our subdivision, and with the school year starting most people who were going to buy already had. Short sales at that time were seen as a big problem by the real estate market. The banks didn't really know what to do with them or how to handle them. The process was slow and unorganized. It could easily last a year, or more. Most buyers in our price range did not have the kind of flexibility to wait without certainty for months on end for a short sale. A short sale required waiting for the bank to decide if they would accept the offer and release the house for sale, and the banks were in crisis. My realtor frowned at our entire situation. She told us not to get our hopes up. I informed her directly that her way of thinking was not going to work for me. I told her, "Our house will get a contract quickly and easily. The short sale process will be the smoothest and quickest she had ever seen." (Step 1 Know What You Want). I think she silently thought I was nuts. To my face, she smiled and said, "I sure hope so."

The house went up for sale on a Wednesday. Not surprising to me, we had a contract on it five days later. My realtor about dropped a load. Her shock and happiness were short-lived. She soon went into Negative Nancy mode, reminding us that the short sale process could be a deal breaker. "If the bank drags their feet, you will most likely lose your buyer." Those kinds of thoughts were nowhere in my mind. I stayed on the path and kept my thoughts in line with my vision of the future. It was going to be quick and easy (Step 2 Watch Your Thoughts).

Lo and behold, the month I was dealing with the bank, the government launched its new incentive program. It was the same program that I had read about in the August article. It wrote off both first and second mortgage balances and paid you $3,000 to move. My realtor definitely thought I was crazy. This program was so new that the banks involved with my mortgages and my realtor had never heard of it. I researched and gathered the information and presented it to the banks and my realtor. The application process began, and now all there was left to do was wait. Multiple roadblocks and detours showed up. We kept a positive attitude, knew it was going to sell, and believed it was happening, despite all the negative thinking of the realtor, our mortgage advisor and the people at the banks. I contacted the bank every two weeks to make sure things didn't get put on the back burner or lost on someone's desk. I also watched my thoughts relentlessly. In September, I decided to start thinking of a nice low amount of money that we would need to bring to closing. Based on what I heard about short sales I thought we would come to the closing with $30,000. In my mind, that would be awesome! It sure sounded better than $240,000.00!

Things were progressing through November. We hadn't lost our buyer, and I was feeling really good. I reevaluated my $30,000 number. Why not believe we would only be out of pocket $10,000? Knowing what I knew, why would I set the number so high? (Step 3 Change Your Thoughts). All the while, friends and acquaintances who were familiar with the short sale process thought I was on a one-way trip to crazy town. They had never heard of such a thing. One friend had to pony up $50,000 and the process took a year and a half! I just let them lecture me about the fantasyland I was living in. They pleaded with me to be realistic. While they whined, all I heard was "blah, blah, blah." Selling our home quickly and easily and having a smooth short sale process where we were out of pocket only $10,000 as opposed to $240,000 was all I heard in my head.

The bank wasn't giving us much information. While others worried about rejection, I decided to change my final closing payout amount to $0 in December. We would pay nothing out of pocket and get approved for that program that would pay us $3000 in moving costs. HAHA. My friends and family now thought I needed medication. I was in Lala Land. I didn't care. I knew it was happening (Step 5 Believe). Even my husband was skeptical. He did his best to play along and say the right words so I would feel supported in the process. Deep down he didn't think it was possible. I didn't care. I thought it, I believed it, and I felt it. It was on!

The bank scheduled a tentative closing date for February. The realtor was very cautious, telling us not to get our hopes up, that banks often do this, but most times short sales got pushed back months. To everyone's disbelief the closing went off without a hitch on the day it was scheduled. We found out that we qualified for the government program that erased the balances on the first AND second mortgages. We owed nothing, zero, zilch. And $240,000 worth of debt – erased! They also presented us with a check for $3000 to move. Score (Step 8 Receive)!

One year and one month after we set our intention to move to Austin, we sold our house and we were on our way. I was ecstatic! Here's the kicker. In order to qualify for that government program that wiped off our balances, my husband's income had to decrease significantly over the previous year. Those losses had to be well-documented in tax returns. All those months of his sales number tanking, all that fighting and worry about not making enough money, turned out to be exactly what was needed to qualify for the program. Without that hell, we never could have qualified. We never would have consciously agreed to losing more than half our income in order to be able to sell our house. That would have been crazy and counterintuitive to the direction we thought we should head. Had my husband continued to "do it his way," he would still be trying to sell more to pay down the balances on our mortgages. Had we gotten caught up in the details of trying to control how it was going to happen, we wouldn't have been able to perceive the signs and take advantage of a program that only existed for a few short months. We would still be stuck in Florida under a mountain of debt. The moral of the story: set your intention, follow your road map, and trust that everything is as it should be. Let go of how you think it will happen. It never happens the way you expect! Hello, Austin!

Shortcuts

→ Live by the Rules of the Road in your daily life.

→ Practice the steps of the Road Map to manifest your intentions.

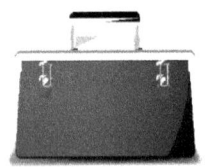

Tool Kit

→ Master the book *Life's a Trip: Shortcuts to Making the Most of Your Journey.*

> "Thought allied fearlessly to purpose becomes creative force: he who knows this is ready to become something higher and stronger than a mere bundle of wavering thoughts and fluctuating sensations; he who does this has become the conscious and intelligent wielder of his mental powers."
>
> ~ James Allen

23
HAPPY TRAILS

Dr. Seuss asserts, "You have brains in your head. You have feet in your shoes. You can steer yourself any direction you choose. You're on your own, and you know what you know. And you are the only one who'll decide where you'll go." Our journey together is almost complete. It has been a pleasure to be your back seat drivers. Now it is time to make the decision to continue down the path of change on your own. The difference between knowing how to change, and actually doing it, starts with a decision. If you truly want to make the most of your journey, you have to decide to change. Vehicles as magnificent as you weren't meant to sit in the garage. They were meant for the open road. Once you have committed to change, the adventure begins. If we can do it, you certainly can do it!

Practice your shortcuts and continue to use your Tool Kit. Tony Robbins says, "A real decision is measured by the fact that you've taken a new action. If there's no action, you haven't truly decided." The days traveling down your path may not always be bright and sunny. As you begin to watch your thoughts and pay more conscious attention to your life, you may be disturbed by what you see. That is OK. Nothing has really changed, except your willingness to come out of the shadow of unconsciousness and denial. It is a necessary part of shedding the past and charting a new course. No darkness can survive the light.

When you are in the midst of change, and you are practicing your new way of being, you may have moments of doubt. You may try to rationalize your way back into your old thought patterns. This is normal and natural. The path is always right in front of you, waiting for you to jump back on. Teri Groves, LCSW, reminds us that it takes practice to assimilate new information into action and behavior. We assume that once we know something we can just do it, like an arrow moving from point A to point B. This is not usually the case. Groves says the assimilation of knowledge travels instead in an upward spiral pattern, circulating between new knowledge and old behaviors. The good news is that the low points on the spiral are still higher than our beginning point, as long as we keep trying and learning.

Buckle up! The road might not always be smooth, but it will all be worth it. Knowing what you want and committing to it by practicing the Rules of the Road and the steps in the Road Map will set forth a vibration of being that may not match your old self. It may feel uncomfortable at first. Things you used to tolerate may become intolerable. Your likes and dislikes may shift. It is just part of the process. People who like the "old you" may not want you to change. Loved ones may be threatened or scared of the "new you" and attempt to hold you back. Stay your course. If you are changing for the better, for your higher good, everyone around you will be well served. People will accept it – or not. They will change with you – or not. Hold your center and be true to yourself. Be your True Self. Let people, opportunities, and events vibrate toward you and away from you.

Wise men throughout the ages have proclaimed that consciousness expands. You can decide to play along or let life's circumstances force change on you beyond your control. One way or another it is already happening. Consciousness is expanding. Why not take the trip and enjoy it? Amma, "The Hugging Saint" from India, says, "When you behold the entire universe as a play of consciousness what is there to do but smile."

All the instruction you need, you already have. All the strength you need is already within you. Access it and free yourself to experience life as the wonderful and mysterious trip that it is. No one can do it for you. It has to be done by you. Make the most of your journey. We wish you Happy Trails!

> "Remember life is a journey. If you got everything you wanted all at once there'd be no point to living. Enjoy the ride, and in the end, you'll see these "setbacks" as giant leaps forward, only you couldn't see the bigger picture in the moment. Remain calm, all is within reach; all you have to do is show up every day, stay true to your path and you will surely find the treasure you seek."
>
> ~ Jackson Kiddard

ACKNOWLEGMENTS

Continued by Karen:

I would like to start by giving a heartfelt thank you to my co-author Amity. She has shown me what true friendship is in my life and has been a wonderful teacher and soul sister. She helped me understand what I wanted to say and has continued to guide me in the best way to say it. She inspires me to be a better person, and I am forever grateful for our friendship. I would also like to thank Carol Albee, who has been a huge support system for my personal growth. To have the inner wisdom and guidance of one so insightful has been a huge blessing in my life. I would also like to thank my ex-husband. Without the struggles we went through, I would not be the person I am today. I am sincerely thankful for the lessons we learned together and the ones I continue to work on to this day.

To my daughters, who are my number one priority: My focus in life is to inspire you to see all the greatness that lies inside each of you. My biggest wish is for you to dream big! I look forward to watching all your dreams come true. Thank you for inspiring me and challenging me everyday to be the best mother I can be.

Continued by Amity:

No amount of gratitude could account for how deeply I appreciate the love and support of my husband, Kevin. Thank you for allowing me the freedom to fully express myself and create this book. Your companionship is my favorite thing. I'd also like to thank my two wonderful kids for forcing me to practice what I preach. These years of your childhood have been the sweetest of my life. I admire you both so much. I am eternally grateful to my parents for setting an example of lasting love and continued learning, two ingredients for a wonderful life. My expression of gratitude would be incomplete without mentioning my two favorite artists, Jason Mraz and Allen Stone. Your music provides me with an instant route to an open heart. And lastly to Karen, my co-author, thank you for your patience in completing this project. It was a vehicle for personal growth for both of us, and I am grateful to have shared this experience with you. You are a perfect example of someone who is committed to personal growth and actually does something about it. Thanks for trusting the process.

THANK YOU

It is with great pleasure that we have opened up our hearts and shared our personal trials and triumphs with you. We would be delighted and grateful if you found our narratives entertaining and our shortcuts useful, but our deepest desire is that you use the information in *Life's a Trip* to make deeper connections with friends and family, find your True Self, take care of YOU, and make the most of ***your*** journey.

If these stories touched or inspired you in any way and you would like to share your own story, ask a question, or connect with the authors, please send an email to: **lifesatrip.shortcuts@gmail.com**

Works Cited

Abraham, Esther Hicks, and Jerry Hicks. *The Law of Attraction: The Basics of the Teachings of Abraham*. Carlsbad, CA: Hay House, 2006. Print.

Abraham, Esther Hicks, and Jerry Hicks. *Money, and the Law of Attraction: Learning to Attract Wealth, Health, and Happiness*. Carlsbad, CA: Hay House, 2008. Print.

Aldrich, Zach. "Overweight America: More than Half of Us Could Be Diabetic or Pre-diabetic." (2011): n. pag. Web. 17 Nov. 2011. <news.medill.northwestern.edu.com>.

Ali, Muhammad. "Muhammad Ali Quotes." *Muhammad Ali Quotes*. Publisher Unknown. Web.

Allen, James. *As a Man Thinketh*. Virginia: Wilder, 2007. Print.

Anderson, Lori. *Divorce with Grace, A Book of Hope and Healing*. Publisher Unknown. 2013. Print.

Attwood, Janet Bray, and Chris Attwood. *The Passion Test: The Effortless Path to Discovering Your Destiny*. New York: Hudson Street, 2007. Print.

Aubrey, Allison. "Poor Sleep May Lead to Too Much Stored Fat and Disease." (2012): n. pag. Web. 17 Oct. 2012. <npr.org/blogs/health/2012/10/17/163018568>.

Author Unknown. "Historical and Cultural Perspectives of Sleep." *Healthy Sleep*. Division of Sleep Medicine at Harvard Medical School, 2008. Web.

Author Unknown. "Medication Relieves Anxiety?" Web Log Post. *Wild Medidation News*. Wildmind Buddist Meditation, 6 June 2013. Web.

Author Unknown. "Neuroplasticity." *NICHD - The Eunice Kennedy Shriver National Institute of Child Health and Human Development Official Home Page*. Publisher Unknown. Web.

Author Unknown. "Unintentional Drug Poisoning in the United States." *Centers for Disease Control and Prevention*. Centers for Disease Control and Prevention, July 2010. Web. <http://www.cdc.gov/homeandrecreationalsafety/pdf/poison-issue-brief.pdf>.

Bach, Richard. "Quotes." *Goodreads*. 04 Feb. 2008. Web. <http://www.goodreads.com/quotes/2126>.

Beattie, Melody. *Codependent No More: How to Stop Controlling Others and Start Caring for Yourself*. Minnesota: Hazelden Foundation, 1986. Print.

Beecher, Henry Ward. "Henry Ward Beecher Quotes." *Iz Quotes*. Web. <http://izquotes.com/quote/14625>.

Berlin, Leslie. "We'll Fill This Space, but First a Nap." *Nytimes.com*. Publisher Unknown. 27 Sept. 2008. Web.

Brown, Jeff, Mark Fenske, and Liz Neporent. *The Winner's Brain: 8 Strategies Great Minds Use to Achieve Success*. Cambridge, MA: Da Capo Life Long, 2010. Print.

Brown, Michael. *The Presence Process: A Journey into Present Moment Awareness*. Vancouver: Namaste Pub., 2010. Print.

Brumfield, C. Russell., James Goldney, and Stephanie Gunning. *Whiff!: The Revolution of Scent Communication in the Information Age*. New York, NY: Quimby, 2008. Print.

Calvino, Italo." Italo Calvino Quotes." *BrainyQuote.com*. Xplore Inc. Web.

Caro, Dan, and Steve Erwin. *The Gift of Fire: How I Made Adversity Work for Me*. Carlsbad, CA: Hay House, 2010. Print.

Carter, Karen Rauch. *Move Your Stuff, Change Your Life: How to Use Feng Shui to Get Love, Money, Respect, and Happiness*. New York: Simon & Schuster, 2000. Print.

Childre, Doc Lew, Howard Martin, and Donna Beech. *The HeartMath® Solution*. San Francisco, CA: HarperSanFrancisco, 1999. Print.

Chopra, Deepak. *The Seven Spiritual Laws for Parents: Guiding Your Children to Success and Fulfillment*. New York: Harmony, 1997. Print.

Chopra, Deepak. *The Seven Spiritual Laws of Success: A Practical Guide to the Fulfillment of Your Dreams*. San Rafael, CA: Amber-Allen Pub, 1994. Print.

Chopra, Deepak.(@DeepakChopra) "*If You Want Something , Give It*". 30 Dec. 2011. Tweet.

Choquette, Sonia. *The Answer Is Simple--: Love Yourself, Live Your Spirit!* Carlsbad, CA: Hay House, 2008. Print.

Christakis, Nicholas A., and James H. Fowler. "The Spread of Obesity in a Large Social Network Over 32 Years." *New England Journal of Medicine* 357.4 (2007): 370-79. Web.

Cooper, Anderson. "Sixy Minutes." *Michael Phelps on Making Olympic History*. 25 Nov. 2008. Television.

Cortman, Christopher, and Harold Shinitzky. *Your Mind: An Owner's Manual for a Better Life: 10 Simple Truths That Will Set You Free*. Franklin Lakes, NJ: Career, 2010. Print.

Cromie, William J. "Does It Have a Prayer." *The Power of Healing*. The Harvard University Gazette, 11 Sept. 1997. Web.

Dennison, Paul E., and Gail Dennison. *Brain Gym: Simple Activities for Whole Brain Learning*. Glendale, CA: Edu-Kinesthetics, 1986. Print.

Desai, Panache. *Discovering Your Soul Signature: A 33-day Path to Purpose, Passion, & Joy*. Publisher Unknown. Print.

Diamond, Jed. "Irritable Male Syndrome." *MedicineNet*. Publisher Unknown. 10 Nov. 2004. Web.

Dispenza, Joe. *Breaking the Habit of Being Yourself: How to Lose Your Mind and Create a New One*. Carlsbad, CA: Hay House, 2012. Print.

Dolan, Eric. "Interesting Behavioral Effects of Ovulation on Women - PsyPost." *PsyPost*. Publisher Unknown. 15 Jan. 2010. Web.

Durante, K. M., N. P. Li, and M. G. Haselton. "Changes in Women's Choice of Dress Across the Ovulatory Cycle: Naturalistic and Laboratory Task-Based Evidence." *Personality and Social Psychology Bulletin* 34.11 (2008): 1451-460. Web.

Dyer, Wayne. *Excuses Be Gone!: How to Change Lifelong, Self-defeating Thinking Habits*. United States: Hay House, 2009. Print.

Dyer, Wayne W. *Change Your Thoughts, Change Your Life: Living the Wisdom of the Tao*. Carlsbad, CA: Hay House, 2007. Print.

Dyer, Wayne W. *The Power of Intention: Learning to Co-create Your World Your Way*. Carlsbad, CA: Hay House, 2004. Print.

Easton, John. "Even Your Fat Cells Need Sleep, According to New Research." *UChicago News*. Publisher Unknown, 17 Oct. 2012. Web.

Emoto, Masaru, and Shizumi Nagayasu. *Xin Fu De Zhen Yi, Shui Zhi Dao = Water Knows the Answer*. Taibeishi: Ru He Chu Ban She, 2004. Print.

English, Jason. "What Bill Buckner Said 19 Days before Game Six of the '86 World Series." *Mental Floss*. 25 Oct. 2011. Web.

Evans, James R., and Andrew Abarbanel. *Introduction to Quantitative EEG and Neurofeedback*. San Diego, CA: Academic, 1999. Print.

Evans, Patricia. *The Verbally Abusive Relationship: How to Recognize It and How to Respond*. Holbrook, MA: Adams Media Corporation, 1996. Print.

Fair, Virginia Sara. *The Art of Forgiveness: A Practical Guide*. Monongahela, PA: Threesie Publication, 1996. Print.

Fowler, J. H., and N. A. Christakis. "Cooperative Behavior Cascades in Human Social Networks." *Proceedings of the National Academy of Sciences* 107.12 (2010): 5334-338. Web.

Fowler, J. H., and N. A. Christakis. "Dynamic Spread of Happiness in a Large Social Network: Longitudinal Analysis over 20 Years in the Framingham Heart Study." *Bmj* 337.Dec04 2 (2008): A2338. Web.

Fox, Emmet. "Great Thinkers of the World." *Living Fully*. Web. <http://www.livinglifefully.com/thinkersfox.htm>.

Haefner, Joe. "Mental Rehersal and Visualization." *Breakthrough Basketball*. Publisher Unknown, 05 June 2010. Web.

Hawthorne, Jennifer Read. "Change Your Thoughts, Change Your World." *Inspirational Speaker*. Publisher Unknown, 2009. Web.

Hay, Louise L. *You Can Heal Your Life*. Santa Monica, CA: Hay House, 1987. Print.

Huffman, Mark. "Quantifying Options for Reducing Coronary Heart Disease Mortality by 2020." *Pubmed.gov*.13 June 2013. Web.

Jefferson, Thomas. "Famous Quotes." *BrainyQuote*. Xplore, Web.

Katie, Byron, and Stephen Mitchell. *Loving What Is: Four Questions That Can Change Your Life*. New York: Harmony, 2002. Print.

Kübler-Ross, Elisabeth, and David Kessler. *On Grief and Grieving: Finding the Meaning of Grief through the Five Stages of Loss*. New York: Scribner, 2005. Print.

Kessler, R. C., W. T. Chiu, O. Demler, K. R. Merikangas, and E. Walters. "Prevalence, Severity and Comorbidity of Twelve-month DSM-IV Disorders the National Comorbidity Survey Replications." *Archives of General Psychiatry* 62.1 (2005): 13. Web.

Kiddard, Jackson. "The Living Book." *One Journey*. 30 Aug. 2012. Web. http://onejourney.net.

Kingma, Daphne Rose. *The Ten Things to Do When Your Life Falls Apart an Emotional and Spiritual Handbook*. Novato, CA: New World Library, 2010. Print.

Knotts, Ronnie, Father. "Sample Prayers." *Thoughts About God*. Publisher Unknown. Web.

Lautenschlager, Nicola. "Effect of Physical Activity on Cognitive Function in Older Adults at Risk for Alzheimer Disease." *JAMA* 300.1027-37 (2009): n. pag. Web.

Lehrer, Jonah. *How We Decide*. Boston: Houghton Mifflin Harcourt, 2009. Print.

Lipton, Bruce H. *The Biology of Belief: Unleashing the Power of Consciousness, Matter and Miracles*. Santa Rosa, CA: Mountain of Love/Elite, 2005. Print.

Marsh, Jason. "Should Lottery Winners Share with Colleagues?" *CNN*. Cable News Network, 01 Apr. 2011. Web.

Mcgill, Bryant. "Today's Quotes." *The Daily Love*. Publisher Unknown. 6 Feb. 2013. Web.

McLaren, Karla. *The Art of Empathy: A Complete Guide to Life's Most Essential Skill*. Publisher Unknown. Print.

Meier, J.D. "Buddha Quotes." *Sources of Insight*, 22 Jan. 2012. Web.

Miller, Michael Craig, Md. "Exercise and Depression." *Harvard Health Publications Report* (2011): n. pag. Web. <http://www.health.harvard.edu/ud>.

Myss, Caroline M. *Sacred Contracts: Awakening Your Divine Potential.* New York: Harmony, 2001. Print.

Neighmond, Pattie. "Losing Weight: A Battle against Fat and Biology." Web Log Post. *Shot's NPR Health Blog.* Publisher Unknown, 31 Oct. 2011. Web.

Neville. *Your Faith Is Your Fortune.* Marina Del Ray, CA: DeVorss, 1941. Print.

"New Study Shows People Sleep Even Less Than They Think: Whites, Women and Wealthy Sleep Longer, Better." – *The University of Chicago Medicine.* ScienceDaily, 3 July 2006. Web.

Northrup, Christiane, Md. "The Wisdom of the Menstrual Cycle - Health Conditions & Advice - Dr. Christiane Northrup." *Drnorthrup.com.* Publisher Unknown. 21 Aug. 2009. Web.

Nørretranders, Tor. *The User Illusion: Cutting Consciousness down to Size.* New York, NY: Penguin, 1999. Print.

Oprah. N.D. Television

Orloff, Judith. *Positive Energy: 10 Extraordinary Prescriptions for Transforming Fatigue, Stress, and Fear into Vibrance, Strength, and Love.* New York: Harmony, 2004. Print.

Peck, M. Scott. *The Road Less Traveled: A New Psychology of Love, Traditional Values, and Spiritual Growth.* New York: Simon and Schuster, 1978. Print.

Posner, Michael. "Meditation and the Brain." *ScienceFriday.com.* Publisher Unknown, 20 Aug. 2009. Web.

Richardson, Cheryl. *The Art of Extreme Self Care: Transform Your Life a Month at a Time.* London: Hay House, 2009. Print.

Robbins, Tony. "Tony Robbins Quotes." *BrainyQuote.com.* Xplore Inc, 2014. Web.

Rohn, Jim. "Jim Rohn Quotes." BrainyQuote.com. Xplore Inc. Web.

Rohn, Jim. "Jim Rohn Quotes." *The Quotes Toolbox.* Web.

Rubin, Gretchen Craft. *The Happiness Project.* New York: HarperCollins, 2010. Print.

Sears, Al. *P. A. C. E.: The 12-minute Fitness Revolution.* Royal Palm Beach, FL: Wellness Research & Consulting, 2010. Print.

Seuss, Dr. *Oh, the Places You'll Go!* New York: Random House, 1990. Print.

Shimoff, Marci, and Carol Kline. *Love for No Reason: 7 Steps to Creating a Life of Unconditional Love.* New York: Free, 2010. Print.

Siddharta, Gautama. "Buddha Quotes."*Thinkexist.com.* ThinkExist, Web.

Siegel, Daniel J. *Mindsight: The New Science of Personal Transformation.* New York: Bantam, 2010. Print.

Singer, Michael A. *The Untethered Soul: The Journey beyond Yourself.* Oakland, CA: New Harbinger Publications, 2007. Print.

Sobel, David, Md. "Guided Imagery Speeds Surgical Recovery." *Alternative Health, Wellness and Healthy Living Information, Articles and News*. Publisher Unknown. Web.

Tagg, John. "Shoulding Yourself, Shoulding Others." *Reflections on Learning*. 1996. Web.

The Holy Bible: New International Version, Containing the Old Testament and the New Testament. Grand Rapids: Zondervan Bible, 1978. Print.

Thie, John F., and Matthew Thie. *Touch for Health: The Complete Edition: A Practical Guide to Natural Health with Acupressure Touch and Massage*. Camarillo, CA: DeVorss Publications, 2005. Print.

Tolle, Eckhart. *A New Earth: Awakening to Your Life's Purpose*. New York: Plume, 2006. Print.

Tolle, Eckhart. *The Power of Now: A Guide to Spiritual Enlightenment*. Novato, CA: New World Library, 1999. Print.

Tolle, Eckhart. *Practicing the Power of Now Essential Teachings, Meditations, and Exercises from the Power of Now*. Novato, CA: New World Library, 1999. Print.

Tracy, Brian. "Brian Tracy Quotes." *BrainyQuote.com*. Xplore Inc. Web.

Tse, Vivian. "Good Night's Sleep Key to Beauty: Swedish Study." *The Local.se*. Publisher Unknown, 16 Dec. 2010. Web.

University of North Carolina at Charlotte. "Brief Meditative Exercise Helps Cognition." *Science Daily* 328.5976 (2010): 293. 19 Apr. 2010. Web.

University of Oregon. "Integrative Body-mind Training (IBMT) Meditation Found to Boost Brain Connectivity." *ScienceDaily*. ScienceDaily, 18 Aug. 2010. Web.

Vitale, Joe, and Haleakalā Hew Len. *Zero Limits: The Secret Hawaiian System for Wealth, Health, Peace, and More*. Hoboken, NJ: Wiley, 2007. Print.

Weiss, Brian L. *Many Lives, Many Masters*. New York: Simon & Schuster, 1988. Print.

Welsh, Joan. "Joan Welsh Quotes." *Thinkexist.com. Quotations.* ThinkExist, Web.

Williams, Kayse. "Essential Oils." *Sacred Alchemy*. Kayse Williams. Web.

Williams, Robert M. *PSYCH-K...The Missing Piece/Peace In Your Life!* Crestone, CO: Myrrdin Publications, 2004. Print.

Williamson, Marianne. *A Return to Love: Reflections on the Principles of a Course in Miracles*. New York, NY: HarperCollins, 1992. Print.

Wong, Jj. "Lao Tzu Quotes." *Inspiration Boost.* Web.

Work, Rich. *Proclamations of the Soul*. Mosinee, WI: Asini Pub. 1999. Print.

www.ingramcontent.com/pod-product-compliance
Lightning Source LLC
Chambersburg PA
CBHW071304110426
42743CB00042B/1163